SERMONS

ON

THE PRAYER-BOOK AND THE LORD'S PRAYER

THE PRAYER-BOOK

CONSIDERED ESPECIALLY IN REFERENCE TO
THE ROMISH SYSTEM

Nineteen Sermons preached in the Chapel of Lincoln's Inn

AND

THE LORD'S PRAYER

*Nine Sermons preached in the Chapel of Lincoln's Inn in the
months of February, March, and April,* 1848

BY

FREDERICK DENISON MAURICE

WIPF & STOCK · Eugene, Oregon

Wipf and Stock Publishers
199 W 8th Ave, Suite 3
Eugene, OR 97401

The Prayer - Book Considered Especially in Reference to
The Romish System: Nineteen Sermons Preached in teh Chapel of
Lincoln's Inn, and The Lord's Prayer: Nineteen Sermons Preached
in the Chapel of Lincoln's Inn in the Months of February,
March, and April, 1848
By Maurice, Frederick D.
ISBN 13: 978-1-60899-713-8
Publication date 6/28/2010
Previously published by Macmillan and Co., 1893

THE PRAYER-BOOK.

Contents.

SERMON I.
INTRODUCTORY (1 *Corinthians* i. 2) . . . . . PAGE 1

SERMON II.
THE CONFESSION (*Isaiah* ii. 11) 15

SERMON III.
THE ABSOLUTION (*Luke* v. 21) 30

SERMON IV.
THE LORD'S PRAYER AFTER ABSOLUTION—THE GLORIA PATRI (*John* iv. 23, 24) 47

SERMON V.
THE NINETY-FIFTH PSALM (*Psalm* xcv. 11) . . . 60

SERMON VI.
THE PSALMS (2 *St. Peter* i. 20, 21) 74

SERMON VII.
THE FIRST LESSON (*Psalm* cxix. 144) 90

SERMON VIII.
THE SECOND LESSON (*Ephesians* iii. 4, 5) . . . 107

SERMON IX.
THE SONGS OF THE CHURCH (*Revelation* xv. 3) . . 121

SERMON X.

THE CREED (*Psalm* ix. 10) 138

SERMON XI.

EJACULATIONS AND COLLECTS (*Matthew* vi. 7, 8) . 149

SERMON XII.

THE LITANY (*Ezekiel* i. 26) 161

SERMON XIII.

THE COMMUNION SERVICE. (1).—THE COMMANDMENTS (*Hebrews* viii. 10) 176

SERMON XIV.

THE COMMUNION SERVICE. (2).—THE EPISTLE AND GOSPEL, AND NICENE CREED (*Ephesians* ii. 20) . . 190

SERMON XV.

THE COMMUNION SERVICE. (3).—THE OFFERTORY, AND PRAYER FOR THE CHURCH MILITANT (*Philippians* ii. 12, 13). 207

SERMON XVI.

THE COMMUNION SERVICE. (4).—THE EXHORTATION AND CONFESSION IN THE COMMUNION SERVICE (*Acts* xiii. 46) . 223

SERMON XVII.

THE COMMUNION SERVICE. (5).—THE ABSOLUTION, AND SENTENCES, AND TRISAGION (*Matthew* xi. 28, 29) . . 238

SERMON XVIII.

THE COMMUNION SERVICE. (6).—THE CONSECRATION PRAYER (*John* x. 17, 18) 252

SERMON XIX.

THE COMMUNION SERVICE. (7).—THE EUCHARIST (1 *Corinthians* xv. 45) 266

THE LORD'S PRAYER.

Contents.

SERMON I.

AFTER THIS MANNER THEREFORE PRAY YE: OUR
FATHER WHICH ART IN HEAVEN (*Matthew* vi. 9) . 283

SERMON II.

HALLOWED BE THY NAME (*Matthew* vi. 9) . . . 294

SERMON III.

THY KINGDOM COME (*Matthew* vi. 10) 304

SERMON IV.

THY WILL BE DONE, AS IN HEAVEN, SO IN
EARTH (*Luke* xi. 2) 317

SERMON V.

GIVE US THIS DAY OUR DAILY BREAD (*Matthew* v. 11) 331

SERMON VI.

FORGIVE US OUR DEBTS, AS WE FORGIVE OUR
DEBTORS (*Matthew* vi. 12) 348

SERMON VII.

AND LEAD US NOT INTO TEMPTATION (*Matthew* vi. 13) . PAGE 363

SERMON VIII.

DELIVER US FROM EVIL (*Luke* xi. 4) 375

SERMON IX.

FOR THINE IS THE KINGDOM, AND THE POWER, AND THE GLORY. AMEN (*Matthew* vi. 13) . . 387

THE PRAYER-BOOK

DEDICATION.

To those who understand the Prayers of the Church best, the sufferers on sickbeds; to those who often feel the need of them most, men toiling in the daily business of the world; to those who turn from them with the greatest aversion, persons harassed by doubts and confusions which seem to be mocked by their tone of calmness and trust; these Sermons are affectionately dedicated, by one who has learnt more of the inner meaning of the Prayer-Book from the first class than from all the instructions of divines; who never appreciated its practical substantial character till he felt that the callings of the second class were as sacred as those of the recluse and devotee; and who by converse with the last, by experiencing their difficulties, by seeking to sympathise with them, by discovering his own incompetency to help them, has been led to know what guidance and comfort there is in it for such as never have found or expect to find a home in any religious party, rest in any religious theory.

PREFACE.

In the Chapel of Lincoln's Inn the prayers of the Church are read every day. If certain popular notions respecting these prayers are true, it seemed to me that I had no right to offer them to God myself, or to ask honest men to join me in offering them.

Those notions assume that the Church of England is the result of a compromise; that the Articles embody the opinions of one party to the bargain, the Liturgy those of the other; that every time I put my hand to the former document I proclaim myself in the strictest sense a Protestant, that every time I use the latter I act as a Papist; that, in fact, I am neither, but one of those who, as the poet has affirmed, are equally hateful to God and to his enemies. Such statements are put forth again and again, not by eager opponents, but by politicians who are disposed to regard us as useful, however feeble, safeguards against the zeal of Puritans and Jesuits, and who allege passages from divines not of one party, but of all, not of other ages, but of our own, in proof that we rather prize this view of our position, as a compliment to our sagacity and moderation, than reject it as an imputation upon our sincerity. It is time, surely, for every one to say whether this is what he understands when he calls himself an English

Churchman; whether it is in this sense he desires to fulfil his office as the minister of a congregation.

The members of the legal profession have an especial right to demand an answer to this question from one who ministers among them. We are very ready to accuse them of straining truth to serve the purposes of the advocate; how dare we insinuate such a charge, how dare we exercise the right which we claim of admonishing them of their temptations, if we habitually commit a much graver sin— if our holiest acts involve a kind and an amount of falsehood which I am sure they would not tolerate in the common transactions of life?

In delivering these Sermons, I endeavoured to tell laymen why I could with a clear heart and conscience ask them to take part with me in this Common Prayer. In publishing them I would address myself with equal earnestness and affection to another class, to the younger part of the Clergy, and to those who are preparing for Orders. I would beseech them to reflect that the Clergy may be either the restorers or the utter destroyers of English morality.

If they will manfully determine to begin a reformation from the root, to set right their own thoughts and practices first, before they denounce the sins of the laity and find fault with the oppressions of the State; if they will ask God to cleanse their hearts of all false conventional notions, and to put truth in their inward parts; if they will determine to be the servants of God, and cast off their allegiance to every faction and coterie; if they will ask strength of Him to give up all their high thoughts and proud imaginations and beautiful theories for Christ's sake; they may, they will, impart new honesty to trade; may rescue the merchant from his devotion to Mammon; may force the statesman to cast his politic deceptions to the winds, and to deal manfully with facts; may bring hardworking suffering men to the conviction that God is with them, and that His kingdom is a true kingdom, and that He will set the world right better than they can. Or they may carry all that is corrupt on the surface of society down to its foundation; they may be as conventional in their faith and devotion as the frequenter of clubs is in his social arrangements; as suspicious of their brethren as the man whose soul is in his trade, is of a rival; as fearful that the ark of God will fall as the jobber is that his house of cards will tumble; as savage and reckless partisans as any one who has not renounced the world, the flesh, and the devil. Being men of this stamp, they must bring down judgments upon the whole country; for the sins of the priests will be the sins of the people, and the more the people become possessed by those sins, the more reasonably and bitterly will they hate those who have set the example of them.

The evils which we bring with us to the Prayer-Book are charged upon it. I believe that it is the great witness against them. Some of us would use it as an excuse for self-glorification, for boasting of our superiority to foreign nations, or to the sects at home. Many of us would cast it aside that they may be more like foreign nations, or more like the sects at home. If we used it faithfully, I believe we should find it the most effectual deliverance from that spirit which converts our nationality into an instrument of dividing the nation, our privilege of belonging to a Catholic Church into a plea for exclusiveness. We should find not that we must cease to be Englishmen in order to be men, but that we are Englishmen only as far as we claim our humanity.

I am sure the Liturgy will torment us so long as we continue selfish and divided, therefore I would cling to it. I am sure it may be the instrument of raising us out of our selfishness and divisions; therefore I value it above all artificial schemes of reconciliation, all philosophical theories, all inventions, however skilful, for the reconstruction of human society, in which there evidently lies no such power.*

* Since the First Edition of this volume appeared, I have endeavoured to explain in a Lecture delivered at Southampton (published by Bezer, Fleet Street), what I conceive to be the difference between the 'reconstruction' and the 'reformation' of Society.

[1852.]

THE PRAYER-BOOK.

SERMON I.

INTRODUCTORY.

Preached on the Sunday before Advent, Nov. 26, 1848.

With that all call upon the name of our Lord Jesus Christ, both theirs and ours.—1 CORINTHIANS i. 2.

THE Sunday before Advent concludes the yearly services of the Church. It seems right on such a day to ask ourselves what use we have been making of them during the last twelve months. We who come day after day to offer up the prayers which our forefathers offered up generations ago, should especially examine ourselves on this point.—What have these prayers signified to us? Have they helped us to know ourselves better? Have they helped us to know our fellow-creatures better? Have they helped us to know God better?

I have another reason for speaking of these prayers to-day. In the Lecture this morning* I was obliged to inquire into the characteristics of the Papal system,

* One of the Lectures on the foundation of Bishop Warburton.

B

and to consider in what sense the word Apostate is applicable to it. Our Prayer Book, as you all know, has been called Popish. Lord Chatham, among others, gave it that title, opposing it, as you may remember, to our Calvinistic Articles. His saying has passed from one mouth to another; it has been eagerly quoted against us. Some Clergymen, it would seem, are quite ready to adopt it as their own.

So eminent a man must have had some reason for a sentence which he delivered very authoritatively. Those who have learnt the maxim from him must have felt that there are facts which justify it. The reason is obvious, the facts notorious. There are most conspicuous differences between the Liturgy and the Articles. Only a few of our prayers belong to the age of the Reformation: the Articles were the work of that age. The Prayers do not allude to any Romish tenet for the purpose of denouncing it; the Articles deal with all the peculiar portions of that system, distinctly and formally. There is nothing in the Prayer Book which reminds us of any controversies; the Articles could not have been written till all the questions which occupied the schools between the ninth and sixteenth centuries had been thoroughly discussed. Except the prayers for the Sovereign and the Royal Family our daily Service contains nothing which belongs to England more than to any other country in the world. The Articles have a markedly national character. In short, these formularies differ generically; the one appertaining to worship, the other to theological study; the one spiritual, the other intellectual; the one for teachers and people, the other especially for the teacher.

These contrasts must strike every one. It is on the last I would especially dwell. The Prayers, be they good or evil, are evidently meant for all, the Articles are meant for a class. Whether that class uses them well or ill may affect mightily the interests of all. But this we may say boldly: They cannot but use them ill, if they turn them to a purpose for which they were not intended. The student in every profession must have his text-books: but if he merely repeats the phraseology of his text-books instead of bringing it to bear on the common business of life, he is a pedant and no workman; he has not really mastered his craft. His professional knowledge is only good so far as it enables him to serve people who are not professional, but who are just as much interested in the realities of life as he is. The jargon of a Physician does not make him better able to cure sicknesses; he has been studying medicine that he may not be entangled with this jargon, that he may find his way through the confusions which the equivocal use of words, or the elaboration of theories has brought into the investigation of facts. The Divine who will manfully turn our Articles to this account will, I believe, find them quite invaluable for the method into which they will guide him; for the deliverance from systems which they will enable him to work out for himself; for the tracks of thought which they will teach him to enter upon and to avoid. I do not think that their benefit to the student of theological facts and principles can be easily overrated; I do not think it has yet been appreciated, or that it will be appreciated, till we make the same distinction here which is recognised in every other department of thought between that which is common, real, living, and that which is special, dogmatical, technical. There ought to be such a difference; if none such exists amongst us we are unfortunate: if it does exist, it may explain why Lord Chatham and others have perceived that our Articles and Prayer Book are documents of a widely different character.

But no such observation can explain why these Prayers should be Popish while the Articles are formally directed against Popery. If that assertion is true, we are living in a lie, and have been living in one for three centuries. And it is the blackest of all lies. The moment we take for practising our falsehood is when we profess that we are coming into the presence of the Searcher of hearts, when we are about to worship the God of truth. Who can estimate what the state of a society would be which had been cherishing a falsehood of this kind in its inmost heart for three generations, a falsehood deliberately abetted by those who were called the messengers and witnesses of truth? What plagues and pestilences would not be needful for a body so rotten, what could be effectual?

If it be true, as grave persons—even Divines—are said recently to have affirmed, that the Reformers tempted the people of their day into our national Churches by giving them prayers which would not greatly offend their feelings—leavened as those feelings were by the superstitions to which for so long they had been addicted—no language can be found strong enough to denounce policy so worldly and so infamous. Men are to be beguiled into the service of God by being permitted to mock Him! And this mockery is to be perpetuated in forms which, as the compilers expected, would be used when the paltry excuse for it had disappeared. At all events the fraud now must be not more wicked than useless. What plea have we for perseverance in a course which we have so often been conjured by nonconformists to abandon, and which would seem from this showing to have outgrown the miserable necessity which produced it?

This is a point upon which I must needs feel strongly, for I endeavoured to show you this morning, that the malignity of the Romish system lies in this, that it has defiled and degraded *Worship*, denying man's direct access to his Creator, turning the service of the Living and Invisible Being into the service of that which is visible and earthly. Here was the great mark and token of Apostasy. If then it is just in our worship that we are popish, we are so in the most inward vital sense. We may protest as we please about other points; we have adopted into our hearts the essential poison of the system. All evil doctrines imply this principle, terminate in this result—they rest our approaches to the Eternal God upon a ground inconsistent with His revelation of Himself, they make the worship of Him false. Whatever else our Reformers conceded, here they were bound to make their stand. Here was that which affected the root of every man's life, that which concerned the whole community, that which robbed humanity of the privilege Christ had claimed for it by His death, resurrection, and ascension. There is no question about it; if we are wrong here we are wrong altogether. No dogmatic articles, let them be the best ever framed by man, will heal this wound; they may show how deep it is, they cannot prevent it from leading to death.

Now precisely the claim I put forth on behalf of our Reformers is that they *did* make their stand at this point. My reverence for the Prayer Book rests precisely on this ground, that it asserts and embodies the principle of worship which the Roman system contradicts. If God permit, I will in some future discourses examine the different parts of our Service, that you may see whether they deserve this character or no. To-day I will speak of the Service as a whole, always keeping in mind the object with which I began, that of showing how it bears upon our own hearts. I hope you will never hear from me any such phrases as our 'excellent or incomparable' Liturgy, or any of the compliments to our forefathers or ourselves which are wont to accompany these phrases. I do not think we are to praise the Liturgy, but to use it. If we find that it has been next to the Bible our greatest helper and teacher, we shall shrink with the modesty and piety of pupils from assuming towards it a tone of patronising commendation. When we do not want it for our life, we may begin to talk of it as a beautiful composition: thanks be to God it does not remind us of its own merits when it is bidding us draw nigh to Him.

I. I said this morning, that the main guilt of the Romish system, as it affects worship, is this—it throws us back upon a time when the Gospel of God's reconciliation had not been proclaimed, when the Covenant 'I will be to them a Father, and they shall be to me sons and daughters, and their sins and iniquities will I remember no more,' had not been actually established. It invents ways of access to God, instead of telling us that we may all approach him with clean hearts as His adopted children. The virus of the system lies in this denial; take it away, announce the Gospel, tell men that their Baptism is a reality and not a fiction, and, as Luther constantly affirmed, the axe is laid to the root of the system; the different contrivances for recovering a lost state become inapplicable; the priest must feel that he has another office than to invent such contrivances, or that his occupation is gone. I claim it as the first and noblest distinction of our Prayers, that they set out with assuming God to be a Father, and those that worship Him to be His children. They are written from beginning to end upon this assumption; every other makes them monstrous and contradictory. It confronts you in the first words of the Service; it is so glaring that you almost overlook it; but the further you read the more earnestly you meditate, the more truly you pray, the more certain you are that it is not only on the surface, but reveals the nature of the soil below. That God is actually related to us in his Son, is the doctrine which is the life of the Prayer Book, and apart from which it becomes the idlest and profanest of all documents.

And there is no opportunity for special pleading about the word '*us.*' The compilers of these Prayers knew not who would frequent the churches in which they were to be used. I do not believe they decoyed men into these churches by unfair arts, but I do believe that they expected men of all kinds to be there— Pharisees and Publicans, decent people and conscious sinners—and that they provided a language for each and all of them. And this language was, 'Almighty and most merciful *Father.*' It was a very bold step to take. There was that in their own minds, and in the minds of all about them, which must have been revolted by it. But they did it. Not a vulgar calculation, which lowered them to a level beneath that of their ordinary lives, but a wisdom which carried them above themselves—above their own schemes, notions, and theories—led them to feel—'We have a right to do this : we are honouring God and His covenant by doing it.' But most of all, this thought must have possessed them, 'We are not *Reformers* unless we do it.—We cannot assert the truth of an accomplished salvation, of a perfect Mediator, unless we do it. We cannot put an end to the idolatry into which men have fallen, through ignorance that they can draw nigh to God as a reconciled Father, unless we do it. If there are to be prayers at all, there is positively no course open but this. And if there are not to be prayers, and common prayers, we are bearing no real practical protest against false worship. For it is not a practical protest to be talking against it, or ridiculing it; the one effectual process is to bring back the high and blessed truth which has been taken from us, and to incorporate that truth into the thoughts, feelings, and daily life of our countrymen.'

They were not disobedient to the heavenly intimation—they did not compile prayers after the notions and forms of their own minds, or of their own time. They claimed, indeed, the gift of the Spirit; they had a right to speak, and could speak for themselves. But they delighted to believe that they could use a common language, that the men of their day were the children of God, as the men of other days had been, and therefore that they might take the words of other days with them, when they prayed with the same Spirit, through the same Lord, to the same Father. They would not let it be thought that just then, in consequence of what they had done, some new right or capacity had been acquired for mankind; they only asserted its privileges against those that denied them; ay, against the tendency to deny them which they found in themselves. Prayer to God gave them a property in the words of all holy men who had confessed Him.

II. This is the second characteristic of the Prayer Book I would speak of. It is expressed in the words of my text—'With all that in every place call on the name of our Lord Jesus Christ, both theirs and ours.'

The Romanists asserted that the Church was bound together by the common adherence of its members to a visible Person and a visible Centre. How was this notion to be refuted? Can you overthrow it by calling the Bishop of Rome Antichrist? By denouncing the Church to which he belongs as the Babylonian Harlot? Or by setting up an Anglican system in opposition to this Roman system—by determining that the centre of our fellowship shall be at home instead of in Italy? Or is exclusiveness best defeated by Catholicity, cruel anathemas by an universal fellowship, a mimic ecclesiastical centre, by turning to that invisible spiritual Centre which was made manifest when Christ rose from the dead and ascended on high? Our Reformers adopted the latter form of protest as the most reasonable, and they made it in this way. They found prayers which were based on this universal principle, many of which had been narrowed and debased by the local and idolatrous principle; they removed the outgrowths, they took the substance of the petitions. So they claimed for themselves and for us a fraternity with other ages and other countries, with men whose habits and opinions were most different from their own, with those very Romanists who were slandering and excommunicating them. They claimed fraternity with men who in every place were calling on the name of our Lord Jesus Christ, whether they were tied and bound by the chains of an evil system, or had broken those bonds asunder. They claimed fellowship with men hereafter, who on any other grounds should repudiate their Church and establish some other communion—with men of every tongue and clime, and of every system. If they will not have a Common Prayer with us, we can make our prayers large enough to include them. Nay, to take in Jews, Turks, Infidels and Heretics, all whose nature Christ has borne. For He is theirs as well as ours. He has died for them as for us, He lives for them as for us. Our privilege and glory is to proclaim Him in this character; we forfeit our own right in Him when we fail to assert a right in Him for all mankind. The baptized Church is not set apart as a witness *for* exclusion, but against it. The denial of Christ as the root of all life and all society—this is the exclusive sectarian principle. And it is a principle so near to all of us, into which we are so ready at every moment to fall, that only prayer to our Heavenly Father through the one Mediator, can deliver us from it.

III. Once more. Romanism co-operates with the sensual tendencies of those whose minds are chiefly busy with the outward world—co-operates equally with the morbid self-conscious tendencies of those whose inclinations are towards abstraction and mysticism. No protest can be effectual for any moral purpose which does not counterwork its influence in both these directions. But how are Articles to counterwork it in either? What food do they offer to the craving of those who long for show and ceremonial, or to those who feel that there is an unseen and mysterious world near them into which they are meant to penetrate? 'Take away these husks of words, give us symbols,' is the cry of one, 'Take away these husks, let us have some spiritual food,' is the equally vehement cry of the other. Both have been heard in other days—they are raised with exceeding loudness in our own. You may denounce them, but you cannot stifle them. The Reformers knew they could not. But this they could do. They could treat men—not a few here and there with special tastes and tempers of mind—not easy men with plenty of leisure for self-contemplation—but the poorest no less than the richest, the busiest no less than the idlest, as spiritual beings, with spiritual necessities, with spiritual appetites, which God's Spirit is ever seeking to awaken, and the gratification of which, instead of unfitting them for the common toil of life is precisely the preparation for it, precisely the means of enabling them to be clear, straight-forward, manly; to fulfil their different callings in the belief that each one of them, be it grand or petty, sacred or secular in the vocabulary of men, is a holy calling in the sight of God. But to assert that man is a spiritual being in this sense, you must claim for him a right and power to pray—you must give him a common prayer—*common prayer* in every sense of the word, not *special* prayers adapted to special temperaments and moods of character, but human; not refined and artificial, but practical; reaching to the throne of God, meeting the daily lowly duties of man. If our spiritual people will have their spirituality to themselves, if they do not like to acknowledge that all men have spirits, if they think that they bring a set of spiritual feelings with them, when they should come to be quickened and renewed by God's Spirit, they must go empty away. 'Blessed are the poor in spirit, for *theirs* is the kingdom of Heaven.'

What Englishmen chiefly want is a clear recognition that the spiritual is also the practical—that it belongs not more to the temple than to the counting-house and the workshop. This the Reformers provided. They were not equally concerned to provide us with a satisfaction of that love of art and symbol, which, though genuine and human, is not characteristic of all nations in the same degree, of our own perhaps less than any. It was their duty however, I conceive, to testify, clearly and strongly, that the whole realm of nature and art belongs to the redeemed spirit, and that it must not abjure its inheritance. The old places of worship, the old forms of worship, had endeavoured to bear this witness. They had been turned into witnesses that man is a slave of the senses and of nature. From this horrible degradation it behoved the Reformers, at all risks, to raise their countrymen. But it was no vulgar expediency to believe and act upon the conviction, that they would not be raised out of it, or would be in the greatest danger of relapsing into it, if worship was wholly separated from sensible associations—if the Priest of Creation did not present the first fruits of nature, as well as himself, to the Lord of All. Quaker-worship has its own meaning and truth. Romanist-worship has its own meaning and truth. A sound national worship should not be a compromise between them, but should justify the principle of each, and prevent them from leading, by opposite routes, to the same fatal issue.

It is not willingly, my brethren, that I have given these remarks an aspect of controversy. In the question which has recently drawn forth a comparison between the Articles and the Liturgy, I take exceedingly little interest. Which supplies the best test of heresy I do not know; for I have never looked upon either of them as designed for this purpose. If we use the Articles to find out the errors of other men, and not to help us out of our own, I do not think we shall ever know what they mean, or in any real sense believe them. If we use the Prayer Book, not that we may worship God, but that we may lay snares for men, I am sure that it will prove our curse and damnation. I am greatly afraid of heresy, but I believe it is most prevalent amongst those who are ever on the search for it; who are continually denying some portion of truth in their eagerness to convict their brethren of denying some other portion of it. I claim the Prayer Book and Articles both, as the protection for those who repudiate the parties into which our Church is divided, from their common assaults. I claim them for the protection of these parties from the ferocity of each other. I claim them as a protection of the Truth from their distractions and mutilations. But most of all, dear brethren, I claim this Prayer Book as a witness against your sins and mine. As that, which, while we try to use it faithfully and simply, will lay bare to us falsehoods which have been hidden from ourselves, as that which will show us how we may be set free from them, as that which God designs to be a mighty instrument, and which He will yet make a mighty instrument, of restoring real christian Godliness to a disputatious, hypocritical, Mammon-worshipping land.

SERMON II.

THE CONFESSION.

Preached on Advent Sunday, Dec. 3, 1848.

The lofty looks of man shall be humbled, and the haughtiness of man shall be bowed down, and the Lord alone shall be exalted in that day.—ISAIAH ii. 11.

THE words "Prepare to meet thy God" which occur in one of the Minor Prophets, have been used again and again as motto to Sermons on preparation for death. I will not dispute the propriety of the application, but assuredly they had no such meaning in the mind of him who originally spoke them. Like all the Prophets he is calling upon his countrymen to meet their God, who was about to reveal himself in fearful judgments upon their land. It was not death which would first bring them into the presence of the Lord whom they were forgetting. They were in his presence then. The forgetting of His presence was their great sin, the cause of all their other sins. To cure them of that forgetfulness, He was coming out of his place to punish them. He was awakening their conscience to feel that

He was there. Let them listen to his voice, interpret it rightly, and prepare themselves to meet him.

This is the spirit of every prophet, of that one especially and characteristically whom we have begun to read on this day. Our Advent lessons are taken from him for this very reason. A day of the Lord is at hand; this is the language of Isaiah. A day of the Lord is at hand; this is the language of the Church from year to year. Was the Prophet deceiving his countrymen when he said so? Assuredly they did not find that he was. They were trembling at an expected invasion from Samaria and Syria. That came to nothing, as he told them it would. But the armies of Sennacherib, which swept away the enemies they were afraid of, came down also upon the fenced cities of Judah, and laid siege to Jerusalem. The hypocrites among them felt that it was a day of the Lord, that He was indeed looking at them, looking into them, and calling them to account for the sins which they had hidden from the eyes of men. The faithful men felt also that it was a day of the Lord, and therefore strengthened their hearts, knowing that He would not forsake any that trusted in him, and that the end of his judgment was to establish righteousness in the earth.

The effects were different, as the effects of the same tree or meadow would be on two persons, one of whom connected it with the discourse and look of a dear friend, and the other with some midnight murder. But both alike bore witness to the truth of the Seer's language. The event might be called an Assyrian invasion, or by any other name; but 'the Judge is here, the books are opened'—this was what each understood to be the meaning of the event; it could not be interpreted otherwise.

That some event or series of events will be continually bearing witness to the everlasting truth of God's presence with us, that these events or series of events will be striking and portentous in proportion to the degree in which the truth has gone out of men's minds, that each day of the Lord carries in it the foretaste of a final day, when no spirit in the universe shall be able to evade the sense and certainty of its being naked and open before God,—this is the principle which the season of Advent affirms. Only it is impossible for the Christian Church to speak merely of *a* Presence or *a* Lord. She must declare what manner of being He is whom she proclaims to the world as its King. It is He who entered into Jerusalem meek and sitting upon an ass,—He, and no other, who is proving in each age by some signal evidence that he is judge himself, that all powers are subject to Him, and that all which rule for some other ends than His ends must come to naught.

My brethren, if on the Advent Sunday of 1847 any preacher here or elsewhere had tried to impress you with the belief that some signs and wonders were actually near at hand, if he had tasked his imagination or his skill in interpreting the hard sayings in Scripture, to tell you minutely what these signs and wonders would be,—are you not sure that his anticipations would have been poor and cold when compared with the things which you have heard of and almost seen in the interval between that day and this? The flourishes and exaggerations of rhetoric, puerile always, become absolutely ridiculous when they are set side by side with the experiences through which Europe has been passing and is passing. Do you really think the invasion of Palestine by Sennacherib was a more wonderful event than the overthrowing of nearly all the greatest powers, civil and ecclesiastical, in Christendom? And yet we know—do not we all know?—that it is possible, yes and most easy, to read of all these transactions, to talk about them, to be interested in them, and yet not to feel appalled and confounded, not to be interrupted in any business or pleasure by them, not to think as much about them as about the most insignificant troubles or gratifications of the passing hour. Whence comes this strange indifference? How may it be cured? There is everything to give impressiveness to the events we hear of. We get the report of them from eye-witnesses; we meet those who have taken part in them; we have no doubt that they have taken place; no doubt that we are greatly affected by them.

All this is not sufficient. The thunder is not near enough yet. We are not really convinced that the voice is meant for us. If I dared to say how we shall be taught that it is meant for us generally and individually, as citizens of the state, and at our own hearths and homes during the next year, you would rightly condemn me for my presumption. But may it not be that those who survive till the Advent Sunday of 1849, will regard all,—even the most seemingly extravagant of such predictions,—just as we now regard any which attempted twelvemonths ago to define what would come upon us?

To speak such words in the ears of persons who have weak nerves and would be merely frightened by them, is foolish and wrong. Men who are living and mixing in the world's bustle are not very susceptible of such terrors; perhaps they would be no better if they were. The prophets, instead of exciting the timidity of their countrymen, sternly rebuke it, and diligently cultivate the opposite temper in themselves. 'The Lord,' says Isaiah, 'spake thus to me with a strong hand, that I should not walk in the way of this people, saying, Say ye not, A confederacy, to all those to whom this people shall say, A confederacy; neither fear ye their fear, nor be afraid.' But how were they to avoid this danger? how were they to meet coming evils with a prepared and manly spirit? 'Sanctify the Lord of Hosts himself in your hearts, and let Him be your fear, and Him be your dread.' This is the needful, the only effectual discipline; whatever leads you to consider dark events as the signs that He, in whom is light and no darkness at all, is coming forth to scatter the darkness, will cause the indifference of your minds and their cowardice to disappear together: without this they will dwell together; the first, sometimes the more obvious, sometimes the other; but doubt and unbelief nearly always at the root of the dread, a base shrinking from the future always mixed with the careless defiance of it. To be thoroughly persuaded that the lofty looks of men will be humbled, and the haughtiness of men laid low, and that the Lord alone will be exalted in that day; to be persuaded that so it must be, and to be thankful for the persuasion, this is the secret for meeting pestilences, famines, revolutions, whatever may be in store for us in the days that are at hand.

If so, the Church which gives us this lesson at the

opening of her year, should provide us with the means of deepening and making it effectual throughout that year. To talk to us about judgments, and the preparation for them, and the sin of being indifferent to them, and the advantage of owning God's hand in them,—how little of real help lies in all this! A wise teacher who knows that we need so much, must know that we need something more. We need to be put in the way of humbling our own lofty looks, of laying low our own haughtiness, of exalting the Lord alone. It is not a habit which we find specially easy of acquisition, not one which comes by merely wishing that we had it, not one which we can afford to practise awhile and then discontinue. It must be wrought into the tissue of our lives, or the day will come upon us unawares, and we shall be found high and lifted up at the moment when we shall most wish to hide ourselves in the dust.

Now, I apprehend that our daily Confession is given us for this end; and that, if we use it aright, it will answer this end. The Church, like the Bible, does not say, Prepare to meet thy death, but, 'Prepare to meet thy God.' She does not say, Come, and perform certain services because there is a future world, and only by such services can you avert the perils or earn the rewards of it; but she says, 'Come, because God is with you now—because intercourse with Him now is essential to your life here as well as hereafter—because without it you cannot do the works of men, and possess the rights of men. You are spirits, and you have been redeemed by the Father of Spirits, for his service: only from Him can you gain strength to act as if your existence was a reality, and

not a dream? But how can your approach to Him be a
reality, and not a dream? Has it not often seemed to
you that worship was the merest form and delusion? Had
you not good ground for thinking so? Were you not
conscious that you were merely going through a form
and a delusion while you were engaged in it? How
was this? Was there some obstacle to be removed
between you and Him upon whose name you were
calling? You are sure there must have been such an
obstacle. Was it distance of place? Your reason
and conscience assure you that it was not. Was it
the reluctance of God to hear your prayers? A very
natural and nearly inevitable conclusion, if the Gospel
of Christ be a lie; impossible, if it is true. Or some
inherent absurdity in the notion of a creature holding
intercourse with a Creator? Yet it is an absurdity
which you never have been able to clear your mind of,
and never will be able, till you have reduced yourself
to the condition of a mere animal. Look as deeply
into the subject as you may, and you will come back
to the old conclusion. The hindrance is a moral and
not a physical one; it is in the creature, and not in
the Creator. It is the sense of evil; the consciousness of having done insincere, false acts; of having
lived in an insincere, false state. This consciousness
indisposes the heart to feel that an eye which cannot
behold iniquity is beholding it. The man goes out of
the presence of God, and dwells apart from Him as
Cain did; and yet he is haunted by that presence
whithersoever he goes. He cannot put it away from
him, yet he cannot enter into it. Converse with God
seems incredible, impossible; and yet there is a
witness within that it ought to be, that it must be,

the deepest of all verities; and that if it is transformed into a lie, all things else must suffer the same change. What a web is here! what an infinite complication and contradiction! but a complication and contradiction in which we have all, in one measure or other, been actually involved. What way is there out of it? Still, says the Church, the old way—you may try many—you will find but this, 'I will confess my sins unto the Lord. I will say that I am in a complication, a falsehood, and that I cannot deliver myself from it; that all my thoughts, efforts, contrivances, only bring me further into it. I will say, O Thou who knowest what I am, and where I am, bring me out of these mists, these false confused lights, into the open day.' A reasonable prayer if God is merciful, and man is weak—if God is our Father, and we are his children: the only prayer oftentimes which it is possible for man to offer: the one which he offers, because he feels that he cannot pray. And surely there is no humbling of man's lofty looks—there is no lowering his haughtiness like this. He brings nothing; he casts himself in mere dependence and despair before One who must raise him, if he is not to sink further and further; who must make him true, if he is not to become falser and falser.

I press this thought upon you. Our daily confession of sins to an Almighty and most Merciful Father, our prayer that He would restore us, is a daily witness against our insincerity, a daily cry to be delivered from it. You know how continually it is charged upon these Prayers, that they lead to insincerity; that the repetition of them is an insincere act. You know with what vehemence men cry out in our day, as they did in former days, 'No more of this mockery; we are weary of it; we will be sincere, whatever else we are.' By all means let such words be spoken; it is good for us that they should; it is needful that we should hear them, for they have an awful truth in them. We have contrived to make acts of confession, as well as all other acts, profane and unreal. It cannot be denied. We have done it, we and our fathers. We, our priests, our princes, our people, are all in this sin. Therefore God is sending judgments upon us; therefore He will send yet more. To show what are the special sins which provoke Him, is not our function; but we know that we are right, when we say it is falsehood—falsehood in the ordinary transactions of ordinary life—falsehood in our holy things. Against this the prophets of the Jews lifted up their voice; against this we believe God is uttering His voice in every age. Unreal profession—feigning to be what we are not—this must be the most hateful of all things in His eyes. And which of us can say, I am pure of this crime? Those who accuse us think that *they* can. They *will* be sincere. How? By talking of sincerity? By proclaiming what a good thing it is? By saying to yourselves and others, 'How very sincere we are?' Oh miserable delusion! Lie beneath all lies! Lie which must ever multiply and reproduce itself, till it converts the whole man in whom it dwells into its own likeness! Be sure of this; till you have done trusting in your own sincerity, you will never be sincere. Till you know how much insincerity is in you, and frankly confess it, and have found some one to whom you can confess it, and who will set you right, you are not in the way to be sincere.

But to have a confession set before us which
brings this guilt to our minds; which tells us that it
has been the guilt of our forefathers as well as our
own; that though our circumstances have changed so
greatly, our temptations and dangers have not changed
—this is not to make us insincere. To be told that
though we have wandered ever so far from God's
truth He is not changed, that He is still Absolute
Truth, and is still willing to raise us out of our falsehood, is not to make us insincere. To be shown that
though our conditions in life are different, though
each has a peculiar temperament and constitution,
though each is conscious of a multitude of thoughts
and acts which no other man knows, though none can
tell what is going on at any moment in his neighbour's
heart, yet that the radical evil is the same, and that all
may confess it together, and that each may feel it
and confess it for the other, is not to make us insincere. For our cheating and hypocrisies one towards
another, and for the deep hiding of our counsels from
God, the Prayer Book is not answerable. Let each
ask himself, whether, if he had used the Prayer Book
as his conscience bids him use it, according to its
natural signification, it might not have been the
mightiest means of preserving him from these evils.
In every world, in the religious world especially, we
find people busy in persuading their own circle
and coterie that they are right, and that all others
are wrong—busy in assuring us that the highest
Christianity consists in our setting at naught our
Lord's command, by taking motes out of our brother's
eye, while a beam is in our own. Why has not this
vile hypocrisy utterly destroyed us? How is it that

any life is left? May not these words which have lasted on through three hundred years of use and abuse, and which must have gone up to heaven from many thousands of burdened and earnest hearts, have had a counteracting power; may we not owe it in a great measure to them that our national faith and honesty have resisted in any degree the influences secular and religious which have been undermining them?

The Reformers had one special form of falsehood which it behoved them to encounter, one which struck equally at the root of the common life and of the solemn acts of the English people. The sense of sins committed, of good deeds left undone, drove them to the confessional; there each conscience was dealt with according to its separate misery; there acts were prescribed external and internal for the removal of the special burden; thence the sinner went forth, it might be with reverence, it might be with hatred, for the person who had imposed the task or granted the indulgence, it might be to live in wretched fear, it might be to plunge more deeply into unclean living— certainly with no feeling that the conscience itself could be set free, that the favour of God was given not purchased, that He had himself broken the chains which bind men to earth, and had commanded them to come boldly into his presence through the one Mediator, and enjoy perfect freedom. To teach that lesson was the great business of the Reformation; I ask, as I asked last Sunday, Could any mere dogmas teach it? Could denunciations of Rome and the Confessional teach it? Alas for those who make the experiment! They have to war with some of the strongest instincts of human nature, and they go to the fight with no armour but one of phrases and sentences. 'It is cruel,' they say, 'to bind chains on the conscience, to appoint penances and mortifications which cannot take away sin.' But the sin-sick conscience craves this treatment. It asks for impositions. It meets the priest half-way; it compels him to do what he would not himself have thought of doing. You find this to be the case, and you talk about the corruptions and delusions of the unregenerate heart. Very good language, if you will only show how these corruptions may be thrown off. But the effect of your teaching is to leave the impression upon the mind of your pupil that it is very sinful in him to obey these impulses, and yet that they cannot be disobeyed till some great crisis takes place in his mental history. Before that crisis comes, can you blame him if he goes elsewhere, if he betakes himself to those who profess that they understand all the diseases of the conscience, and who are ready to administer the medicines which it desires for itself? The truth must be spoken. Those who think that they can exorcise the spirit of Romanism will find that it is lurking very near them when they are denouncing most furiously its external and distant appearances; in themselves or in their children the symptoms will appear with more than their old virulence.

Would you try what seems a more decisive remedy? Would you revolutionise the whole mind of a country, banish faith, canonise Atheism? That experiment has been made. Has it answered for this end? Has it got rid of the Confessional? Has it made the Confessional less mischievous? The modern literature of France makes answer; Confessors are scattered over the land like locusts; no house is safe from their invasions; they destroy the authority of the husband, of the father; their ranks are so close that we cannot break through them; their influence so secret and invisible that we cannot grapple with it. I do not inquire how much of this statement is exaggerated; it is often put into forms too rhetorical and passionate to be credible; but it is surely an acknowledgment from philosophers and sceptics that philosophy and scepticism have not found themselves able to cope with this antagonist. Men who would be most inclined to preach the feebleness of theological influences, at all events in this nineteenth century, leave us with the impression that a system of religious fraud is almost omnipotent.

That doctrine, my brethren, we are solemnly pledged not to receive. How then, if not in either of these ways, may the spell be broken? We may answer in the words which the Attendant Spirit in Milton's poem addresses to the two brothers when they had let the 'foul enchanter 'scape:'

> 'Oh! ye mistook: ye should have snatched his wand,
> And held him fast; without his rod reversed
> And backward mutters of dissevering power,
> We cannot free the Lady who sits here
> In stony fetters, fixed and motionless.'

We cannot banish the evils of the Confessional till we have initiated men into the meaning and mystery of confession; we cannot lead them to cease from men whose breath is in their nostrils, till we have persuaded them to go up to the Mountain of the Lord, to the house of the God of Israel, that He may teach them of his ways, and that they may walk in his paths; we cannot bid them cast the idols which they have made each for himself to worship to the moles and to the bats, till we have shown them what blessing, what deliverance there is in fearing the Lord and giving glory to him. Thus is 'the wand snatched,' the 'rod reversed;' here are 'the backward mutters of dissevering power.' We are tied and bound with the chain of our sins, we know that we are; but even in these chains we may arise and go to our Father. That name has not lost its truth and power, because we have been rebellious children, because we have erred and strayed from God's ways like lost sheep, and have broken His holy laws, and have left undone what we ought to have done, and have done what we ought not to have done. We are not to expect crises in our lives before we take up our rights; we are not to wait till an angel troubles the water before we obey the command of the Lord of Angels, 'Rise up and walk.' There is no strength—no health in *us*. But 'thou O Lord, have mercy upon us, miserable offenders: Spare thou them which confess their faults,' all who come before thee; all of every creed, in every condition of suffering or evil, who are redeemed by the same blood, with whom the same spirit is striving. Restore thou them to their true estate. Enable them to show forth what they are in all they do, and think, and speak; to live a godly, righteous, and sober life, to the glory of thy holy Name. And this for His sake who is the head of the whole family in heaven and earth, the bond of peace between God and man, between man and man.

The words are large and simple; they belong to

the time in which they were written and to our time; to Advent Sunday and to all Sundays; to days of work and days of rest. They do not go into the minutiæ of your experience just because your comfort will consist in laying that experience before Him who understands it all; because your consciences are seldom the better, often much the worse, for the probing of human instruments; because we ought to understand that when each man comes with his own spirit's burden, with the plague of his own heart, before the Great Deliverer, he is surely surrounded by a multitude of sufferers with whom he may sympathise, for whom he prays; seeing that Christ came in great humility to sympathise with them, seeing that He lives in the glory of the Father to make intercession for them.

SERMON III.

THE ABSOLUTION.

Preached on the Second Sunday in Advent, Dec. 10, 1848.

And the Scribes and the Pharisees began to reason, saying, Who is this which speaketh blasphemies? Who can forgive sins, but God alone?—LUKE v. 21.

THE Scribes and Pharisees did not merely pretend to feel horror when our Lord said to the paralytic man, 'Son, thy sins be forgiven thee.' Such horror as they were capable of they did actually feel. They could not doubt that the formula was a correct one—'None can forgive sins, but God only.' And if it was correct, it could not safely be trifled with. If sins could be forgiven at once, and so easily, what security was there against the continual commission of them? If the people began to fancy that they might at the word of a man be discharged from the apprehension of future punishment which haunted them, what would become of religious awe? What need could there be for any religious practices? All arguments of civil and spiritual policy were against the tolerance of so monstrous a claim.

We cannot deny that there may have been something more in their minds than this calculation of consequences. A recollection that sin was that against which Sinai had uttered its thunders; against which the whole Divine Word had been directed; which was the contradiction to the Nature of God; which only He knew, and only He could remit—this no doubt was in their minds, a witness of truth, not yet extinguished by all the dryness, selfishness, cruelty, which dwelt beside it. The two convictions together—mingling strangely with rage at one who was exercising a secret power of which they knew nothing—led them to say in their hearts, 'Who is this that speaketh blasphemies?'

Was their fear unreasonable that men might contract an indifference to the civil penalties of crime, if they could hope for a pardon from some one who, they believed, was higher than the Law? Certainly not: experience has justified it. Were they wrong in thinking that there was a danger of spiritual influences being weakened, if men learnt to think lightly of the evil they had done, or might do? There is every warrant in the history of individuals and nations for such an opinion. Is it an idle notion, that if sin is not directly connected with rebellion against God—if He is not regarded as our deliverer from it, there will be a low appreciation of its hatefulness? Far from being an idle notion, it was a truth which the Scribes would have done well to meditate upon far more deeply than they had ever yet done.

For this is the true charge against them—They had never fairly grappled with any of these thoughts—Sin, Forgiveness, God. They had read about them in their sacred books; they had studied all traditions which turn upon them; they had discoursed upon them to the people; but they had never understood that those sacred books were speaking of realities; they did not know that those traditions, if they were not the merest trifling, or in direct violation of the Divine commandments, were the results of the actual experience of living men. They did not know that the people were not machines, made to obey a penal law, or to go through a set of religious exercises, but were actual men, who felt the burden of sin, needed forgiveness, were crying out, if ever so confusedly, for a living God. 'Their fear of me is taught by the precepts of men.' This was the charge which the Prophets brought against the Jewish teachers and people of their day; this was the charge which our Lord applied to those who denounced him as a blasphemer. They had the notion of Sin accurately defined; a multitude of rules for ascertaining the weights and measures of particular sins; numerous distinctions respecting the possibilities and degrees of pardon, and the means of obtaining it. And every rule of the law about the way of approaching the Most High God, the whole scheme of sacrifices, and which was suitable in each case, they had learnt perfectly by heart. But that it was needful to be free from Sin in its root and principle; that all pardon which does not lead to this result is vain and mischievous; that God is in very truth the Deliverer and Absolver; these convictions were wholly alien from their state of mind. Yet, if there was one truth which was written with sunbeams in the Law and Prophets, it was this last. How had the Lord revealed himself to Moses in the bush, when he trembled and durst not behold? As one who had heard the cry of his people against their taskmasters, and would deliver them. How had He spoken on that dreadful day of Sinai, when the Law was proclaimed?—' I am the Lord thy God, who have brought thee out of the land of Egypt, out of the house of bondage.' How did he declare himself after the great sin of the golden calf had been committed? —' I am the Lord, the Lord God, merciful and gracious —forgiving iniquity, and transgression, and sin.' What was it that every Israelite was to tell his child, when he was asked, ' What meaneth this feast that ye keep from generation to generation?' He was to say, ' It is the memorial of the Lord's deliverance of us and of our forefathers.' By what name does the Psalmist, crushed under the sense of evil without and within—of enemies bodily and spiritual—and possessed with the most awful sense of God as a hater of evil— invoke Him? As a refuge, and high tower, and Saviour, to whom men may escape, as one who compasseth his people about with songs of deliverance. And, be it observed, that this character is not opposed to that of a Judge; as if the two, though not actually incompatible, yet suggested two most different trains of thought and feeling. On the contrary, they are identified. ' Arise, thou Judge of the Earth,' is again and again taken as an equivalent expression to 'Arise, thou who wilt set the Earth free from its bondage and its curse.' Such were the testimonies of their own Scriptures—testimonies lying on the surface of them —going into the depths of them—pervading and explaining the whole of the Divine Economy—and yet by these accurate and laborious interpreters wholly overlooked. God, in their conception of Him, was not a Deliverer or Absolver at all. That which awakened the awe of Moses, and David, and the Prophets, seemed to them utterly destructive of awe. The only way of keeping up reverence in their own minds or in the minds of the people, was to regard Him as one who willeth the death of the sinner, but who might be persuaded, by certain methods, to give up that will, and to sell him forgiveness.

Another consequence followed inevitably from this. As the Old Testament is throughout a history of God's deliverances of men, so it is throughout a history of His deliverances of them by men. Every Jewish lawgiver, patriarch, chieftain, judge, prophet, and king, is said to be called out for the purpose of filling some part in the scheme of God's deliverance: so far as he understood that he was to be a deliverer, so far he fulfilled his vocation; so far as he fancied that he had some other or higher work than this, so far he did evil in the sight of the Lord. You will find no exception. Joseph, Moses, Joshua, Samson, Gideon, Samuel, David, Hezekiah, Ezra; all are deliverers; all break some yoke of bondage from off the neck of the people; all do it in the name of the Invisible Lord; all confess themselves to be acting as His servants, to be doing the task which He has given them to do. God was the Deliverer, man was the instrument and agent of His deliverance. But seeing that there is one kind of emancipation which is the highest, the most necessary, the most universal of all, that without which other freedom is impossible, that of which all other freedom is either the foretaste or the fulfilment—that which concerns every human being, that which most directly and intimately concerns him as he feels that he is related to God,—the deliverance or absolution of the conscience or inner man, the breaking of the fetters by which it is tied and bound in order that it may be able to offer up a true and acceptable service to its unseen Lord; therefore is the *Priest* set apart by a more special consecration, by a more continuous ordinance, to reveal God in this high character, to be the instrument for imparting His inmost mind to His creature, for working out the thorough redemption of that creature. And as every one of the appointed deliverers of whom I have spoken, by that which he did and that which he could but do, by the witness which he bore that all his inspirations were of God, that he was only in an imperfect way showing forth His character and mind to men; by the witness also which he bore that this character and mind could only be revealed in a man; that a man only can be the true image of God, and that to be that he must have entire sympathy with the whole race and with every one of its members; as each was thus declaring that there must be a perfect Son of God, and a perfect Son of Man, and was preparing the way for His manifestation; so did the Priests still more especially and remarkably declare that only such a one could carry out the meaning of *their* mission, and show that they had not been sent into the world to deceive it. When the Scribes and Pharisees said, 'This man blasphemeth,' because he had said to a sick man, 'Thy sins be forgiven thee,' they did but express in one instance their general feeling. It was but part of the general assertion, 'By our law he ought to die, because he made Himself the Son of God.' But they perceived, and the instinct was a true one, that if there were a number of proofs to make up the charge, this was the highest and most capital one. And there could be no hope that this would be a solitary exercise of such a power. Our Lord spoke in every discourse of a Kingdom; a Kingdom of God, a Kingdom of Heaven, a Kingdom of His Father. What could such words mean if they did not indicate that the society, whatever it might be, which He was establishing would recognise more distinctly than any other had ever done, that Men and God are not separated but united, and that in some higher sense than before men can utter forth God's will as an Absolver?

Must not even the distant dream of such a state of things have been most revolting to the Pharisee? He was exercising a power—a very great power—over the minds of his countrymen. They looked up to him as a teacher at once and a specimen of righteousness. They received his doctrines to a certain extent, at least they obeyed his decrees. But it was not an absolving power; it was directly the reverse of such a power. The Pharisee was riveting all chains of custom and tradition upon the hearts of his disciples, he was bringing their consciences day by day into a greater bondage and contradiction, he was keeping them more and more from any trust in God. What must he have thought of the proclamation of a Law of Liberty? of a Gospel which would enable men to serve God without fear? of a covenant with men not as servants but as sons? He had no notion of a morality which does not proceed from a dread of penalties, or an expectation of prizes; from the fear that the one will probably be incurred, the other assuredly not won, if certain acts and services are not performed. He had no conception that the people, at all events, could be kept from evil courses in any way but this. Whatever led them to believe and hope in God, instead of regarding Him as an object of terror, would, the Pharisees believed, lead to the dissolution of society. And yet they must have known what kind of morality they had succeeded in producing. Every page of Josephus testifies that domestic crimes of the blackest kind, suspicion in all classes of society, insurrections, murders, so far from being hindered by the religious sanctions to which the Pharisees resorted, were often very clearly traceable to them.

It was precisely because the Apostles of our Lord proclaimed a *Gospel*, because they preached forgiveness of sin, because they declared God to have made a new Covenant with men, of which this was the tenor, 'I will be to them a Father, and they shall be to me children, and their sins and iniquities will I remember no more,' that they did provide any effectual remedy for this corruption, that they did lay the foundation of a high moral state. They attacked evil in its first principle; they said, 'How can ye, *being* evil, *do good* things?' They told men that they were not meant to be evil, that they were created in Christ Jesus to good works, that He was the real root of humanity; that they might be reunited to that root and receive sap from it, and so might bring forth living fruits. They proclaimed God, the Father of Jesus Christ, to be the great Absolver, to have given His Son for men that He might take their nature, and might claim those who bore it as His brethren, and might endue them with power to be like Him, pure, brave, gentle, loving one another as *He* loved them who had called them to be His friends and ministers and fellow-workers, loving the world as He loved it who had died for it. This was the regeneration of humanity, the reconstitution of it upon its true ground, the acknowledgment of it and of those who would be content to show it forth as truly formed in God's image. The Gospel is the great absolution of the race; the Christian kingdom embodies the principle of that absolution. That kingdom stands in the name of the Father, from whom the absolution proceeds, who is its author and ground; of the Son, the High Priest of the race, in whom it is accomplished, and who ever lives to claim it for men; of the Holy Spirit the Comforter, who endows the Christian family with the life and sense and fruits of it. Under this economy surely, not less than under the last, must every man look upon himself as God's servant in his especial work and office, to secure for his brethren the freedom which has been obtained for them, to explain the nature of it, to educate men into the living apprehension of it, to resist every invasion of it, to clear his own mind of every notion that is inconsistent with it, to labour for the reformation of every society that has lost the belief of it, or has never yet realised the benefits of it.

And if so, and if each man is not to intrude upon the work assigned to his neighbour, but simply in his own work to act as God's servant for the deliverance of his fellows, we should surely expect to find in this economy, as much as in the last, an order of men who, from generation to generation, would set forth God as an Absolver, not only in the lower and subordinate senses, but in the highest sense of all—as the Absolver of the conscience and spirit of man, as the Deliverer from the essential evil.

I should be much shaken in this conclusion by the vehement language in which able and excellent men have expressed their dissent from it—denouncing the idea of a priesthood as a relic of the old world, and as quite unsuited to this;—if it were not clear to me that they regard the elder priesthood in quite a different way from that in which I have represented it, and from that in which, I think, it is represented in the Old Testament. They speak of it as an expression of man's desire to find his way into the presence of God; Moses and the Prophets speak of it as the expression of God's character, and of His will to bring men into His presence. If the Priest's office stood on the first ground, it must of course be obsolete when the way into the Holiest Place is revealed; if it be the utterance of the mind of Him who is the same yesterday and to-day and forever, there is no reason why it should be less needful in one time than another; when He has bestowed the highest glory of which the race is capable upon us than when He was only educating us for that glory. Worship does not cease when it becomes in the full sense possible. God does not remove from man the witness that He is really present with him, because He has fully revealed that He is.

But perhaps in the latter days that witness has ceased to be needful. Men understand their privileges so well, there is no call for any of the charters and signs of freedom: slavery has become altogether impossible. The facts on which the writers I have spoken of rest their main arguments against a Priesthood, are a satisfactory refutation of *this* dream. They say, and say most truly, the Christian Priesthood may become—has become—an instrument of binding the consciences, just as the heathen or corrupted Jewish priesthood did. There is the same peril now as before in this institution; if we love Christian liberty, we must be continually on our watch against it.

Certainly, other instruments were contributing to rob men of their rights, but this was the most efficient instrument. And why was it the most efficient? And why does the conscience rise up against *this* tyranny, and denounce it with *more* righteous vehemence than any other? And why did Priests—Priests especially— feel that it was *their* work to put this tyranny down? Precisely because this was the most flagrant contradiction of the purpose for which the order existed; because, when the priest became merely or chiefly the oppressor of his brethren, it was certain that society was corrupt at its very core; that faith in God was departed from those who professed it most; that God would raise up some witnesses for Himself. And it was most probable that those witnesses would be among the men whom He had commissioned to be the absolvers of His people's hearts and consciences. The fact that such an order did exist was the perpetual protest against its abuse—against the infinite disorders of which its members were guilty. The Reformers in the sixteenth century felt the contradiction more vividly, more intensely, than we feel it; not more, however, than we should feel it. It was no doubt their first business to assert, by all means, that God was the Absolver; every other assertion was subordinate to that. Priests, they said, must perish if they interfere with the truth, that men of every class have the right of drawing nigh to God through faith in Christ.

It was easy to say this; but did the mischief which some of them saw lurking in the name of Priest disappear out of their communities? No! it was necessary to have teachers who could explain what kind of faith, what amount of faith, constituted man's right to claim God as his Father, and approach Him. An order of Protestant Priests, or, if you like the word better, Scribes, organised itself for this purpose; a new form of slavery appeared; a new set of men to pervert the truth that God is the great Absolver in Christ; that men are sent into the world to carry out this object of His government. Protestant divines have maligned God's character as much as Popish divines; they have acted on the notion that it is blasphemy to suppose that the Son of Man does now on earth forgive sins; they have put the Article in the Creed to death which first gave life to Luther. So that poor men and women, as well as cultivated men, have fled back to Romanism, hoping to find there the pardon and peace which their own communion could not give.

In the seventeenth century Milton discovered that New Presbyter was but Old Priest writ large. What has been our experience since? Men have denounced the idea of Priesthood—ridiculed it—argued against it—invoked the wise in their bright minds to kindle such lamps as would make its pale name shrink and shrivel back to the Hell from whence it first was hurled. But it clings to them still. They cast it off in one shape—it reappears in another. The Encyclopædist succeeded to the tyranny of the Middle-Age Priest in the last century; the Journalists possess it in ours. Talk as you please of a Universal Priesthood; each class, faction, coterie, does set up its own special Priest, whom it invests with mysterious authority, and from whom it expects some tidings of the invisible world, whether these tidings be that it is peopled with bright or dark forms, or that it is utterly desert and inaccessible. To deny that there is any true form of a belief which by such an evident necessity haunts human beings, in all possible circumstances and conditions of their existence, is certainly strange. Those who propagate such a denial cannot simply in that character be welcomed as helpers of their kind. To bring out the true form of this belief—to present it from age to age as a witness against the different perversions of it—would seem to be an act of real benevolence, one which might well be attributed to a divine guidance and inspiration.

Such an act it seems to me our Reformers accomplished. They placed an absolution immediately after the Confession in the daily Service. They appointed that this Absolution should be read only by a Priest. Hereby they declared this to be his especial function. All his other acts were to be referred to this one— 'God the Father of our Lord Jesus Christ,' he says, 'who desireth not the death of a sinner, but rather that he should turn from his wickedness and live, and hath given power and commandment to his Ministers to declare and pronounce to his people, being penitent, the Absolution and Remission of their Sins: He pardoneth and absolveth all them that truly repent, and unfeignedly believe His holy Gospel.'

THE ABSOLUTION.

These are no doubt mighty words. For a man to utter them not thinking them to be true, not thinking that God has pronounced them, and that he has a right to pronounce them in God's name; not feeling that it is his highest privilege and glory to be permitted to pronounce them, not feeling that he is bound to carry them out in his other acts and utterances, is shocking. But whether we have done this or not, these words coming from the most unworthy lips, have testified to hundreds and thousands of hearts in every time since they were adopted into our service, of a true God, an actual Deliverer, in whom it is not a sin but a duty to trust. They have encouraged many humble hearts to hope in Him when all seemed darkest in their own hearts, and in the world, and in the Church. They have borne witness against a multitude of notions coming forth from opposite quarters, Romanist and Protestant, foreign and English, orthodox and heretical, which slander the character of God and war against the freedom of man. Such notions it is just as necessary to fight against in London as in Rome, in the nineteenth century as in the sixteenth, or the thirteenth, or the third. Notions respecting the differences of sins which overlook the nature of sin; notions respecting God as a forgiving Being under the old and imperfect Covenant, but not under the new and perfect one; notions which make a certain measure of faith and experience the condition of drawing nigh to God; notions which practically set at naught the truth that God has redeemed men in His Son, and has claimed them for His own by His Spirit; notions which make united worship a lie, and which throw us back upon all the methods for securing a special individual pardon of sin which Romanism has devised. Of such notions, I believe despondency to be the first result, superstition the second, open infidelity the third.

I have spoken of the first words of the Absolution as explaining the ground of the priest's office. They show that he is not first an utterer of man's wants, but first an utterer of the mind of God. He is not making a way from earth to Heaven, but bringing a message from Heaven to earth. The end and result of that message, I admit, is to bring men to God; and the priest, I doubt not, is to guide them on the road. So the Church teaches with great emphasis in the latter part of the Absolution: 'Therefore, let us beseech Him to grant us true repentance and His Holy Spirit, that those things may please Him which we do at this present, and that the rest of our life hereafter may be pure and holy; so that at the last we may come to His eternal joy; through Jesus Christ our Lord.' These words are the proper introduction to those acts of the priest which he performs 'for man in things pertaining to God.' Of some of these acts, and the way in which our Liturgy appoints that they shall be performed, I propose to speak next Sunday. But I have one word more to say now. In the Second Lesson this evening were these awful words: 'Behold the Lord maketh the earth empty, and maketh it waste, and turneth it upside down. And it shall be, as with the *people*, so with the *priest*; as with the servant, so with his master; as with the maid, so with her mistress; as with the buyer, so with the seller; as with the lender, so with the borrower; as with the taker of usury, so with the giver of usury to him.'

I believe that this passage belongs to the time of

the Prophet who wrote it. I have no doubt that his threats were accomplished very literally in the great Assyrian invasion which was then at hand. But I believe, also, that there is in it a note of even greater terror for our days than there was for his. There is described the breaking up of a society, a convulsion which begins at the centre and penetrates to the extremities. It ends—ominously enough for our land— with 'the lender and the borrower; the taker and the giver of usury.' But it begins with the words 'It shall be, as with the people, so with the priest.' I dare not shrink from the strictest application of this language. If we think that we have less to answer for than you have, that we are better in any respect than you, God will find out the falsehood of our boast, and will lay it bare before our eyes. We have most to answer for; the judgments which are going on in the world are especially against us. Against us for not having acted out our part as absolvers more faithfully; for having hid our talent in a napkin, and charged God with being an austere Judge, who reapeth where he sows not. We have been sent into the world to do it good, and we have oftentimes been Jonahs in the vessel, the very causes of the storms which were shaking it. This sin we are bound to confess, and to ask more humbly than any others for God's forgiveness. But we cannot listen to those who come to us saying as the steward said to the debtors in the Gospel, 'How much owest thou unto my lord? A hundred measures of wheat. Take thy bill quickly, and write fourscore.' We cannot disclaim powers for which we are sure we shall have to give account; we cannot pretend that these priestly gifts have not really been bestowed upon us. It would be a pleasant way of escaping a dreadful responsibility—therefore we will not be tempted to take it. Rather would we plead for ourselves and for you. 'Absolve, we beseech thee, oh Lord, thy people and thy priests, that they all may be delivered from the bands of those sins which they have committed. Teach us all to stand fast in the liberty wherewith Christ hath made us free. And if we have proved ourselves unworthy to be the instruments of carrying out thy great purposes of redemption for mankind, yet accomplish these by thine own mighty power, for the sake of him who is worthy, and for the glory of thy great Name.'

SERMON IV.

THE LORD'S PRAYER AFTER ABSOLUTION.
THE GLORIA PATRIA.

Preached on the Third Sunday in Advent, December 17, 1848.

The hour cometh, and now is, when the true worshippers shall worship the Father in spirit and in truth: for the Father seeketh such to worship him. God is a Spirit: and they that worship him must worship him in spirit and in truth.—JOHN iv. 23, 24.

THAT the woman of Samaria expected our Lord to decide the question whether the true temple was that in Jerusalem or that on Gerizim, is evident. That His answer was meant to give her the apprehension of a higher Covenant, which would make the settlement of that controversy needless, all will admit. Nor will it be doubted that he meant to speak of this Covenant as connected with a more complete and spiritual Revelation of God. But these first vague impressions about the passage require to be often reconsidered before we arrive at any clear understanding of its intention.

I. Our Lord says that the hour is coming when the true worshippers shall worship the Father in spirit and in truth. It is surely consistent with the whole tenor of the New Testament to lay an emphasis on the word *Father*; and to assume that it contains a key to the difference between the time that was coming and the time that was passing away. Not as if men had not been worshipping the same Being in the old time as they would worship in the new; but that in the old time He was not revealed as a Father, and that it was in this character precisely that the only begotten Son came to declare Him. Till that name was spoken fully out by Him who alone could speak it, men must worship at Jerusalem or Gerizim. The limitation of place was not a cause of superstition, but a deliverance from it. If they were not to worship a host of visible things, or to conceive of God as a presence in those things, they must be taught that He was a distinct living Person. The Tabernacle, the Temple testified of this. They saved the Jews from thinking of the Most High as separated by any conditions of space from His creatures; they educated the devout worshipper to feel that he who would ascend into the holy place must be of clean hands and a pure heart, who had not lifted up his eyes to vanity, nor sworn to deceive his neighbour. The idea of a moral Being who looked into the heart, and spied out man's ways, drove out the blank and dreary notion of a physical Omnipresence. Even the heathen received an advantage of the same kind, though in a less degree, from the same cause. How much more did the idea of righteousness attach to the Jupiter of the Capitol than to the Zeus of Olympus, though the latter was clothed by the Greek imagination with so many more attributes of external splendour and sublimity!

THE GLORIA PATRIA.

And yet the Most High did not dwell in Temples made with hands. Those who loved the Temple-worship best, and cultivated it most faithfully, knew better than all others that he did not. There was to be a greater manifestation, though this was the needful and blessed step to it. The body of a man was the Temple (so the volume of the book had foretold) in which the Fulness of the Godhead would please to dwell. When that body was offered up, and he who bore it was declared to be the perfect High Priest of the Universe, the only-begotten Son who had perfectly fulfilled his Father's will, then was another, a perfect, a universal way of worshipping God made manifest; men could draw nigh to the throne in Him who was the brightness of the Father's glory, and who was not ashamed to call them brethren.

II. But this new revelation of God is also a new step in the elevation of Man. The time is coming, and now is, when the true worshipper shall worship the Father in *spirit* and in truth. The former dispensation had been working to this end—working mightily. From first to last it had been opposing all idolatry, that is to say, all sensual worship. The sign of the Covenant had been a token that God separated his people from the flesh to serve Him with the inner mind. The holy men who lived in the age of Moses apprehended man's spiritual condition better than the patriarchs; the prophets better than either. You may trace a gradual evolution of the doctrines that the spirit and the flesh are contrary to each other; that the flesh is not subject to the law of God, neither can be; that if we live after the flesh we shall die, that if with the spirit we do mortify the deeds of the body we shall live. These truths had been gradually unfolding themselves in the minds of those who were not merely Jews in outward appearance; but the complete discovery and enunciation of them was reserved for the time that was then and was more fully coming. Then only could men fully believe themselves to be spirits when they fully believed God to be their Father, when they fully believed that He had sent His Son to redeem and absolve them from the tyranny of sin and the flesh, when they felt that they were united, not in belonging to this or that country on earth, not in worshipping with their face towards this or that hill, but in Him who was their invisible Head and Mediator, who had bound them to Himself, not by carnal bonds, but by bonds which held their hearts in subjection. Then would they really worship the Father in spirit, not as creatures of earth endued with some soul or intellectual principle, but as citizens of an invisible kingdom, whose bodies were held down for a time by earthly trammels, from which they also should at length be set free.

III. So worshipping the Father in spirit, they would worship Him in *truth*. It was impossible that they could know Him truly while they did not truly know themselves, who were made in His image. As they attained to this sense of their own spiritual condition, they would have a continually-growing apprehension of the height and depth and length and breadth of His Divine Nature. They would know that He was not less personal because He was spiritual; but that personality belongs to spirit. They would not contemplate Him any more under the limitations of space and time. They would not be distracted by the impossibility of thinking of Him as at once absolute in Himself, and as holding communion with them through one who possessed their nature.

IV. This sense of His glory and His condescension was possible, only because the Father *seeketh* such to worship Him—because He has sent forth His Spirit to teach us what we are, and for what end we have been created; to draw up our spirits towards Him in all the solemnities of united worship, in all the acts of daily life.

Such is the principle; how denied and set at naught by priests and people, the annals of Christendom sufficiently testify. It has been found that there is the mightiest inclination still to select some holy place, Jerusalem or Gerizim, as the central seat of divine awe and worship; the mightiest inclination to forget that God is a Father, and to deny that man is a spirit; to act as if God would be worshipped otherwise than in spirit and in truth; as if He were not seeking us, but we Him.

How shall these tendencies be opposed? How shall the truth of the text be asserted? 'Most easily!' cry thousands of voices. 'Let there be no holy places; let men believe in the perfect Fatherly kindness of God to them; that He craves no sacrifices, that he appoints no Priest, that He has no grudge against men for their evil doings; let men only pay Him secret inward homage; let them ask Him for no mercies or forgiveness, but give Him credit for willingness to grant all.' Plausible methods assuredly; calculated, it would seem, exactly to meet the mischief. Let us see how they work. The particular place is destroyed, the Universe becomes God's Temple. But the Universe is still filled, as it was in days of old, with innumerable pictures and images; with things in heaven above, in earth beneath, in the waters under the earth. And to some of these, men worshipping in the Universal Temple *did* bow down in the times of old, *will* bow down now; will not be prevented from bowing down, because you tell them that they are not to have any special fancies, for that there is one great soul going through them, and through all things. They have their special fancies, and will indulge them; common men will—philosophers will; let their notions and theories be what they may. For this soul of the world is not a Father, call it so as much as you please. It does not care for the things and men whom it pervades, does not sympathise with them, does not seek to raise them. There are no affections in it; none that satisfy yours, when they are alive, or kindle them when they are dead. You say it does not ask your prayers; certainly not, for it is indifferent to your miseries: it does not demand Sacrifices; why should it? seeing it heeds not your sense of loneliness, of sin, and despair. But men *are* miserable—they crave for they know not what—they do feel sin and despair. They must have something besides this universal dream. You know they must. You believe in much more than this, else why do you talk of a Father?—why dare you not give up the old language? —why do you cleave to it, in spite of all your reasonings and conclusions? If you ever do give it up, see what will become of your belief in man as a spiritual creature! See whether all your boasts of his glorious nature and high destinies will keep him from crawling, whether your entreaties to him to believe that he is a God, will save him from becoming a beast. See whether he will not sink lower and lower; and if anything stops him in his downward course, whether he will not make some frantic and desperate effort to reach Heaven—and, for that end, whether he will not call back all the superstitions which, it was hoped, had been banished for ever—with Priests in every high place to carry on these superstitions!

Is this the way of fighting with the grovelling tendency of our nature?—this way of mere negations?—Or is it this, First, to assure him that God the Father of our Lord Jesus Christ pardons and absolves all who repent and believe His Gospel, and then to ask the Lord to grant us at once true repentance and His Holy Spirit: to ask in other words, that as He has sent forth His Son to make us freemen, He will enable us to take up our freedom, and really to turn to Him, the Universal King and Deliverer, that as He has claimed us as His spiritual children, He will enable us by His Spirit to serve Him, not in the oldness of the letter, but in the newness of the Spirit—as those who are born again of the Word, who liveth and abideth for ever. And so the things will please Him which we do at this present; our acts of worship will be spiritual acts: we shall worship Him who is a Spirit in spirit and in truth, because He himself is seeking us to worship Him. And then the rest of our lives hereafter will be pure and holy. For we shall believe in a pure and Holy being, who is with us when we rise up and when we lie down; who has created us to be holy as He is holy—pure as He is pure. We shall not believe in a dark Being made after our likeness—nor in a shadow or abstraction. We shall believe that we are spirits, capable of conversing with that which the eye hath not seen, or ear heard; spirits which have a desire for that which is right and true, an impatience of the confusion and corruption which they feel very close to them; spirits which may be delivered from that which they know to be their curse, because their Father hath promised to give them His Holy Spirit, that they may attain their native liberty, and that they may become capable of an eternal life, which life consists in an ever-unfolding knowledge and love in the joy into which Christ our Lord, after enduring the cross and despising the shame, entered for us.

I think, brethren, that a priest who in this belief invites us to join in a prayer of this kind and then acts as our spokesman and interpreter, bears a better witness for the spiritual condition of man, for his deliverance from the fetters of time and place, for the unity of the whole body though composed of the most different elements in an unseen Head, than that which is borne by those who maintain that worship is only free and comprehensive in woods or upon mountains. Worship there as much as you please; the more the better. But take care that you do not fly thither to be out of the way of those who live in close alleys, damp cellars, dark garrets. Take care that you are not running from your kind to be easy and comfortable in your own grand thoughts. If you do so, you may worship a spirit of the air, but you will not worship GOD who is a Spirit. You may exalt yourself, but you will not feel that you are a spirit; for a spirit seeks for a real fellowship with all other spirits. Churches were not built as signs of exclusion, but of reconciliation. They do not say, We are the only places in which you ought to worship; but they say, We are devoted to God that every hovel and prison may become a holy place, may possess its own secret and wonderful consecration, and that it may be known how God prefers before the Temple of the Universe, or any other, the upright heart and pure. Therefore we desire the same Spirit for the rest of our lives which we desire for the immediate service in which we are engaged.

And therefore this is the form in which we express the prayer that we have just been invited to offer up: 'Our Father which art in Heaven, Hallowed be thy name.' Neither on Mount Gerizim nor at Jerusalem do we worship; not as belonging to a place, not as members of a sect, a school, or even a nation, but as belonging to the great Family which God has adopted in His Son; yea, to the great Family of Spirits in this world and in any other of which that Son is the Head.

In this way we ask that we may offer an acceptable sacrifice, in this way that we may live pure and holy lives. We ask it by desiring that the Name of the Everlasting Father may be hallowed; that His Kingdom may come; that His Will may be done. For we are certain that He does will our highest freedom and blessedness; that in his Kingdom, all from the prince to the beggar, have their vocations—their thrones and their priesthoods; we are certain that in His Name is the perfect Unity for all the creatures whom He has formed. We know that He seeks to give and to forgive, to bring us out of temptation, and to deliver us from evil. Here therefore we find the true sacerdotal prayer, that which Christ presents within the veil for the Universal Society, and which the priest presents in the name of one Congregation, but really for all mankind through Him.

Then the priest says, 'Lord, open Thou our lips;' not as if he were separate from the congregation; not as if he had any power given him for himself. His glory is to be one with them; to represent their fellowship, to feel their weakness, to receive the strength which ever flows forth for him and them. The congregation answer, 'And our mouth shall show forth Thy praise.' With one heart and one mouth we will praise Thee, when Thou hast opened our lips; not as a set of separate atoms, but as a real living organic body—possessed with one spirit, inspired with one language. Next goes out of the lips of the priest a cry which expresses the secret sense of helplessness to pray, to think, to speak, to act, in thousands of human spirits—'Oh God, make speed to save us'—and the congregation echoes that cry, 'Oh Lord, make haste to help us.'

Do you think, brethren, that the most vehement and scornful discourses against the arrogance of priests when they exalt themselves above their brethren, and establish a guild of their own, are more effectual protests against this evil and wickedness than simple utterances in which the shepherd is taught that he is nothing except as he identifies himself with the flock, as he follows the Chief Shepherd, the great High Priest, in feeling and bearing what each of them feels and bears, in sympathising with all the groans of humanity? To be self-conceited, self-satisfied, self-glorifying, is the continual peril of the priest, because it is the continual peril of the man; and he must experience the temptations of other men in their most terrible forms. But as he who yields to this temptation forsakes the true privilege and glory of Man, and cuts himself off from the divine type of humanity, so the priest who yields to it becomes—you all feel it, your words of indignation and contempt show that you do—more than all others an apostate from his rightful and appointed calling.

Finally, he and the whole congregation say as they rise, 'Glory be to the Father, and to the Son, and to the Holy Ghost.' 'As it was in the beginning, is now, and ever shall be, world without end.' Here is the Name which men in all ages had been trying to utter, of which some had muttered one syllable, and some another. These asked for an absolute, self-concentrated Being; those, for one who could hold communion with them; others for an Inspirer to dwell in them. All were divided, broken, incapable of fellowship, drawn apart by that which should have held them together, yet sure that they could be held together in nothing else. This was the name which the Father who had been seeking men to worship Him in spirit and in truth, had been educating them to know; the Name with which, when the Son had been glorified, and the Spirit had descended on different kindreds, and tribes, and tongues, people of every race might be sealed; their highest spiritual treasure, near to each—common to all. And here the absolved spirits, delivered from material notions, from sensual apprehensions—the united family who have prayed together—those whose lips have been opened, whom God has helped out of their ignorance and darkness, can feel the reconciliation of their awe and their sympathy, of their sense of distinctness and their sense of Oneness, of Him whom the Heaven of Heavens cannot contain, and of Him who dwelleth in the humble and contrite heart. To discuss all notions and theories concerning this Name in the schools is easy, but to utter it in worship, O how difficult! Difficult not to the Reason which confesses the Name, and glories in it, and bows to it; but to the heart, through want of meekness, of purity, of charity. Our pride of ourselves and contempt of others, and unbelief in the largeness of God's grace, these cause the ascription to die upon our lips; these confound the Persons and divide the Substance more than all errors of the understanding. A divided Church cannot give glory to the Father, and to the Son, and to the Holy Ghost. If we dare to speak it, the *Gloria* must be turned into the prayer, ' Unite our hearts to fear thy Name.'

The answer to that prayer may come in ways that we think not; in the whirlwind and the earthquake and the fire at first, in the still small voice afterwards. The Prophet whose dirges over a fallen country and a shaking world we have been listening to for the last three Sundays, bursts into a more hopeful song to-day. He sees lofty cities laid low, defenced cities becoming a ruin, palaces desolated. But he sees that God is a strength to the needy and a refuge to the poor; a strength to the needy in his distress, a refuge from the storm and heat. He foresees that God will destroy the covering which is cast over all people, and the veil that is spread over the nations, that He will swallow up death in victory, and wipe away tears from off all faces. Even thus, brethren, should we look upon that which is passing around us. We have had the

Prophet's vision of terror; it will come still nearer to us, we cannot turn away from it. But we may also have his vision of hope; we may see a light coming through darkness, a veil about to be taken from the nations; out of chaos the birth of a universe; out of endless divisions a more glorious unity. Such thoughts many are still cherishing. God forbid that we should check them, or not strive by all means to strengthen them! The expectation is feeble, it seems to me, because those who speak of the veils and vestures of the past—notions, opinions, systems, forms—being torn off, know not what is beneath them; because they only expect to see these vestures exchanged for others—the rags of the past for the rags of the present.

The Scriptures speak otherwise. They say, 'Of old Thou hast laid the foundations of the Earth, and the Heavens are the work of thy hands. They shall perish, but THOU shalt endure. Yea, they all shall wax old as doth a garment, and as a vesture shalt Thou change them, and they shall be changed. But THOU art the same, and Thy years shall not fail. The children of Thy servants shall continue, and their seed shall be established before Thee.'

And the Church takes up exactly the same Confession. Systems, opinions, forms of society, may go, but glory be to that which has been from age to age the refuge of the poor, the help of the needy, the Name of Truth and Love when they seemed banished from the world below. 'Glory be to the Father, and to the Son, and to the Holy Ghost. As it was in the beginning, is now, and ever shall be, world without end. Amen.'

SERMON V.

THE NINETY-FIFTH PSALM.

Preached on the Fourth Sunday in Advent, Dec. 24, 1848.
(Christmas Eve).

Unto whom I sware in my wrath, that they should not enter into my rest.—PSALM xcv. 11.

WHY should this Psalm hold such a prominent place in our daily Service? There are many others which speak more directly to our human sympathies. The 23rd brings out more touchingly the idea of God as a shepherd, and of us as the sheep of his pasture. The 25th is a more simple and childlike utterance of a sinner's trust in One who is good and upright, and who will therefore guide him—though not good and upright—in the way. The 34th Psalm contains the inmost mystery of thanksgiving, the 51st of penitence. And if these have too individual a character to be the regular expression of a common worship, the 103rd expands, 'Bless the Lord, oh my soul,' into 'Bless the Lord, all his hosts, in all places of his dominion.'

Those to whom I alluded last Sunday, who say that the Universe is the great Temple where we

THE NINETY-FIFTH PSALM.

should offer the worship which has been confined by priests to buildings of stone raised with earthly hands, might almost suspect that the compilers of the Prayer Book, when they made this choice, had forgotten their wonted prejudices, and were transported for a moment into some high conception of a God of Nature. For certainly this Song, more almost than any other, seems to claim the mountains and the sea as partakers in our devotions. Though such language is not strange but quite familiar to all readers of the Bible, though sympathy with the outward Creation is at least as characteristic of the Hebrew poetry as of any in the world—the sun going forth as a bridegroom out of his chamber, and rejoicing as a strong man to run his race, the earth breaking forth into singing— though there is no one human feeling of which the sacred writers do not seem to have heard an echo in the sensible world, yet we shall find no Psalm so entirely pervaded with this spirit as the 95th. It is as if the Hebrew singer had indeed heard those two voices of which the English poet* speaks, and as if they were in his ears proclaiming the same message of freedom.

I should be very unwilling to overlook so leading a characteristic of this Psalm, or to suppose that it had nothing to do with determining the Reformers in the 16th century to adopt the practice from some other liturgy, or on their own responsibility, of making it the introduction to the rest. Nor if the view which I have taken of the Absolution be the true one, if the

---

* See Wordsworth's noble sonnet:
  Two voices are there, one is of the sea,
  And one is of the mountains, etc.

word means what it appears to mean, if it is the declaration of deliverance to the enchained spirit of man, if the acts of worship which follow are its first free exercises, would it be at all strange that the sea and the mountains should be acknowledged in our service as the chosen music of liberty ?

But then of a *spirit's* liberty—of that liberty which the worship of Nature not only does not give, but of which it seeks to rob us, of that liberty which is possessed only when we feel that we are meant to be above Nature, and that He whom we serve is enabling us to rise above it. Our confession was, that we had not claimed our position as spiritual creatures, but had acted as if we were the thralls of Nature and the world; our absolution was God's acknowledgment of us as His children, and His invitation to us to resume that dignity by yielding to His spirit. We do resume it when we say, 'Our Father,' when we ask Him to open our lips that our mouth may show forth His praise, when with that mouth we say, ' Glory be to the Father, and to the Son, and to the Holy Ghost.'

It would be a strange inconsistency and fearful fall surely if having recovered these rights we were instantly to cast them away, by doing homage to natural things or pretending to be a part of them. But it would be carrying out the very principle that we had been asserting before, if we took it upon us to lead the songs of the Universe, to interpret its unconscious language, to use it as God's minister and witness instead of his rival. Still more should we be maintaining this principle, if with the summons to mountains and seas we joined a higher and more imperative, and more awful summons, to our brethren—to all who bear God's image, whom He has redeemed, whom He absolves, that they will not deny their high estate, their mighty privileges, but will join with us in asserting them. And this we do when we call upon men to enter into God's rest, and when we forewarn them what is implied in the refusal of it. This I think is the central idea of the Psalm, that which explains all the parts of it; and herein lies its fitness to follow the portion of the service which has gone before it, and to introduce that which follows it.

Considering it thus, we shall be able, I think, to feel what it meant to those who first joined in it, and what it means to us. When the Israelites knew themselves to be a nation, a song was the utterance, the only fitting utterance, of that knowledge. 'Sing ye to the Lord, for he hath triumphed; the horse and the rider are gone down into the sea.' Some one man must first have spoken the words, but he spoke them as an Israelite; his voice was the voice of a whole people. He could speak, because he felt that chariots and horses, sea and deserts, were not his masters. He could speak, because he felt that the God of Abraham, and Isaac, and Jacob, was the Lord, the God over all the powers of Nature and Man. And there has been no other, there is no other, and there never will be any other, genuine expression of a nation's freedom and a nation's unity but this. If there is not a sense in the mind of a people that enemies have been overcome, that it has a real, living, personal Deliverer, that He has cared for it and broken its bonds, the chains are still upon it; they may have been shaken off some limb, but only that some other may be more fast bound, and that the heart within may feel its bondage more bitterly.

The first words of this Psalm express for the Israelite of every day that which his fathers felt in the moment of victory. The conviction realised then was true always; Pharaoh's yoke had been broken for the ages to come as much as for that age; every one who kept the passover, every Jew who spoke to his children of the wonderful works of God, every Jew in exile and in prison, had a right to believe that neither visible human tyrants nor the powers of Nature were lords over him; 'The Lord was his God.' The Lord who had cast down the oppressors from their seat, who when they dealt exceeding proudly, had shown that He was above them.

Now these words thus transferred from the celebration of a special victory to the general life and history of the chosen people, and of each man who belongs to it, we hold to be capable of a yet further expansion. Not by any straining of their meaning, but of mere necessity, they unfold themselves into a thanksgiving for our human deliverance, so soon as we believe that deliverance to have been effected. It is not that the history of the Old Testament may by some ingenious scheme of types and allegories be distorted into applications for our use. If He in whom the Jews believed was the Lord; if He was the Deliverer; if the witness which they bore to the whole earth, not by words half so much as by the facts of their history, was, 'He may not be known by any other Name than this, Woe to those who worship Him except as a Deliverer;'—we must twist their words, not to make them fit, but to make them unfit, for our worship. If, indeed, what we want are some forms of language which will endure adaptation to the fashions, conceits, and affectations of a particular age, or to our individual exclusiveness, we shall find Scripture—and no Scriptures more than the Psalms—exceedingly intractable. They will not give up their own becoming costume to clothe themselves with ours—they will not shut out other men from a share in the blessed truths which they proclaim, to please us. But if we desire to be human beings—if we are not hunting for individual comforts and assurances, but wish to have done with all such morbid selfishness, and to take our stand upon a ground which is as firm for every creature whom God has redeemed as for ourselves—here we shall find it. 'Oh come, let us sing to the Lord, let us heartily rejoice in the strength of our salvation,' in the Lord who was in the beginning, is now, and ever shall be; in the Lord whose name is the Deliverer, and who will not be invoked by any other name. Let us whom He has redeemed and justified, and claimed for His own children, not in virtue of any work or merit of ours, not from any partiality in Him, but in that Son whom He made heir of all things, and who has taken the nature of all men, let us whose spirits He has absolved that we may draw nigh to Him in spirit and in truth, let us with these spirits rejoice in Him who is the strength of our salvation. This is true Jewish language, and it is also the highest Christian language. You do not find David or the Prophets making out any claim or title to salvation, and on the strength of *that* calling upon God and fearing Him. You find them declaring that the Lord *is* their salvation. They have no other theory or scheme of salvation. They know that He has revealed Himself as their Deliverer; they trust in Him, and so are delivered from their enemies. And alas for the Church of Christ when it begins to adopt another language than this! Alas for it when it puts a set of notions between men and their Father in Heaven, or substitutes these notions for Him! Against such wickedness the Church protests by her use of this Psalm, as she does by every one of her services. Against it Christmas-day raises its solemn yearly witness, declaring that One who hath taken our nature upon Him and been born into this world, is the living bond which God hath established between His creatures and Himself, and that notions and theories are no such bond, and cannot create one.

'Let us come before His presence with thanksgiving, and show ourselves glad in Him with Psalms.' The Jew felt assured that worship was entering into God's presence. He could form no other conception of it. He was not required to go through a series of services, for the sake of obtaining certain benefits here or hereafter. He was invited to draw near to the Majesty of Heaven and Earth; to Him whom Moses durst not behold; and yet to Him of whom Moses besought that he might see his face, and behold his glory; to Him who, as the Tabernacle told him, was in the midst of his people, for if he were not, all would be feebleness, and misery, and darkness. The priest's office was to show that in His presence was fulness of joy, and that it was there for the whole nation, and for each of its members. Is this lesson obsolete? The writers of the New Testament affirm that the words, instead of being obsolete, have acquired a meaning which they had not for the minds of those who first spoke them. Deep as was the conviction of the Jew that he was in the presence of the Unseen God—near as he felt that presence to be—he had also a testimony in his heart, which the symbols of his worship repeated and confirmed, that there was a veil which hindered him from fully coming into His presence—that the way into it was not yet made manifest. The removal of that veil, the opening of that way, is declared to be the characteristic glory of the New Covenant. The Son of God and the Son of Man has not come at all, or he has come for this, that there might be a communion between God and Man which the former ages saw afar off, but could not partake of. This Christian worship therefore, if we understood it, would surely be thought of as something much more real and awful than that of the Temple. More real, because more spiritual—because it is, in the very highest sense, intercourse between spirits and their Creator. The absence of sensible indications of that intercourse from our ordinary services, the simplicity of forms, the substitution of the plain altar and the bread and wine for all the solemnities of the holy place, are not witnesses that a glory has departed, but that a glory has come—that we are permitted, with open face, to behold that countenance which the Prophets could only see through a veil. They are witnesses of the truth, which St. Paul was not afraid to speak in the ears of the worshippers of Minerva—which we should not shrink from speaking in the ears of Christians—that He is not far from any one of us; for that in Him we live, and move, and have our being. Words which the Athenians probably listened to with much contentment, while they seemed only the expression of a Pantheistical sentiment, that was quite familiar to them, but which acquired a new and very revolting significance when St. Paul connected them with his declaration of a Man by whom God would judge the world, and when he bade them turn from sensible idolatries to Him of whom their own Poets had declared them to be the offspring. And yet what a dreary doctrine it is without these additions! To think that men are living, moving, having their being, in the All-righteous and Perfect One, yet that the earth is to continue a habitation of cruelty and misery for ever! To think that man has One all Pure and Holy near him, and that he himself is never to become pure and holy! To think that we are God's offspring, and that He cares not the least whether we are growing into every habit and principle which is at war with His nature! No! this is a good faith for men who are spending their time in nothing else but in telling or hearing some new thing—a good faith for sophists, and orators, and idlers. It is no faith for working, suffering men—no faith for those who care for their kind, and do not wish themselves to be the instruments of more deeply degrading it. Such men must believe that if they are living and moving, and having their being in God, He will reveal Himself to them: that if they are not far from Him, He will show them how they may really enter into His presence : that if they are His offspring, He will teach them how He is their Father. And such will feel the words really spoken to them, 'Let us be glad in him with Psalms.' Let us confess His Name to others by praising and blessing His Name ourselves. Let us not think of Him as dwelling in Nature, but think of Him as the Father of our spirits. Let us not isolate those spirits one from another, but draw nigh to him as *our* Father, in Him who is the only Lord of our spirits, and in whom only we can feel that we are one. This is the meaning of common worship—of that worship which, because it is most spiritual, must be also most general. 'For the Lord is a great God, a great King above all gods.'

We are not serving a power, or a multitude of powers; that is the misery and slavery of the Idolater; that is the misery and slavery to which the Pantheist, by another route, is rapidly coming back. Natural powers become objects of his sage adoration; a King of kings and Lord of lords, he cannot endure to think of. The words are so low, so anthropomorphic, so unsuitable to his grand notions of a Divinity. And therefore he must ascend into a region of mist, till he arrives at pure Nothingness. He must eschew all human symbols, till in sheer weariness he throws himself back upon them, declares there are nothing else, welcomes back again Egyptian, or Greek, or Hindoo forms of Idolatry, as refuges (and they are refuges) from utter vacancy. But, dear brethren, the old language was good, wholesome, honest language, after all. This human language is the true expression for what is divine; you will find no other. If you want to save it from degradation—if you want it to be an instrument in raising you—think of yourselves as made in God's image, not of Him as made in yours. Believe that you do not by searching find Him out, through the persons and forms which you are conversant with, but that He reveals Himself to you in the person of a Man, in whom He has created all things, and by whom all things consist. Believe that his Kingdom is that by which all Kings stand—that they are raised up by Him, and reign by His grace, and are cast down at His word. Believe that He is the great King, above all human and natural gods.

And then will you learn Nature's harmonies, and be able to join in them. 'In His hands are all the corners of the earth, and the strength of the hills is His also. The sea is His, and He made it, and His hands fashioned the dry land.' The corners of the earth are not in the hands of some Divinity or Deity, but of Him who gave His only-begotten Son for us. The sea is His, and He made it, who made us after His own likeness. His hands prepared the dry land whose Word is the light of men. Therefore, 'Oh come, let us worship and bow down, let us kneel before the Lord *our Maker*.' Let us think of Him and speak of Him by that name; let us use no vague dreary phrases, which put a whole world of space between us and Him. He is the Lord *our* Maker, our spirits are his earliest handiwork. The children of the house are nearer to Him than the servants. 'For He is *our* God, and we are His people, and the sheep of His pasture.' He cares for the world; not a sparrow falls to the ground unheeded; but He is emphatically our God; our Shepherd. He feeds the raven with that food which he needs, but He feeds us with a higher nourishment, which He has made necessary to us, and which He will not suffer us to want. We are the sheep of His pasture; He guides each one of us, and brings us from our wanderings, and binds us as a flock together, in spite of our wild desires to be separate and alone.

Then comes the thought which the rest of the Psalm expresses; which has been latent in the whole of it. 'To-day if ye will hear the voice of this Shepherd, harden not your hearts.' To-day He is speaking to the heart of each one of you; to-day He is proclaiming Himself your King and Deliverer, the guide of your spirits. Therefore harden them not; do not determine that this voice, which is repeated by all Creation, but which He is addressing directly to you, shall be lost. Do not determine that you will not be under this Shepherd—that you will live apart from this fold. For assuredly you will have a huge inclination to do so. All history proves it—the history of men in all respects like you. Forty years He had led His chosen people through the wilderness, testifying to them of His presence, feeding, guiding, teaching them. But they did not understand Him. The visible had such an intense hold upon them that they could not recognise an invisible Leader. They could not believe that He really cared for them—was really helping them hour by hour. They could not perceive that they were living by the words which proceeded from His mouth —that their bread would be given them, and their water would be sure. It was a time of provocation. Their Teacher was not like them, selfish and cold. He felt their hardness of heart. He was grieved by their distrust. Such language is offensive to the worshippers of an abstract Deity, whose glory is to be exempt from all which we admire most in human beings; to possess all that indifference which we most abhor in them. But it is and must be true language if we believe in a God of Love. When the Apostles speak of grieving the Holy Spirit, they are not, they cannot be, using an idle and profane metaphor. They must mean what they say. They must mean just what is said here, that God is beseeching men to enter into His rest. A gracious Friend, ever nigh to us—ever persuading our hearts to trust Him—ever inviting us to give up that suspicion which has been the cause of our sin, and is the fruit of it; this is He of whom the Scriptures preach to us. As clearly do they present to us what the result of distrust is—' I sware in my wrath, they shall not enter into my rest.' 'They *could not* enter into rest because of unbelief,' says the writer of the Epistle to the Hebrews, commenting upon these words. The punishment is not one which God devises for them. It is what they devise for themselves. The punishment is *not* resting in Him, in whom alone a creature who is formed to know Him, to love Him, to depend upon Him, can rest. Our consciences tell us how certain the judgment is—how accurately this language defines the nature of it. We know that restlessness has been and is the great curse of ourselves, and of all human creatures. We know that we distrust God through love of visible things— through superstition—through the Atheism which denies that He is, or that He has anything to do with us. And the consequence has always been, always must be, the same. Growing restlessness, willingness to try all methods; new failures leading to new experiments; the impostor who promises help to-day succeeding the impostor who left us more miserable than he found us yesterday; at last an incapacity of understanding how there can be any blessing left for us— is not this what we have felt?—what we see around us in individuals, in families, in nations? Are not the words, 'They cannot enter into rest,' written deep upon the struggles, the confessions, even the seeming triumphs, of multitudes?

But is there nothing better for us than this dark prospect? Is the Love of God baffled by the unbelief of Man? Are the kingdoms of the Earth to be always seeking rest and seeking it in vain? Not so. 'For unto us a Child is born, for unto us a Son is given, and the Government shall be on His shoulder; and His name shall be called Wonderful, Counsellor, the Mighty God, the Everlasting Father, the Prince of Peace.' The ninety-fifth Psalm becomes this day a Christmas Carol. It bids us to enter into His presence, who took our nature upon Him, that we might be made the Sons of God; it bids us ask for His Spirit to renew us, that we may rest in Him who is God with us, now and evermore.

SERMON VI.

THE PSALMS.

Preached on the First Sunday after Epiphany, Jan. 7, 1849.

Knowing this first, that no prophecy of the Scripture is of any private interpretation. For the prophecy came not in old time by the will of man: but holy men of God spake as they were moved by the Holy Ghost.—2 St. Peter i. 20, 21.

This passage has caused some trouble to commentators, perhaps because they were contradicting it in the effort to make it clear. They *were* resorting to private interpretations; determining that some view which struck them as plausible should be regarded as the adequate and satisfactory one. For I think all agree that this meaning is contained in the text, though much more, which I do not perceive, may be contained in it likewise. The Apostle does certainly tell us that we are not to limit the language of Scripture by our peculiar experiences—by the habits and accidents of the time or place in which we live. It may meet those experiences, it may adapt itself to those habits and accidents; but it is not confined by them. It may take in many others, and be just as suitable to them. Our private solution may not be without its use; it may point at one side of a great truth; but if we idolise it, and set it up against every other, and search for no further light, we shall find that we are ourselves claiming to be higher oracles than those which we profess to consider divine.

The application of this remark to the subject of prophecy (which was evidently uppermost in St. Peter's mind) I endeavoured to illustrate this morning.* But the Prophet in Scripture, I need scarcely remind you, is not merely the Seer, or even the Preacher of Righteousness. David is said to be a Prophet; the Psalms are felt to be as much the utterance of a prophetical spirit as the words spoken by Jeremiah or Ezekiel. And these Psalms illustrate the text perhaps more remarkably than any other part of the Bible. They enable us to feel the force of St. Peter's reason. No Scripture prophecy is of private interpretation, 'For holy men spake of old time as they were moved by the Holy Ghost.' If the Bible had been written, as some people, mistaking it for the Koran, suppose it was, by mere *dictation*, it would not have refused—it would have demanded—one peculiar, definite, rigid, interpretation. There would have been in it no elasticity —no vitality—no perpetual power of expanding to meet new cases. These qualities it owes to the fact, that holy men spake, not when certain words and letters were given them to write down, but as they were moved by the Holy Ghost. That which worked in them was a mighty quickening power, which first stirred the depths of their being before it found for itself any expression in language.

In one of the Warburtonian Lectures.

It was an *Inspiration*—which belongs not to sounds, but to men; to conscious voluntary beings; to spirits formed in the image of God. It was an inspiration which went lower than the conclusions of their own understanding, than the determinations of their own wills; it found out that which lies at the root of these, their true essential humanity; that which they had not merely as David or Isaiah, not merely as living in this or that age; not merely as Jews, but as men. It was the inspiration of Him who had created them for this very end, that they might set forth his mind, not in the deadness and extinction or suspension of their own; but in its freedom, fulness, highest activity.

The creature sinks into nothing before the Majesty of Him who has chosen it, but it sinks that it may rise; it becomes conscious of powers to which before it had been a stranger; of sympathies stretching into infinity, and going down to the lowest insect; of a citizenship in the visible and the invisible world, in ages past and ages to come.

The words of men thus speaking *cannot be* of private resolution. They were most truly individual men; they had their own circle of feelings, hopes, and interests; they were no abstract dreamers, living for all time, and not for a particular time; cosmopolites instead of patriots. If they had been such, men would have left them to enjoy their lofty thoughts and independence, and would have claimed no fellowship with them. They were truly men, not shadows; and through the strength of their feelings and sufferings, not through their indifference, were they fitted to be the spokesmen of the race. Each portion of it feeling them to be so, tries to fix and appropriate their language to its own use; but they break loose from the fetters thus imposed on them. 'We speak,' they say, 'for you, but for hundreds of thousands besides, whom you have never seen or heard of; whom you dislike, whom you would exterminate: we were not permitted to confine our words within the limits of our own apprehensions, therefore we cannot confine them within the limits of yours. We uttered more than we knew or meant; is it likely that we should only have uttered just what you know or mean? We cast our bread upon the waters, believing that it would be found after many days, by those who needed it. If you are hungry, eat and live; but know that you cannot get more than food for the day, and that he who gathereth much will have nothing over, and that he who gathereth little will have no lack.'

Now these truths which the simple and poor in spirit readily apprehend, but which our pride and vanity are perpetually robbing us of, have, I believe, been especially brought home to the hearts of people by the Book of Psalms. Let a man hold his theory about the dictation of Scripture ever so strongly, it must break down with him when he begins to read that book, or at least in any manner to enter into the spirit of it. Is it possible, he must say to himself, that these prayers, these songs, these confessions of sin, were repeated in the ears of a man that he might write them down for the good of the world? What! he did not actually pray, actually rejoice, actually confess! It is deception throughout! We shudder at the blasphemy into which we have been betrayed by an apparent homage to Scripture; we feel how much more safety there is in the witness of our conscience, than in the schemes of our understanding. Wherever the Psalmist learnt these words, they did come fresh and burning from his heart; they must; or how could they go fresh and burning into other men's hearts? Is it difficult to understand then, how they can have been *inspired*, how God can be the author of them? Difficult truly, if we are determined to know what praying, and giving of thanks, and confessing are, without praying, and giving of thanks, and confessing. Difficult! say rather impossible. But if we have ever tried to perform these acts, tried because we felt we could not live without them; tried with this conviction, and yet have been disappointed; we do and shall learn that prayer, if it be man's utterance of his own wants to God, has yet its beginning and first spring in Him; that He gives songs in the night; and that He awakens repentance. A man reflecting upon these discoveries in his own experience naturally exclaims, when he reads what he recognises as a true outpouring of the heart, 'This is not of the earth, earthy; it comes from the Lord of Heaven; the holy man spake it not of his own will, the Holy Ghost moved him to the feeling and the utterance.' And if so, he learns also how it is possible that such an utterance should become his; why myriads who have passed out of the world should have felt it was theirs, why myriads yet unborn shall feel it to be theirs. The Holy Ghost who spake by the Prophets is He who proceedeth from the Father and the Son; He who dwells in the Church and in each of its members, who strove with our fathers and who is striving with us; He who stirred up all the good and heroic deeds and thoughts in the days of old; He who only can inspire us with any of them. Whatever words have been most spoken under this teaching; whatever words He has drawn out of the deepest caverns of man's spirit, these must be enduring: the accidents of space and time clothed them; but they have a substance altogether unaffected by these accidents. It offers itself to the heart of the worshipper most when he is most willing to seek God and to forget himself, when he is most ready to confess his position as one of a family, not to stand upon rights from which others must be shut out.

This I conceive is the reason why the Psalms have asserted such a place for themselves in our daily worship. In Matins and Vespers they form the chief part of our devotion; we go through them month after month. Unquestionably we are following the same bad examples in this case which are supposed to have misled us in others. Those who look into any breviary will easily be able to convict us of gross imitation. There they will find numbers of Psalms set down for repetition; even in the modern books wherein Litanies to the Virgin are the main charm, this characteristic remains. There are some who may be inclined to say, If it be *Scripture* it is well; the use of that cannot be injurious, whoever may have set the fashion of it. But I cannot avail myself of this argument. I think a fashion of using Scripture may become a mischievous fashion; nay, the very word *fashion* in such a case almost condemns itself. There may be as much superstition in the stringing of texts as of beads; the superstition may be more evil because it is the degradation or perversion of a holy thing, not the mere playing with an indifferent one. The Reformers knew that the people were in this danger; the words of Scripture even in an unknown tongue seemed to possess a mysterious significance; when they were translated the danger of turning them into amulets would not be less. If they ministered to this corrupt tendency, they were not helping to emancipate their countrymen from a heavy bondage, but imposing it in another form; they were not showing respect for Divine Inspirations, but making light of them.

It seems to me that by incorporating the Psalms in our daily worship they were taking the very best course which they could take to interpret their real sense; to bring out their latent power; to unfold their various applications; to guard against the peril to which they, more, perhaps, than any book, have been exposed of private interpretation. It seems to me that they took the best course they could take to redeem the words from a carnal, superstitious, artificial use, and to make them of practical worth and reality for men in all conditions and circumstances.

I will illustrate briefly each of these remarks. Nothing is more puzzling to the person who reads the Psalms merely as a student than the questions, Which of these refer to the condition of the individual writer? which to the condition of the Church generally? which may the individual Christian adopt without dishonesty or irreverence, as the utterance of his own experience? which must he refer directly to Christ? After centuries of commentaries on these questions one is often inclined to think that they are more unsettled than ever. The divine rests upon his distinction of Messianic and non-Messianic. The philologer brings to light facts in the records of the

Hebrew people which determine them to a particular age. The popular reader resolves that he will read himself into them, making Edom, Moab, Israel, and Zion, just what he likes them to be. And yet beneath all these perplexities of the understanding, there has, through all these ages, been a strong and general conviction, that every historical fact respecting the time in which the Psalm was composed is of the greatest value; that David must have written what he did write as David, and not in some fictitious character; that Christ must in some sense be the subject not of a few of them, but of all; that they do of right belong to each human being. Whence has come this settled and harmonious conviction apparently so much at variance with that uncertainty, and contradiction, and restlessness, in the midst of which it exists? I answer, Men have got it from worship. So far as they have felt that these Psalms were the best and most perfect expressions they could find for a public united devotion; so far has there been a reconciliation of difficulties which other experiments only made more hopeless. For they could not have anything to do with our worship if the writers of them did not refer themselves and the whole universe to one Centre. While they do this, and we do it, we feel that they are meant for us. But it is just the doing this which makes them so strongly the property of their original owners. They are driven about and tormented by innumerable enemies—personal enemies —they betake themselves as their only help and refuge to one who is their friend. They are crushed under a weight of oppressive accidents; they must find one who is always the same. They are crushed under giant human evils; Death and Hell are close to them, and are mightier than themselves. What can they do but trust in Him who has said to Death and Hell, 'I will be your plagues'?

'These words must be real; they must have been felt by those who spoke them,' cries the worshipper, because they are so real to me, because they so exactly express the burden under which I am groaning. Personal enemies are pursuing me; a load of petty anxieties is pressing upon me; these giant universal foes are threatening me every moment. I have come to Church to fly from one as much as the other. And there I find that I am not alone. My groan has been uttered before; men thousands of years ago sought the deliverance I am seeking. And they did not pour out a wild shriek into the ear of some unknown power. They took refuge in a Being in whom they were sure they should find a refuge; One who, they say, had awakened their longing for Himself; who had declared that there was a bond, an everlasting bond, between them and Himself. What was that bond. It seems as if the men who were pouring out these prayers had a glimpse of it, and as if they were feeling their way into the full apprehension of it. Does not this Church to which I have come, signify that I may have a fuller apprehension of it? Does it not say that the mystery has been revealed? Does it not tell me of an actual Living Person who is the bond, the perfect bond of Peace between God and His creatures, and between these creatures as brethren of the same Family? Does it not tell me of a Daysman in whom we are reconciled, and can meet? of One in whom God looks upon us and is satisfied? This truth is working itself out in the mind of the Psalmist, as it must work itself out in ours. The mere notion is nothing; here we have the living process of discovery; its stages of doubt, clearness, vicissitude, fear, hope, rejoicing. The Psalmist is rising through worship, into a perception of the right which he has to call us and all in every age of the world, his brothers; we, through worship, come to understand his difficulties; in claiming that right he becomes our interpreter; while yet we are better able to understand his words than he was himself.

This wonderful reciprocation of benefits, this magnetic communication between distant ages, is simply a fact. The commonest experiences of our lives imply it. We could not sympathise with Homer or any writer who grew up in circumstances altogether different from our own, if it did not exist. Christianity interprets the fact; Christian worship substantiates it for us; teaches us that the magnetism is a spiritual, not an animal, one. It is not produced by the excitement of meeting together; it is grounded upon that purpose of God which He purposed when He created us in Christ Jesus, and which He will accomplish when He shall gather all things together in Him. By acts of worship, then, we come to understand how that which is David's becomes ours in Him who is the Son of David and the Son of God. The Service brings before us on the same day Psalms written in the most different states of mind, expressive of the most different feelings. If we have sympathised in one it often seems a painful effort to join in the rest. And so it must, as long as we look upon prayers and praises as expressions of our moods, as long as we are not joining in them because we belong to a family and count it our highest glory to lose ourselves in it and in Him who is the head of it. We must be educated into that knowledge. It may be slow in coming, but till it comes the Psalms are not intelligible to us; our Christian position is not intelligible to us; we do not more than half enter into the parts of the service which we seem to enter into most. They touch certain chords in our spirits, but not the most rich and musical chords: these do not belong to ourselves; they are human; they answer to the touch of that Divine Spirit who holds converse with the spirit of *a man* which is in us.

But there is another difficulty in the Psalms which affects the conscience more seriously, and has often been said to make them unfit for the purposes of Christian worship. I spoke of the allusions in them to *enemies*. 'It is very well,' you may say, 'to talk as if David meant secret spiritual enemies. But what does his history tell us? Did he not cause the Ammonites who had insulted him to pass under saws and harrows of iron? Did he not give up the sons of Saul to pacify the Gibeonites? Did he not command his son to bring down the hairs of Joab and Shimei to the grave with blood? Do not these facts interpret the spirit of the man, and of his prayers?' I will not stop to argue how many of these acts were righteous acts of a Sovereign, who is not to suffer his land to be polluted with blood through any vague feelings of clemency; how many unjustifiable acts of personal vengeance. I believe some of them belong to one class, some to the other; and that the Bible helps us by its teaching to make the distinction; not forbidding us, but encouraging us to condemn every act of any

one of its heroes and saints which we find, after deep
and earnest meditation, to be incompatible with the
divine law as Christ interprets it. I may make
mistakes, of course, in the application of principles;
I may acquire light which makes me see acts differently
at different times. I am to be cautious in forming a
judgment about a man of other days, as well as about
a contemporary; but there is no special check arising
from the circumstance that the acts of the person I
am speaking of are recorded in Scripture.

But let me ask you this question, Do you think
the writers of the Psalms were *worse* than the men
you ordinarily meet with in the world? And do you not
think they would be worse if it made no change in
their feelings that they were engaged in solemn
prayers to God? Would you not think very ill indeed
of a man, who, when he was drawing near to the
Majesty of Heaven, was not somewhat more subdued,
mellowed, softened, than in the common jars of life?
If he were not, could not you say with perfect confidence, 'That man's words *cannot* live; they are the
utterances of temporary excitement; they are the
utterances of momentary ferocity; he will himself
long to blot them out before he is a year older—if he
does not, they will perish through their own fearful
and monstrous contradictions'?

But these Psalms have lived—have continued to
be the expression of the thoughts, not of the
cruellest, but of some of the gentlest and purest
creatures, that ever dwelt upon this earth. How do
you account for it? I say, if you listen to your consciences, you will find no difficulty. You will not
force yourselves to suppose that David forgot the

actual people who were fighting with him, and trying to extinguish him, when he poured out his heart to God. You will not think he puts himself into a strained artificial state of mind when he was approaching Him who looks into the depth of the heart. But you will suppose that the contact with a perfectly holy, and true, and loving Being, may not have had less effect upon him than intercourse with an imperfect friend of the same character would have had. If a wise teacher, or tender wife, or sister, may change the whole tone and character of a man's feelings towards one who has grieved him, not by insisting upon his hiding them, not by refusing to sympathise with them, but by the very gentleness which expresses itself in that sympathy; do you think that a Divine Being will not have some more effect upon the mind of a worshipper in transfiguring his whole mind, in drawing out the truth which is hidden under his complaints, in severing them from their earthly ingredients? I could not understand worship to mean anything, if I did not believe this. I should look upon it as a mere phantasy and delusion. As I look upon it to be the greatest of all realities, I hold that in it, and in it alone, one is taught what a difference prayer wrought in David's mind—how much David's actions were affected by David's praying, and yet how little we must measure the sense and spirit of his prayers by the inconsistency of his acts. Instead, therefore, of being afraid of hardening my own heart by adopting this language, I do not know how I can so well soften it. I am not likely to indulge in any furious passions against Edomites and Hagarenes, but

I know that I am in danger of feeling very bitterly against particular persons who offend me individually, or who, I think, are enemies of my country and the Church. I do not find that I feel less bitterly by saying that I ought to be charitable, and pretending to myself that I am, or by adopting large and general phrases concerning humanity, or by telling myself that of course such or such an unkind word or unkind act does not really move me. No man who knows himself will trust to these tricks. Stings that he may affect to despise do fester; he knows that they do. A person may call himself a friend of the human race, as the elder Mirabeau did, and torment all individuals of that race who come in his way. Nor is it possible, nor is it right, that we should be without objects of hatred. We cannot be so but by the extinction of some of our deepest and strongest feelings; nay, but by ceasing to love. What we want is to hate the evil in ourselves and in all those who hate us; so we learn really to love ourselves, and to love others as ourselves. To do this we must feel about our enemies as our common worship will teach us to feel; only in praying against them do we understand what they are, and overcome them. I do not want to spiritualise the Psalms, if you mean by spiritualising, to turn them into shadows and abstractions. I want to feel the exceeding reality of that which is spiritual; that to wrestle with flesh and blood is nothing, but that to wrestle with those principalities and powers which may come to me clothed with flesh and blood, or without any such clothing, is work indeed. If you tell me of men who are quick at finding modern substitutes out of some sect and party which they abhor for all whom David besought God to destroy, I say: 'And such you will meet with—more and more of them—till you pray more earnestly for the destruction of God's enemies, and of Mammons and Belials which men are worshipping instead of Him.'

Whoever, then, set us the example of incorporating the Psalms in our daily Service, all thanks be to them for it! By doing so we have struck at the great roots of Papal and of all other superstition. The Psalms teach us that in old times men believed there was a way into the presence of God, and that they sought to know that way, and that they found Him who is the way. The Psalms encourage us to enter through that way into the Holiest of Holies, where the High Priest has entered for us. So they train us, as they trained the Reformers in the sixteenth century, to be impatient of all superstitions, by whomsoever sanctioned or devised, which presume that God has not redeemed and justified us, that we are not warranted in calling upon Him as a reconciled Father.

The Psalms teach us that we are surrounded by enemies, and that God is our stronghold and refuge from them. Superstition proclaims that He himself is our enemy, that it is He who must be persuaded to be at peace with us. It invests Him with the attributes of the evil spirit, and leads us to fly *from* Him— not *to* Him. Deep and subtle blasphemy, ever reappearing in new shapes, the implicit ground of all false religions! the consummation to which they are hastening! Day by day we must encounter it afresh in our own hearts and in the hearts of our brethren.

These Psalms used as the language of our faith and prayers will be mighty helps: it will be extinguished at last, when He who met the spirit of lies here on earth, and prevailed, shall be revealed in the glory of His Father, and of the Holy Angels.

SERMON VII.

THE FIRST LESSON.

Preached on the Second Sunday after Epiphany, Jan. 14, 1849.

The righteousness of thy testimonies is everlasting: give me understanding, and I shall live.—PSALM cxix. 144.

How can these testimonies be called Everlasting? Are they not the records of the Old Covenant to which the Psalmist refers? And has not that Covenant passed away?

It is easy to evade these questions by drawing distinctions between the moral and the ceremonial law, between that in the old Economy which was Jewish, and that which was for mankind, between the earthly parts of it and the heavenly. No doubt there is a meaning in these classifications, but like all classifications, they should not be taken for granted, but patiently considered and tested by facts, or they will become hinderances instead of helps in the discernment of truth and in the practice of life. All these words, Moral Ceremonial, Jewish, Universal, Earthly, Heavenly, require to be sifted and exchanged for real equivalents, before we can safely settle the force of a grave and divine sentence by means of them.

The word 'testimonies,' which the writer of the 119th Psalm and of all the Psalms repeats so often, is simpler than any of these, and may perhaps aid us in understanding them. He evidently looks upon his country's History, and Laws, and the words of its holy men, as testimonies of GOD; witnesses concerning Him; telling what He is, and what the nature of His Government is. Supposing this were *all* He meant; supposing he did not imply further—as we shall agree that he did—that they were testimonies *from* God, His witnesses concerning Himself—still this would be sufficient to justify the use of the word Everlasting. He does not suppose that a testimony respecting an Unchangeable Being can be true to-day and false to-morrow. It was false at first, or nothing can make it false; it was true at first, or nothing can make it true. This was precisely the difference between the Heathen and the Jew. The first recognised a Power about him in Nature, or in the more mysterious region of his own thoughts; a Power which, he must needs confess to be above him. But what this Power was, he determined by Nature and by his own thoughts. It varied with the variations of the seasons, with the variations in his own observations and consciousnesses. It was divided as the objects in Nature were divided—as his heart, when it was under the sway of the most contradictory emotions, was divided. The Jew said, first of all, *He is*. I know Him because He speaks to me. I know Him just in so far as He reveals Himself to me. I dare not measure Him by what I see in the world. That assumes new and different complexions while I gaze upon it. It is His work, His lower work—I am His higher, His chief work. But I deny my own glory while I try to conceive and judge Him by myself. For all that is within me bows before Him—acknowledges Him as my guide, my teacher, the source and spring of my thoughts, my powers, my life. Therefore all that is within me says, 'Thou art everlasting—all thy testimonies are everlasting. *Give* me understanding, that I may live.' The eyes of my body cannot see Thee; of myself I cannot find Thee out. But there is an eye in me which is created to perceive Thee; open it, and I shall possess my true, my highest, life.

The Jew then, so far as he understood his own position at all, understood that he was to bear witness of that which was fixed and permanent. He had no work in the world if he had not this. And he understood that he was to bear this witness not merely by what in any given period he said or did. It was implied in his calling and covenant, that his national history from generation to generation would be the declaration of God to man. Whether individual men, whether priests, kings, prophets, were faithful or unfaithful servants of God, or worshippers of idols, would make no difference in this respect. Their folly as much as their wisdom—their sin as much as their obedience—would be a testimony of Him. Nor could the history be broken up into artificial divisions; this part of it being called essential, or divine, or moral; that accidental, or human, or local. If it were a history at all, it must be what all histories are—it must describe the acts of men; not their transcendental acts, but their common acts; not that which they might have been if they had lived in conditions in which no man ever did live; but that which they were, dwelling as they did in a certain spot of the actual earth, in the midst of ordinary human occupations, relationships, and interests, surrounded by the perplexities, temptations, contradictions, which belong to such and such times and places. But this, you say, is the form of a human history. *Therefore* I answer, if the Scriptures are right, of a divine History. If God is the Lord of Man, if He bids men own Him as their Lord, we must expect that in their common life and business He will make Himself known. To separate any portion of this life or business from His Revelation, is simply to say, that for that portion He is not what He declares Himself to be; that portion lies out of the region of His influence; that is independent of Him. Take away all the part of Jewish Law and History which seems to you—perhaps which rightly seems to you—special and local, conceive the writer to have been guilty of a pious fraud when he said, 'The Lord spake,' 'The Lord ordained this statute or judgment,' and you set at naught the principle of the Book—you deny God to be actually concerned for the wellbeing of His people—to be actually ordering their circumstances, and educating them through these circumstances.

Had the Jew then no power of discriminating between the different acts which were enjoined upon him?—must he regard them all as equally sacred—all as equally binding upon every human being? Far from it. You cannot read a single prophet without being struck by the bold language in which he speaks of what he believed to be ordinances of God. 'What mean the multitude of your Sacrifices unto me ? What mean your Feast Days, and your New Moons; your solemn Oblations ? I am weary to bear with them. Who hath required this at your hands, to tread my courts ? Wash you, make you clean, put away the iniquity of your doings from your eyes; cease to do evil, learn to do well;' this is the characteristic tone of the prophetical exhortation, or sermon. How did the preacher acquire the right and the power to speak thus ? Where did he learn thus apparently to slight one part of the economy and to exalt another, while he looked upon all as divine ? Had he fallen in the way of some heathen philosopher, whose instructions raised him above the traditions of his fathers ? No— he acquired this method of speaking by meditating day and night upon that Law and that History in which he believed God was revealing himself. Thus, and not by any heathen help—thus, while he kept himself most free from heathen pollutions, and observed most strictly the divine commands — he acquired this faculty of distinguishing between means and ends; between what was appointed with a view to the attainment of the divine knowledge and the divine character, and that knowledge and character. He was not hampered by the thought, 'All these things are of God, therefore one is worth as much as another.' He was not forced to say, 'This or that is not of God.' in order to make out the difference. In the light of God he saw and felt it. The purpose of the whole economy revealed itself more and more clearly to him as he distinguished its parts. While his countrymen were turning the divine provisions against sense and idolatry into ministers of sense and idolatry, he could at once point out their real worth, and the wickedness of this perversion; the positive uselessness, nay, mischievousness of God's own institutions, if they were turned against God; if they withdrew His people from seeking His Righteousness, and were made excuses for approaching Him, as if He were one of the dark and evil powers to which the nations round about paid homage. The Prophet, just because he believed that the Unseen God was the real, not the nominal, King and Teacher of His Nation, just because he studied the whole history as the history of his acts and revelations, arrived by safe and experimental processes at the apprehension of those distinctions, which we lay down formally, arbitrarily, scholastically, destroying the life of the subject in our determination to dissect it. He learned to regard the forms of outward service and worship, not as needing to be rudely severed from their moral and spiritual essence; the sin of his countrymen consisted in this, that they did dissever what had a most intimate and blessed connection; thence arose the necessity of showing the insignificance of the accidents, nay, the infinite harm and degradation which reverence for them alone was producing. He did not say, Here is something which is of no consequence, because it only concerns us as an Eastern people, and here is something precious, for it belongs to East and West alike; but by honouring and using that which was manifestly intended for him, whatever other persons it might not be intended for, he came to know what blessings were promised, and would be given, to myriads of people, and how the Jews were the honoured stewards of these treasures. The more he dwelt on these treasures, and delighted in them, the more he perceived that they were such as the spirit only could apprehend, for that they belong to the nature of Him who is the Father of Spirits, and who is educating men to know Him, through the Word, who is the brightness of His glory, and the Light of Men. But that sublime discovery did not make him indifferent to the outward business of the world, to human relationships, to the joys and sorrows of nations and individuals, to laws, wars, trade; to any fact in nature or in human policy. All these acquired a new and divine significance from the fact that man stands in so near and wonderful a relation to his Creator. Human relationships were steps in a ladder, of which the top reaches to the throne of God. When fathers forgot what they owed to their children, when husbands proved unfaithful to their wives, the higher bond was also broken. A cloud came between Earth and Heaven; the multiplication of such crimes showed that the belief in the Covenant, and in the government of the nation by its invisible Lord, was perishing; the domestic adultery, the popular idolatry, were branches from the same trunk. The honesty and simplicity of ordinary dealings depended upon the clearness with which a Lord of Righteousness was acknowledged as presiding over the whole Commonwealth; all acts of fraud and insincerity—none so much as those which were done under a religious pretext—weakened and undermined that acknowledgment. A King who did not habitually preserve the sense of his responsibility to the invisible righteous King, who did not look upon his family as reigning by covenant with Him, and as witnesses of Him, would inevitably become a tyrant; he would degrade his people with sensual and base worship; he would rule them for the gratification of his own lusts; he would bring division and captivity upon them. All national events and phenomena of necessity excited the fear of those who believed in a Sea God, and a Sky God, and a God of the nether world. To confess any powers of Nature as having rule over him was in the Jew a sin; but he must regard them as instruments of the Judge and Saviour of the world, by which He carries on the moral education of his people.

Such are a few of the obvious characteristics of the Old Testament Scriptures—of the Old Testament, I say, as distinguished from the New. That has its own deep and eternal message to us, a message wholly in accordance with this: raising some of the Jewish lessons to their highest power. But it is not occupied mainly and characteristically with the divine government over this Earth; with the conditions of national society, with the discipline of men considered as creatures sent upon the earth to till and subdue it. I do not mean that the New Testament treats principally of a *future* world; that seems to me a very careless and erroneous statement, and one which has greatly perplexed our view of both dispensations. But it does treat principally of a spiritual and mysterious though most real Kingdom; all its other teaching has its termination in this. It does not therefore claim to be self-sufficient; it implies a foregone conclusion; it assumes the existence of the Old Testament. Whatever was already done it pretends not to do again. It brings out that which had been hidden in the Old; it interprets that which in the Old had been indistinct; it makes distinctions which had been asserted clearer;

it unfolds the previously undeveloped form of Universal Society. But it leaves the testimonies of the Old Testament; it confesses their righteousness; it affirms that righteousness to be everlasting; it invites Christians as much as Jews to ask for understanding to take them in and live.

These remarks are necessary to explain the course which the Church has followed in appointing a Lesson from the Old Testament every morning and evening. Evidently the object in this case is not the same with that which I was considering last Sunday. The Psalms are given us to express our thoughts and feelings as members of the Church and of the human family. The word 'Lesson' implies that we are not speaking, but spoken to. Another is teaching; we sit still to learn. Now thoughts of this kind suggest themselves to a great many in every church where the Old Testament is read: 'What have we to do with these? We have been hearing perhaps a chapter out of the Book of Kings, perhaps one of the Jewish prophecy —the first is simple enough, but it belongs to the far-gone past; the other, for aught we know, may belong to past, present, or future, but we do not understand it. We can find something profitable to our souls in the Psalms; some practical instruction concerning ordinary life in the Proverbs. The Commandments we admit are of standing value. But why not make a collection of profitable extracts; why force upon an English congregation, composed of the most various elements, that which cannot be applicable to the condition of one in twenty?'

You will easily conclude that the compilers of our Prayer Book must have gone upon some different principle from any which these objectors recognise. We may as well try to ascertain what it was before we condemn them. They had had several centuries of experience to draw instruction from; this book had met with various kinds of treatment; they had some means of judging (though not of course so good as we have) how far one or another had been profitable. For instance, the plan of making extracts from the Old Testament for spiritual reading and edification in churches and in private, was one with which they must have been quite familiar. What had been the fruit of it? One story might be as good for edification as another. 'An exalted Christian Saint had many advantages above the highest Jew; the acts of such a Saint might surely be as helpful to the people at large or to the individual believer as any that could be found in the old records—why should not one be as much read as the other?' It was not easy to find an answer to such a question; still there was a traditional sacredness about the Bible; it was different from other books; how could the difference be asserted? how could the reverence be maintained? It must be used less familiarly; people must be warned against approaching too near to it; we are safest if it is kept in a learned language. What was the practical consequence? Not merely *this*, that the legends of saints became far more practically and popularly influential than the histories of the Bible, but that the Bible itself began to be looked upon as precious, because it contained a collection of such legends. The idea of it as a book of testimonies concerning *God* was more and more tending to become extinct. The notion of reading it as a book to do the soul good, as one which supplied a set of useful maxims or instructive examples, threatened entirely to supersede this. And the soul got exceedingly little good from its self-seeking; the useful maxims could not be understood, the instructive examples could not be followed; they were sure to be perverted, the meaning of the command being really given by the habits and circumstances of the reader; he bringing the rule with him by which the acts he heard of were measured.

But men were crushed under the consciousness of inward evil. The legends of the saints give no relief from that burden. If the Bible were merely a superior book of legends, it could give none. The Reformers declared that it was not this. It was a testimony of God's reconciliation, it declared His mind. This discovery gave it a new aspect altogether. It was hailed as the book—the divine book. But there was the same temptation now as before to put Self in the place of God. The Bible so far as it ministered to man's comfort, so far as it spoke of peace to the conscience, was exceedingly prized. Soon whatever had not this character was left to the schools; common men had no direct concern with it. Though the watchword of the Reformation abroad was, 'A Bible for the people,' the people did not get a Bible; they had it whole on their shelves; they heard only extracts from it in their worship; it did not directly, habitually connect itself with their thoughts of God; they did not listen to its history as to His lesson. The schools possessed themselves of it, to reduce it into maxims and dogmas as they had done of old, to rend it into fragments when the new analysis became triumphant.

I do not claim it as a special merit of the Reformers,

but I confess it as one of the special responsibilities of our English position, that with us it was otherwise. All the Teutonic people of Europe felt the national impulse strongly in the fifteenth and sixteenth centuries; the revival of Pagan literature, the decline of reverence for the Popedom, made it stronger; the Reformation made it irresistible. But our island nationality had been altogether different in its character from that which could be enkindled in the subjects of an empire pretending to be the successor of the old Roman, boasting a kind of supremacy over Europe, putting itself forth as the rival of that which had its centre in the Vatican, composed of the most incongruous materials, without any hereditary head. Ours had been a nationality like that of the Hebrew, exclusive if you will, but defined and secured by natural boundaries, by unity of language, by the family succession of the sovereigns—the interruptions in which had caused the principle of it to be more strongly felt, and to be referred to an authority which could dispense with it when He pleased for higher ends. The Jewish books spoke to us of an Unseen King reigning over this land; so soon as our king had broken his bonds to a visible Potentate it was felt that he held power by the same tenure as David or Hezekiah held theirs. But for this conviction the arbitrary maxims of the Tudors would have been intolerable; leavened by it, these monarchs became the instruments of imparting a vigour to the heart and intellect of the people which had been unknown before. The Reformers did but interpret the inner mind of their countrymen when they said to them: 'You are to sit and listen to these lessons from the oldest book in the world. They will be lessons to you concerning all your country's policy, concerning all the events that befall it, concerning the commonest events of your daily lives. They shall be mixed with your worship; that you may know that He to whom you have been praying—the King of kings and Lord of lords—is indeed teaching you out of them here; is ruling you according to the principles set forth in them always.'

Now consider how many knots were cut by this simple practice. There was this first and chiefly. Romanism had secularised and degraded common life. It had professed to take every thing under the control of the Church—kingdoms, families, individual consciences. But it had really made the King feel that he was not directly responsible to God; the father of the family, that his children were not his but the priest's; the individual man, that he had no distinct direct inheritance in the divine treasures. It had treated that life as most heavenly which was most separated from earth; so far as the system prevailed —in spite of the ten thousand counteractions which there were in the constitution of the Church itself, in its Creeds, in its noblest teachers—the feeling grew up that what is inhuman, not what is human, is the image of the Divine. Here, out of the book which was felt to be of transcendent authority, the opposite lesson was inculcated day by day. The sanctity and dignity of all social relations; the direct connection of all earthly acts with God himself. Men were divinely taught *not* to touch the things of earth with scrupulous superstitious hands, as if they were unholy; they were told that it was a sin against God to do so;

the thought was forced upon them, 'You are fallen into the heathenism and idolatry out of which God has raised you, if you act thus.' At the same time earthly life was invested with a real and awful significance. Deceitful thoughts, lying acts or words, under whatever pretext, were offences against the Majesty of Heaven, against the Judge and King of the Nations.

Look again at this point. The greatest perplexity of all with which people had been distracted was this, 'How can we interpret the Scriptures? who can interpret them?' 'The Church.' 'Yes; but where is the Church, what is it, who represents it?' 'The Doctors of the Church.' How? Are they above that book which they profess is above them? Can they measure it by their rules, lower it to their standards? 'Sit down,' says the Prayer-Book, 'and listen. Hear this chapter, and this. We tell you it is a lesson. We tell you that it will interpret yourselves to you and the world to you. And again, that the world and yourselves, or, in other words, God's dealings with the world and yourselves will interpret *it* to you. There is no question about private judgment. You are going to be taught; of course you want understanding. You may ask, and it will be given you. Of course you do not wish to put your own meaning into the book; if you do you cannot learn out of it. No difficulty arises, either about the interpreters or your own rights. Get all the interpreters you can, use all the rights you can; only do not make one or the other a contradiction. Remember the end you are seeking, and all things will become means to that end. You will find God to be above His book, above yourselves, above all interpreters. He is the teacher, the teacher in a thousand practical ways. Submitting to Him we shall be shown how to do His will, and so we shall know His doctrine.'

Hereby another perplexity is removed. The English Christian is anxious to distinguish that which is local and transitory in the Scripture from that which is permanent and universal. He can find no rules to help him. But he reads the book as a lesson about himself, and the things which he has actually to do with. If he is not among lepers he will not fancy that the directions about lepers are meant for him. Yet they may not be useless to him because he has no obligation to obey them. They are testimonies of God; the *righteousness* of them is everlasting. God cared for the lepers of Judæa—for the most suffering and loathsome objects; He cared that the community should not suffer from contact with them. He cared equally that they should not be cast out and neglected. The case is gone; the principle lives. He cares for the outcasts in our streets as he did for the outcasts in the cities of Palestine. He would not have cities polluted by that which is physically or morally pernicious. It is the sin of men, their forgetfulness of His presence, if they suffer them to be so. But each man who is spreading the pestilence, who is infecting a people with disease and crime, is still a living man. The Lord of all does not forget him; if we do, it is because we are regulating the world upon some other maxim than His.

I take this instance to illustrate the application of these old testimonies of the outside of life, and specially to show that we cannot afford to dispense with them any more than our fathers could. The mischief is that we *have* dispensed with them. The words have not been heeded, the lesson has not been learnt. Divines and religious people have been too fine to meddle with such things; they have supposed that religion had nothing to do with them. And since religion could not touch them, something else must. Selfishness undertakes this charge; the external world is surrendered to its dominion, provided the internal is saved for God. But they will soon follow the same law. Selfishness will have both worlds if it is not banished from both. Religion will be felt, and rightly felt, to have a hold upon nothing real and human. And this will not be because we have risen into a spiritual and divine region. We shall hover in a misty cloudland, as far from heaven as it is from earth, and never discover that the Son of God when He took human flesh really made them one.

All the temptations which I have alluded to, as connecting themselves with the consideration and study of Scripture among the Romanists, are still ours; and we have others which belong to a later time. I believe, brethren, that we shall find one of the most powerful deliverances from them lies in this practice of the Church, if we do but ask grace to profit by it—if we do but pray, 'Give us understanding that we may feel the righteousness of thy testimonies.' And more and more while we use that prayer we shall find that the hard passages of the Old Testament explain themselves, and present themselves to us as everlasting, and as life-giving. I am sure we may, if we will, understand Isaiah's prophecies, which we are reading now, far better this year than we did last year. I am sure that what were dead letters to many of us have been found quick with meaning; there is scarcely any one who has not, at times, a startling sense of their reality and power.

How has this happened? Have commentators been very active? I do not know: I fancy people in general have been too busy to care about them if they have. Has some great discovery been made respecting the language of the Prophet, or the history of the countries in which he lived? Possibly: but this has not been the source of our illumination. We have heard in our own language of what has passed in countries close to our own in our own days. Here are the practical witnesses that the truths he proclaimed are everlasting; that the Righteousness of his testimonies is as applicable to the condition of one age as of another. We ask no evidence of Scripture but this, that it shall teach us how to think calmly and hopefully of events which would of themselves drive us to madness and despair. And that petition the Bible does not refuse. This afternoon it has given us the comforting assurance, 'The Lord is my King of old; the help which is done on the earth He doeth it Himself.'

SERMON VIII.

THE SECOND LESSON.

Preached on the Third Sunday after Epiphany, Jan. 21, 1849.

Whereby, when ye read, ye may understand my knowledge in the mystery of Christ, which in other ages was not made known unto the sons of men, as it is now revealed unto His holy apostles and prophets by the Spirit.—EPHESIANS iii. 4, 5.

ST. PAUL seems to have felt himself more overpowered by the dignity, and more wonderfully enlightened respecting the nature of his office, when he was writing his letter to the Ephesians, than at any other time of his life. In Ephesus he had been obliged to separate himself openly from the Synagogue; in Ephesus he had encountered the first systematic opposition from Greek idolatry. Everything in the position of the city and in his own had led him to regard his labours there as a turning-point in the history of the Church, a kind of proclamation of its distinct substantive existence which had not been made elsewhere.

What a temptation there was in such circumstances to draw out an accurate scheme of Christian doctrine, and to put it forward in formal antagonism, as well to the mythology and philosophy of the Pagan World, as to the Rabbinical lore of his own countrymen! Was it not almost necessary that such a scheme should be propounded if the young Church was to be preserved from the plots of the worshippers of Diana—from the teachings of innumerable sophists, who cared little for her worship, but were quite ready to avail themselves of the prejudices of its votaries, and to offer some ingenious modern explanation of it—and lastly, from the persevering and powerful efforts of unbelieving and believing Jews? Must we not suppose that there was in the mind of St. Paul, more than in that of any other Apostle, a preparation and a capacity for such a work as this? He who had been brought up at the feet of Gamaliel, he who evidently possessed so much of Greek wisdom, had surely the predisposition and the ability to construct a great Christian edifice composed of these materials, or of materials, if such could be found, different from both, which should remain a perpetual monument to the glory of the Architect.

How did he use the opportunity which was offered to him? He does not deny his knowledge in the mystery of Christ. He feels that it has been in a very remarkable and direct manner revealed to him. He earnestly exhorts his disciples to read his letters that they may profit by this knowledge. But what is this mystery of Christ? It is the mystery that the Gentiles are fellow-heirs and of the same body. It is the mystery which all the previous history of his own country had been unfolding; it is the mystery which from the beginning of the world had been hid in God, who created all things by Jesus Christ. It is a mystery which he is now declaring, that all men might have fellowship in it. Here is his difference with the Jew. He believes that God, instead of intending that a certain set of men should know Him and attain to the blessedness which is the consequence of that knowledge, had created all to share in it. He differs from the Gentiles, because they worship a multitude of divided objects, and do not practically recognise a common humanity. He vindicates the Jew from his own determination to shut himself up in a system of notions and ceremonies, showing that so doing he can never attain to the glorious inheritance which was promised to him and to his father Abraham, who was told that in his seed all the families of the Earth should be blessed. He vindicates the Gentile from his determination to shut himself up in his local worship, or in a philosophical system. He invites both to claim the privileges of men. The Gospel, he affirms, is the full discovery of Him who is the Living Centre of the Universe, the assertion that all men are related to Him; the destruction of every wall of partition between Man and Man; the admission of all who desire it into fellowship with the Father of the whole family in Heaven and Earth.

This, according to St. Paul, is Christianity, or the Christian Religion. He does not use the words; they are not New Testament words. In one sense I may say the idea of them is not in the New Testament; we are never taught there to adopt a certain scheme which can be labelled and ticketed Christian, and set up as the rival of every other. The Apostles when they speak of a revelation take a different, a much humbler and yet a much higher ground. They speak of a Person—a Son of God and a Son of Man; one who is Lord of their Spirits and of the Spirits of all flesh, one before whom they must bow, one whom they and all creatures are bound to obey. He was declared to them that they might do Him homage; that they might invite other men to do Him homage. He was declared to them that they might be set free from an intolerable yoke, that they might bid all men claim the freedom with which He had made them free. Is not this a humbler view of their vocation, seeing that it supposes them to be nothing, and Him of whom they are speaking to be all in all? Is it not humbler, seeing that what it chiefly binds them to is practical submission; a sense of their fellowship in the sorrows and sins of all other men; an acknowledgment that they have no blessings in which all men are not partakers with them? Is it not a higher view, inasmuch as it asserts capacities for humanity, and for each man, which never had been asserted before, though all had been dreaming of them and trying to exert them; inasmuch as it claims to set forth the purpose of the Universe, and of Him who formed it?

At all events, the difference is a most serious one. It seems to me, brethren, that the time is come when we must distinctly understand which of these meanings we attach to Christianity. We cannot much longer, I conceive, hover between them: either it is a system which will stand as long as there is an external power sufficiently strong to make it stand, and for which its supporters will always be trembling whenever it loses any props or safeguards in the opinion of society, or in the goodwill of rulers; or it is the revelation of an eternal Order, of a Truth which cannot be shaken by any changes in the external economy of the world, but must be more fully manifested by each one; which cannot be weakened by any new discoveries respecting the physical structure of the earth, or respecting the condition of man, but must receive fresh light from all such; which does not depend for its evidence upon the proof that all who have entered into it imperfectly or not at all, were utterly false, but which recognises all that they have said or done truly, and gathers fresh confirmation from it; which will survive amidst the ruins of all systems, yet does not seek to ruin any, but rather to redeem the divine truth in each from the husk in which it is hidden, and to unite it with all from which it has been separated.

Philosophy has affirmed that this is the great problem—has proposed to solve it. We affirm that it *can* only be solved by a personal Revelation; that by a personal Revelation it *has* been solved; that the New Testament when it is read as the announcement of such a Revelation explains the steps and method of the solution. If this conviction be true, we can safely trust Him to manifest its truth to the hearts and consciences of His children, who has promised that He will guide them into all truth. But we may, in the meantime, inquire what light the past throws upon the question, and what circumstances in our position are favourable or adverse to the consideration of it.

I would appeal to the history of every great religious movement in modern Europe, whether the substitution of direct belief in a Deliverer and King for a general belief in Christianity, or a Christian scheme, was not its main characteristic. I make no exception. I believe the records of the Middle Ages would furnish as decisive evidence of the assertion as those of the sixteenth, seventeenth, or eighteenth centuries—the commencement of the Crusades, the rise of the Mendicant Orders, as the early stages of Puritanism and Methodism. But I will confine myself to the events with which we specially and rightly associate the name of Reformation. The proclamation of an actual Redeemer, of one who could forgive sins and bear sins, was received in Luther's day by tens of thousands of hearts as a new message, one which they had never heard before. Yet this proclamation was, to all appearance, an integral portion of the doctrine which was set forth in every missal, preached in every pulpit, taught in every school. The Reformers appealed to old and familiar documents—to the Lord's Prayer and the Creed, which were repeated by all children, and were their first text-books. Why, but because here they found the full declaration of a Person in whom men might trust; in whom they might find the emancipation and rest which they were craving for. The Bible was welcomed as *the* book—the poor man's book, precisely for this reason. It revealed to those whose consciences were oppressed with the burden of sin, a Lamb of God who took away sin—to those who felt themselves excluded from the presence of God, one who had made peace for them, and had ascended into His holy presence. The Preacher was welcomed, the Creed was welcomed, the Bible was welcomed, as a witness of this Gospel, which had been utterly choked by a scholastic system. If Preacher, Creed, or Bible, had been felt as setting forth a system, and not declaring the Son of Man and the Son of God, the charm would have vanished. This new faith, because it was that which had been from the beginning, because it spoke of Him who was from the beginning, could break chains of custom and habitual reverence from a multitude of hearts. But that custom and reverence were mightier than all the subtleties of Protestant doctors. When they began to use the Bible —still professing the same honour for it as heretofore—to consolidate their theories, the people felt that the meaning of the Reformation was gone. Then came the Romish reaction. The Jesuit body possessed a far more complete organic system than the Reformers in any country could exhibit. But not a bare dry system. With it were all the appliances of tradition and old respect; enthusiasm such as had marked the first preaching of the Reformers; an appeal to the desire for obedience and guidance which are such deep and true principles in the hearts of human beings; above all, that recognition of a personal object of faith and devotion, implied in the name of the Order; a skilful direction of the affections and fancies of the disciples towards secondary human objects in which they might find a refuge from the dryness of divinity, of casuistry, of external formalities. If Christianity was to be a System, here it presented itself in its highest power. Nothing was left out; no one scholastical notion or mystical emotion; nothing which proved that Religion was meant for the Universe, nothing which brought it into contact with the family or the individual. Why was not this Order invincible? Where was the barrier against it? This was its weakness, this was the fortress against it; men never could be brought heartily to believe that the Gospel *was* a system, even the most perfect of systems. In each age, in each country, in each community, amongst Protestants, amongst Romanists, amongst Jesuits themselves, various testimonies were borne that it was not this, that it must be something altogether different from this; yea, something which was to cast it down and trample it under foot. The painful truth became too clear to be suppressed, that when men are leagued in support of a system they will resort to craft and dishonesty in defence of it; that they will feel acts of this kind not sins but duties; that the habit and rule of their life will have more and more tendency to become one of untruth in proportion as they feel more distinctly that Truth and the System are identical. If, therefore, simplicity and truthfulness are the main elements of a Gospel character, if every one departing from them is conscious that he is departing from the Gospel standard, and that he has something to repent of, the inference is certain—the Gospel must extinguish the most circular and satisfactory of human efforts to systematise, or that effort must extinguish the Gospel.

In England we are always ready to sacrifice theoretical consistency rather than commit a practical error. It is our temptation to idolise the practical, and to suppose that we can be right in action, when we are violating not a maxim but a principle. But the temper of mind which is apt to take this evil direction, is, I conceive, in itself a good one, and has produced many blessed results. I only dare attribute it to that temper as a secondary cause or instrument that our Reformers were led to take the course which they did take respecting the reading of the Bible in our Daily Service. How they were probably influenced to adopt a regular series of Lessons from the Old Testament into the Daily Service I considered last Sunday; to-day I will speak of their policy with regard to the New, and of its effect. The word 'policy' may seem scarcely applicable; the course they took was so very simple and natural a one, and so entirely in accordance with their method in other cases. But I cannot think that the profoundest wisdom ever succeeded in procuring for a land so great a benefit. The Reformers abroad, as we saw, declared the Bible to be a book for the people; and the people joyfully received it as theirs. But how can a book continue to be popular?—how can it be really felt to be a part of a Nation's treasure? Not by its being sold in every street, or admitted, as part of the necessary furniture, into every cottage. It is only then popular when it incorporates itself with the inmost feelings of a people; interprets their daily existence; is associated with their most sacred acts. A strong impulse, a great revolution, may give *a* book such a position; a great religious impulse or revolution will certainly confer it on *the* book. But only through worship can it preserve its hold on men's affections. Every reader of Burns knows that through the family worship of the Scottish farmers and peasants it maintained its influence among them. The poet who can scarcely find scorn strong enough for the teaching and practices of the clergy generally, pays a genuine and heart homage to these domestic devotions. I do not suppose that the same class of people in England, or perhaps any class, has felt *this* kind of influence with nearly the same strength; but the introduction of the New Testament into our national devotions has, I believe, tended more than anything else to keep alive a feeling in the minds of our countrymen, that it has some very intimate connection with the lives of individual men, and with human society; that though it does not bear so directly as the Old Testament does upon outward acts, upon the business of nations, it has some mysterious relations to the very springs and sources of morality, to the humanity of each man, and to the condition of the whole race; that in spite of many difficulties, it is essentially practical; that, though it may seem to need interpretation, it is in fact far more simple than the comments upon it. I think that, at all events, these convictions have withstood many opposing influences in the minds of a considerable number of Englishmen; not of those only who partake of religious ordinances, but of those who receive an impression at second hand through them, which affects their conduct and their conclusions in a number of ways unknown to themselves. But I own that I should look upon such results, however valuable, as very unsatisfactory, noways proportioned to the claims which the New Testament puts forth for itself, and to the influences which I believe it should exert upon every community of baptized men. I would rather speak of the multitudes of humble people, men, women, and children, who have drawn in life from these daily lessons, to whom they have revealed evils deeply hidden in their own hearts, whom they have taught how to repent of them, and be delivered from them; in whom they have kept alive the sense of an ever-present friend, guide, helper; whom they have taught to understand their

Bibles at home, and other books, and the intricacies of their own lives; whom they have initiated in that inward righteousness, out of which have come the simple daily love of husbands, wives, sisters; to whom they have given assurance of a Kingdom into which they are admitted, and which will reveal to them new powers and mysteries through ages upon ages.

But neither of these influences could have been produced if the Church had not kept this personal object of the New Testament perpetually before the minds of all who listened to its words. If she had taken beautiful passages out of the Gospels and Epistles —say, the Sermon on the Mount, or St. Paul's discourse on Charity, in the thirteenth chapter of the First Epistle to the Corinthians, or what are called the doctrinal parts of the Epistles—such as the third, or fifth, or ninth chapters of the Epistle to the Romans— or passages out of our Lord's life, which might seem useful as examples, the whole moral and spiritual effects of these Scriptures would have been changed. By reading in the morning the Gospels and the Acts, she has made us understand that the Son of Man and the Son of God, not in part of His life, but in the whole of it, is the object which the Bible is setting before us—not only in His humiliation but in His glory —the self-same Person now as when He was walking beside the Lake of Gennesareth, or teaching in the streets of Jerusalem—still healing sickness, casting out devils, instructing disciples. His Miracles do not come before us as artificial contrivances to prove His mission, but as substantive parts of His work of Redemption. His Parables connect God's work in Nature with His work in us; His Death is the consummation of His Incarnation, the fulfilment of the Sacrifice which He was offering up each day. His Resurrection and Ascension are not strange, perplexing additions to the narrative, but the orderly carrying out of its meaning; events without which all that goes before would be incomprehensible.

Passing from these Lessons to those of the Evening which are taken from the Epistles, we do not feel that we are entering upon a new region. We are not more among abstractions. The subject is still the same— Christ the Son of God and the Son of Man. Viewed as the first-born of many brethren, as adopting men into the Kingdom of which He spoke on earth—a Kingdom having an essential, heavenly, invisible ground, and therefore intended to subdue and subordinate all visible earthly powers to itself. I am certain that there are some who can say, honestly with their hearts, that they have learnt more of the meaning and harmony of the New Testament from these Lessons than from all the Commentators they have ever read, and from all the clearest teaching of pulpits and schools. And such persons, I think, will see in this method something specially adapted to the perplexities of their own time, and will anticipate far greater fruits from it than it has yet borne.

I will speak of one which is closely connected with my text, and with all St. Paul's teaching. Romish and Protestant divines, differing in the upshot of their schemes, have yet agreed in the construction of them. The Fall of Man is commonly regarded by both as the foundation of Theology—the Incarnation and Death of our Lord as provisions against the effects of it. Now St. Paul speaks of the Mystery of Christ as the *ground* of all things in Heaven and Earth, the History as the gradual discovery or revelation of this ground. Such a view, I think, at once presents itself to us as the most reasonable and satisfactory, when we read the Scriptures of the Old and New Testament in a continuous order, as a series of Divine Lessons. We feel that one veil after another is in them withdrawn from our eyes, and that the last step in the process must be that which discloses the full Atonement of God and Man, of Earth and Heaven, and the full Name of God, just because this is that true Original Foundation which sin has been concealing, and denying, and seeking to destroy.

If this is so, the idea of a development of Doctrine in the sense which is given to that phrase by Modern Romanists as well as by Modern Rationalists, is altogether untenable and false. We do not want one giant hill of notions to be heaped upon another until we nearly reach heaven; we do not want all that is old to be cast aside that we may dwell only on the little pin-point of the actual present, or in dreams of a possible future. The Divine Book gives us the promise of a mightier blessing. It tells us that the Name, and Kingdom, and Will, which are hidden from the wise and prudent system-builders, may be revealed to babes; that the past, present, and future, may be seen united in Him, who desires that we should have that eternal life which is in His Son.

In one arrangement concerning these lessons, the compilers of the Prayer Book seem to me to have failed in moral courage, and I cannot but think that their descendants have suffered severely for their cowardice. I do not see that they were justified in omitting the Apocalypse in their courses of Sunday or daily reading. Had they surrounded it with the solemnities of worship, had they taught us to read it like the other Scriptures, as if we were in God's presence, I cannot believe that we should have dared to indulge in the fond trivialities which every commentator, almost every private individual, seems to think he may safely pour out upon a book surely as grand and awful as any that exists in human language. And is not its grandeur and awfulness precisely of that kind which worship, and worship only, teaches us to appreciate? Is it not in the truest sense the winding-up of all previous revelations? Is it not the discovery of Him who is walking in the midst of the golden candlesticks—the true High Priest, and King of the Universal Society, before whose brightness all that have usurped His titles and offices must fade away, and perish? Does it not show how beneath the mystery of Him who was dead and is alive, and who liveth for evermore, lies the still deeper mystery of the Name of the Father, the Son, and the Holy Ghost, which has been the excuse for infinite debatings, heresies, narrowness, which shall be confessed one day to be the expression and the foundation of all Love, Unity, Comprehension?

SERMON IX.

THE SONGS OF THE CHURCH.

Preached on the Fourth Sunday after Epiphany, Jan. 28, 1849.

And they sing the song of Moses the servant of God, and the song of
  the Lamb, saying, Great and marvellous are thy works, Lord
  God Almighty : just and true are thy ways, thou King of saints.
  REVELATION xv. 1.

SOME students of the Apocalypse have believed that they could trace in it the form of a regular drama constructed on the Greek model, with a choral song between each of the acts. This opinion has not been confined to one school of commentators. It was promulgated by the Neologian Eichhorn, who maintained, in opposition to the contemners of the Apocalypse, that it was at least a sublime and elaborate poem ; English writers have agreed with him, who have attributed the book to the divinest inspiration, and have found in it a guide to all history. They were certainly better able to justify their notion than Eichhorn was. To suppose that the writer became a dramatist, because he had a preference for a certain kind of composition, because he had a special skill in it, because he knew how attractive it would be to his readers, is to outrage all reason and probability. Where could he have acquired his taste? who could have trained him in his art? how could a Jew of Ephesus dream of finding an audience for that which must have seemed an incomprehensible subject to all who were in any degree familiar with the form? On the other hand, a divine teacher would certainly impart to the mind which he educated, not only certain profound ideas, but an apprehension of the method in which they could be most perfectly embodied, and could be made most intelligible and impressive to that age and to future ages. That a drama should be the form for tracing the progress and unfolding of a divine purpose, working through human wills and in spite of them; that it should exhibit vicissitudes of hope and fear, exultation and depression; that the action of it should be partly in the visible, partly in the invisible world; that it should be closely connected with the ideas of Mystery and of Revelation, cannot certainly surprise any one who has reflected much upon its nature or upon the most remarkable specimens of it in ancient or modern times. Any one who had considered how many of the deepest and most earnest thoughts of human beings,—of those which belong to their own spiritual nature and to their relations with God—had found this kind of utterance, might have felt astonished and disappointed if he had found nothing answering to it in the Scriptures. He would hail with corresponding delight the discovery of some book which seemed to embody the inmost intent and spirit of the drama, to explain all its ordinary applications, and to raise it to its highest power.

Whether those who take this view of the book be altogether right or not, they have at least the merit of directing our minds to some characteristics of it which are very striking, and yet which have been often overlooked. The choral tone of the Apocalypse, the continual allusions which it makes to songs in Heaven and Earth, cannot be much noticed by those who regard it as a collection of dates, and who value it chiefly for the exercise which these afford to their ingenuity; but a sign which connects it so closely with some of the Old Testament writings, and with the very scheme and form of prophecy, must be prized by any really diligent student; still more fondly by those who read for spiritual edification. It would be strange if they passed over passages which embody the devotion and rapture of the whole Bible, to occupy themselves with speculations turning upon the numerical value of the Greek letters. The words of my text lead us into the heart of this subject. 'And I saw as it were a sea of glass mingled with fire, and them which had gotten the victory over the beast, and over his image, and over his mark, and over the number of his name, standing on the sea of glass, having the harps of God. And they sing the Song of Moses, the servant of God, and the Song of the Lamb, saying, Great and marvellous are Thy works, Lord God Almighty; just and true are Thy ways, Thou King of Saints.' The former verse I quote for the sake of the latter; in truth they cannot be separated. The reason of the Songs, the nature of them, is interpreted by the state of those who sang; what that state is, I believe the symbols, if we look simply at them, and interpret them as we should, if we meet with them anywhere else, very distinctly and emphatically declare. Here are men who have been engaged in a sore conflict. Their enemy has been the beast. Mere brute power has been trying to bring human beings, spirits, creatures formed in God's image, under its yoke. This brute power, it seems from the next words, has not merely sought to crush them by direct means; it has worked by the Circæan cup; its great object has been to reduce them to its own likeness, in the language of Scripture, to write its *Name* upon them. The choir is united; one great effort of the enemy has been to divide it; to break the links which hold its members to each other. The successful resistance to this temptation, I conceive (for various reasons which I have not time now to set forth) is expressed by the phrase 'getting a victory over the *number* of the Name.' Creatures formed to be distinct, formed to be one, are urged to forfeit their *personality*, to become mere dead portions of a mass; they are at the same time urged to cast away the secret of their *Unity*, to receive a mark which shows them to be all separate atoms, even while they have the internal semblance of fellowship.

But they have gotten the victory. They have found that He is on their side in whom they were created to be one, that He has Himself come to deliver them from the tyrant. They have 'His Father's Name upon their foreheads.' In place of a power before which they quail, which they worship because they dare not withhold worship, they have been brought to confess One who claims them as His children, and promises to make them anew in His own Image. And they have received from Him that Spirit who is one

IX.]   THE SONGS OF THE CHURCH.   125

in many members, who holds them all together, who gives to each his proper place and function, who awakens every individual power and energy, who makes it in its highest freedom and exercise most entirely subordinate to the good of the whole.

They have overcome; but they stand 'upon a sea of glass.' There is nothing in the mere ground at their feet to give them security; if they trust in that it will break under them, and they will sink whither they know not. If they look down to see the reflection of their own images in the glass below, they see beneath them an unfathomable abyss and nether fires. But they look up. They sing songs to Him who has created them and the whole Universe; to the Lord God Almighty, whose external works are great and marvellous; to the King of Saints, whose secret ways, whose inner purposes have been revealed to them, and are found to be just and true. Here is their standing ground; here is their confidence. They know in whom they have believed. They know what He has done for them, and what He is. They praise Him in songs of triumph for what He has done and for what He is.

These are said to be the Songs of Moses, the servant of the Lord, and of the Lamb. If you turn to the first Song of the Israelites which is recorded in Scripture,* that which they sung when the horse and his rider went down into the sea, you will see how exactly it corresponds to the idea which the words of this book give us. The chosen people had been set free from a visible oppressor—from a brute tyranny. They carried his name upon their forehead; the animal

* See Sermon V.

tendencies, the animal worship of the masters, were deeply imprinted upon the slaves. They had been a tribe known to their rulers as aliens; known to each other as possessing a common origin, a common enemy; but broken, selfish, heartless. They had been told of an Invisible King. He had claimed the earth as His possession; showing Pharaoh that the locusts and the flies were His; that the firstborn were His, that the sea was His. They had found that this King was a Deliverer. He had used all this power for their redemption. He cared for exiles and outcasts. They had gotten this great victory over the Beast. And in the acknowledgment of this great and divine King, they knew themselves to be creatures of another mould and character. Raised and reclaimed to the acknowledgment of an unseen Lord, and Friend, and Helper, they are for the first time Men. They have gotten this victory over the Name of the Beast—over his image in themselves. And now there was awakened in them such a sense of union—of being indeed a family, a tribe, a nation, as was altogether new to them. They have gotten a victory over the Number of his name—over that spirit of helpless, hopeless selfishness, by which men brutalised and slavish are always possessed. Yet they stand upon a sea of glass. All the worst Egyptian habits and tendencies are in themselves; all lust, animal worship, pride, division, slavery; nether fires ready to burst forth in a moment if they forget who has called them out of the house of bondage, and in whose righteousness they stand. Their Song expresses their sense that He is their one Redeemer, and King, and Upholder. The Lord of Hosts is His Name.

It signifies little which was uppermost in the mind of the writer of the Apocalypse, this song or that in the thirty-second chapter of the book of Deuteronomy. 'Give ear, O ye heavens, and I will speak; and hear, O earth, the words of my mouth,' which we are told Moses spake in the ears of all the congregation of the children of Israel. Both have the same general characteristics which I have noted, only the Song in Deuteronomy brings down the history a stage, or I might say many stages, further; showing how the principle of the first Song was that in which alone the people could live; how infallibly when they forgot it they would sink into idolatry, baseness, slavery. And indeed, with the exception of some Psalms which I have spoken of already, and a portion of which rather exhibit men in the process of conflict than in the hour of victory, and perhaps of the book of Lamentations, we may safely say that there is no Song in the Old Testament which has not this type. All are Songs of Redemption; of Redemption from some tyrant power, which has tried to set itself up against the true righteous power; all are proclaiming the Lord God Almighty to be great and marvellous in His works; all are thanksgivings to the Invisible King, who has for them overcome the Beast, and his Name, and the number of his Name; all are witnesses and prophecies of a complete victory which He shall win over this tyranny for them and for the whole earth.

But the text speaks also of the Song of the Lamb. That Song of Moses and all the Songs of the Israelites had implied that man is not merely a creature of this earth, though he has so great a work to do in tilling and subduing it. The very possibility of praise and prayer showed that he must have some closer and more intimate connection with the unseen world than had yet been declared. The belief that he could execute the purposes of his Maker, and still more the assurance conveyed in direct words, realised to some great extent by every faithful man, that he was made in the image of his Maker, showed that there was some Kingdom more wonderful than that which is spoken of in the words: 'Great and marvellous are thy works;' in which God rules, and with which man has to do. Of such a Kingdom the forerunner of our Lord spoke: 'Repent,' he said, 'for the Kingdom of Heaven is at hand;' of such a Kingdom our Lord Himself spoke after that He had been baptised and declared to be the Son of God, and the Spirit had descended upon Him, and after He had been led up of the Spirit into the wilderness, to be tempted of the devil. He called it the Kingdom of Heaven; the Kingdom of God; His Kingdom; His Father's Kingdom. He said: 'Blessed are the poor in spirit, it is theirs; blessed are they that are persecuted for righteousness' sake, it is theirs.' He spoke of this Kingdom to the multitude in parables, teaching them to notice the Divine operations in all common outward things, and then telling them that there were operations like these, but still more wonderful, which were going on in themselves at the roots of their being. These mysteries He more clearly revealed to the disciples who had heeded His instruction. He chose out some of them to be the heralds of this Kingdom to the world. He led them by various methods to feel their own intimate relation to Himself, to feel that it was not a relation which was produced by His bodily presence with them, or which would be interrupted when He was visibly withdrawn; that it had a deep and eternal ground. He said that they were united to Him as the branches are to the stem and root of the vine, deriving their life from Him. He spoke to them of a Father to whom He was going, and to whom He Himself was the way. He spoke of a Spirit which He would send them from the Father, who would teach them of the Father and of Him, and guide them into all Truth. Much of this discourse they could not understand at the time; a portion of it was made plain to them by bitter experience. They found that they wanted an inward strength which they had not, that their love was feeble, their faith nothing; that without these their intercourse with Christ, and their recollections of His words and acts, availed them nothing. They saw Him who they believed was to redeem Israel betrayed and crucified. He returned from the grave, declaring that He *had* redeemed Israel, and that He was their Friend still, and that He had all power in Heaven and Earth. He went up out of their sight. The promised gift came upon them on the day of the Jewish harvest festival. They felt that the powers of thought and speech, like the powers of the seed in the ground, were made to germinate by an inward and secret power; they felt that this power was a Spirit of Love binding them to men of all tongues and kindreds, because binding them to the unseen Lord of all. They baptized three thousand men with the Name of the Father, and the Son, and the Holy Spirit. They taught these, and all who in different places received the same light, confessed the same Name, that God had adopted them into His Family, that Christ had taken the nature of man, and had in that nature overcome the enemies of man, trampling upon death and all the powers of darkness, claiming for men the privileges of spiritual beings, admitting them into the fellowship of saints and angels. They bade their disciples act in the belief that Christ by His entire surrender and sacrifice of Himself, by entirely yielding Himself to the will of His Father, had conquered the great enemy, and tyrant, and divider of the race, the Spirit of Disobedience and Self-will, and had made a complete atonement between God and Man, between each man and his brother. They besought them to remember that the Spirit of Christ, the Spirit of Love, and Meekness, and Gentleness, was working in them to destroy the works of the devil; to make them obedient and free; to make them entire conquerors over every power that had led them captive, and had brought wars and fightings among them. The Song of the Lamb is the song of this victory; of this victory which is in one sense the consummation, in another the ground, of that which the Israelites celebrated in their song. The consummation, because it completes the deliverance of man and the Revelation of God; the ground, because men had learnt, by slow and painful discoveries, that all triumphs over the earth's visible oppressors are vain, and terminate in fresh discomfiture, unless there be some way of striking at the root of their power, of destroying spiritual wickedness in its high places. The Song of the Lamb is the song of triumph over principalities and powers by Him who was slain that He might endue men with a new, and risen, and divine life. It is like the first, a Song of Redemption. It is like the first, a Song to God as the Deliverer. It is like the first, a Song of Rejoicing from human beings who had received the rights of men, and knew themselves not to be beasts. It is like that, a Song of men who feel themselves to be no longer divided, but one. But it is a Song to God the Father, whom we know to be Absolute and Eternal Love, for delivering us from that devil-worship which lies beneath all bestial worship, and is always threatening to start forth in its nakedness when any form of that worship becomes worn out. It is a Song to the Son, the King of Saints, who has unfolded God's Kingdom, and has shown not only His *works* to be marvellous, but His *ways* to be just and true, for delivering us from that pride of human strength, that desire for independence which destroys freedom, and which is the devils' image in each man. It is a Song to the Spirit who knits the knots of peace and love in all lands for deliverance from that anarchy and sectarianism, that false peace and material unity, which are different aspects of the devil's image in human society.

The Book of Revelation being, as it seems to me, especially intended to wind up the New as well as the Old Testament, and to show how they are reconciled and incorporated in the Christian Constitution, unites both these Songs; that of victory over the oppressors of the earth, that of victory over man's internal enemies, that of his admission to his rightful dominion over the earth and animal nature, that of his admission into the divine or Heavenly Kingdom, that of Man in God's strength triumphing over all that resists him. Both these Songs it calls upon all men to take part in who are baptized into Christ's Church; if they forget either, they do not really understand the redemption which has been wrought out for them.

Upon this principle our Church has acted in teaching us to use those Songs which follow the First and Second Lessons in our Morning and Evening Services. Some of them are taken from Scripture; the two longest, which are not found there, seem to illustrate our text better than almost any existing compositions. The *Benedicite omnia opera* is emphatically the Song of Moses the servant of the Lord—'Great and marvellous are thy works, O Lord God Almighty!' Its traditional connection with the Three Children, however imaginary, illustrates the sense in which it was conceived. 'We will not worship the Golden Image which thou, O king, hast set up.' 'O, all ye works of the Lord, bless ye the Lord, praise Him, and magnify Him for ever.' So must the martyrs have felt, though they spoke no such words; so must the witnesses against all idolatry, and especially against Moloch and Mammon-worship, feel in all ages. The Eternal, Invisible King, the King who dwelleth with men holy and humble of heart, He is the Lord of all those works which men are enthroning in His place. They are all silently paying Him homage. Man is to interpret and utter their praises. The *Te Deum* takes higher ground. The Song of the Lamb mixes in it with the Song of Moses the servant of God. 'Just and true are thy ways, thou King of Saints, is even more distinctly heard in it than, 'Great and marvellous are thy works, Lord God Almighty;' yet both are there. It is in fact the finest transition that can be conceived from the Jewish Scriptures to those of the New Covenant—the noblest assertion of our right to the whole sense of those Scriptures, and of our power to see them by the light which Kings and Prophets longed for, but had not. We praise Thee, O God! Thee of whom we have been reading in the Law of Moses, in the Prophecy of Isaiah, *Thee*, and no other; Thee the I AM, before whom the Shepherd hid his face; whose glory filled the Temple when the Prophet said, 'Woe is me, for mine eyes have seen the King, the Lord of Hosts.' 'We acknowledge Thee to be the Lord'—Thee a living Person, not a shadow—Thee a Deliverer, and not a tyrant. The Confession still continues in what might have been the language of an ancient Hebrew, 'All the earth doth worship Thee;' but quickly there comes in the new Name. The Father Everlasting. A deeper relation has been unfolded to us—a deeper mystery. Yet it is still the *Earth* which worships the Father; yea, all the Earth. We who have been taught that word, claim it for the Universe: we are the spokesmen and priests of mankind. And, as such spokesmen and priests, we unite our voices with angels, and with the Heavens, and all the powers therein. The barriers are broken down. He who is walking in the midst of the golden candlesticks on earth, is also in the midst of the throne, the Lamb that was slain.

Upon this union of the seen and unseen, of the spiritual and the earthly world—of the old and the new—of ages past and ages to come—of the assembly of the first-born, and of each suffering sinner upon earth, the whole hymn turns. But it is a union which is only possible because the name Holy, Holy, Holy Lord God of Hosts, which Cherubin and Seraphin, which Apostles, and Prophets, and Martyrs, and the whole Church throughout the world are adoring, is the Name of the Father of an Infinite Majesty, His Honourable, True, and Only Son, and the Holy Ghost the Comforter. It is only possible because Christ the King of Glory did not abhor the Virgin's Womb, because he underwent the sharpness of death, that he might open the Kingdom of Heaven to all believers. Therefore can all his saints pray together, 'Help us whom thou hast redeemed with thy precious blood,' 'Make us all to be numbered with thy saints in glory everlasting;' therefore can the feeblest, most tempted, most erring member of the whole family say, 'O Lord, in Thee have I trusted, let me never be confounded.'

The Hymn of Zachariah after the Second Lesson is expressly the Song of the New Covenant. It speaks of the fulfilment of God's promise to Abraham and his seed; of the promise being this especially, 'That we should serve Him without fear, in holiness and righteousness, all the days of our life.' It speaks of a Child who was to be the herald of this Redemption to the Jewish nation. It encourages a Minister, who feels that he is sent forth on the same errand with John Baptist to claim the right, to feel the obligation, himself; it encourages every Christian parent to ask, with trust and fear, that, seeing the least in the Kingdom of Heaven is greater than the greatest in the old time, his own child may, into whatsoever sphere of work he is called, go before the face of the Lord to prepare His way. The *Jubilate* is a Psalm of the old time; but it is a Psalm which bids all lands rejoice in God; a Psalm therefore in which a man of the chosen nation, of the former world, bears witness

THE SONGS OF THE CHURCH.

of the throes of humanity and of the Child who has been born to *us* to rule the Nations.

Now if the great crime of every apostate religion is this, that it denies the full redemption which has been wrought out for mankind; if all its other evils are involved in this; and if the chief of these evils is, that the character of God and the relation of man to God are represented either in the terms of an imperfect dispensation, or still more frequently in the language of heathen ignorance and unbelief—I do not know what mightier protest it is possible to bear against such religion, than the continual daily use of these songs. They declare that that has been accomplished once for all which we need, that Christ has consecrated a new and living way into his Father's presence; that in Him all things are reconciled, both things in heaven and things in earth; that we are bound to give God thanks for that reconciliation, and to abide in the belief of it. Our Evening Hymns strike still more deeply at the heart of some idolatrous corruptions which belonged to all times, but had never a greater hold upon any time than upon our own. The *Magnificat* is the true, abiding witness against Mariolatry. 'He hath magnified me, and Holy is His Name. He hath exalted the humble and meek; the rich He hath sent empty away.' Let any man or woman drink in the life and sense of these words, applying them first of all to the Virgin herself, and then, as the use of the Hymn in our Service intimates that we should do, to the whole body of the Church, and you will find that the forms of modern Roman Catholic devotion and flattery, which, in spite of their grossness, are found to have an attraction even for refined spirits if they have been occupied exclusively with their own individual acts, become absolutely revolting and loathsome. And if this Hymn is rightly the preparation for reading the Epistles, the *Nunc dimittis* is the true expression of rest and satisfaction in the full declaration which they contain of the good things which eye hath not seen, nor ear heard, but which God hath given to them that love Him.

These Hymns have all come down to us from other days. We sing that which men sang generations ago. In the use of them we put honour upon the songs that were sung even among the Heathens; for all these, so far as they were true, were songs of freedom—witnesses that we are not meant to be bound by the chains of custom and of our animal nature—aspirations after a spiritual inheritance, and after one who should bring men into it. We put honour upon all genuine expressions of heart-devotion, though in the poorest doggrel; upon all poetry of later days, which embodies any high, earnest, human emotions, or unfolds any secrets of human character, whether it be formally religious or not. We put contempt upon every kind of song which has tended to sensualise and degrade the human spirit, let it assume what airs of religion it may; we begin to regard with some indifference all cold, artificial, exclusive Church-poetry, which does not speak of emancipation from spiritual fetters, and of real spiritual unity.

For, indeed, we have no leisure to indulge sickly fancies, and self-exalting tastes. We, too, stand upon a sea of glass. O, do not let us look for the Church in that mirror! We may see a reflection of its towers and minarets, but the image will be inverted. We shall be gazing on a shadow, not a substance. And how soon, while we are amusing ourselves with a picture, may we be made aware of real subterranean fires, which are ready to burst forth! And how soon may rise up beside us too a form of brute power with which we have no arms to fight, but which will stamp upon us its name, Division or Hatred! If we would win the victory, we must look up, and claim our part in the Church which is risen and ascended with Christ, which is sitting with Him in heavenly places, and which will reign with Him till all enemies are put under His feet.

SERMON X.

THE CREED.

Preached on Septuagesima Sunday, Feb. 4, 1849.

And they that know thy name will put their trust in Thee: for thou, Lord, hast not forsaken them that seek Thee.—PSALM ix. 10.

EVERY one must, I think, at some moment of his life, have been startled by the wonderful force of the words in Scripture with which he has been most familiar, and which had seemed to him most commonplace. For instance, the word 'trust' which meets us at every turn in the Book of Psalms—how soon we came to think of it as a kind of catch-phrase, as once which was characteristic of a peculiar people who lived some thousands of years ago in the East! In overwhelming troubles, in a time of utter weariness, when every calculation has been disappointed, when there seems no fair ground for expecting help from any quarter, when all is dark without and within, how has this little word dawned upon a man, what a witness it has seemed to give of a world of light somewhere, perhaps not far off! To be told that he may trust, or put his trust, in God; that this is not a sin, but a duty; that it has nothing to do with prospects of success, or even with the conditions of his own feelings; that the command is addressed to those who are in the midst of failure, upon whom the world has been frowning, who have found no resources in their own present consciousness, or in recollections of the past; to learn that such persons have best understood the command, and have obeyed it best; this is strange; what was a commonplace becomes a paradox, and yet in that form the man receives it, entertains it, ascertains it to be true. To fear God he knew was right, whether he did it or no; to love God he had always held to be right, if it were possible. But to trust in God, without being certain that he does either fear or love; to trust because all is in God which he has not and feels he has not, in himself, this is precisely what he needs, and precisely to this the book which had seemed a dull repetition of unmeaning sounds is inviting him.

There is another word in my text which has an inseparable connection with this. The great privilege of the Jew throughout Scripture is said to be this, that he knows the *Name* of God. He is not called to trust in some power which has sent him into the world, and which is exercising dominion over him, and with the nature and purposes of which he is unacquainted. It is assumed on the plainest grounds of reason that such trust would be impossible. It might be prescribed, but the rule could not be obeyed; it might be desirable, but no one could practise it merely because he wished it. You cannot trust a *thing*, or a mere *power*, or a mere *law*. Trust must be in a Person; you cannot trust a Person whom you suspect of possible malevolence to you. Therefore this was the feeling which grew with the growth and strengthened with the strength of every Jew who understood his own position : 'If I am to trust in God He must declare Himself to me. I trust Him because He has made me feel and know that He is Righteous, and that He cares for me. I cannot see Him, but I know His *Name*.'

Let us understand this well, brethren, for it is very important in reference to notions that are current in the present day. If there is to be a religion of trust, and not of slavish cowardly fear, that religion must have a Revelation, the revelation of a Name for its basis. A religion which creates its own object cannot be one of trust. I cannot rest upon that which I feel and know that I have made for myself. I cannot trust in that which I look upon as a form of my own mind or a projection from it. To suppose this is merely to practise a fraud upon myself; a fraud which is concealed from me while I am speculating, but which will force itself upon me the moment I begin to act. Neither can I trust in any shadowy impalpable essence, or in any Soul of the world. If this be the God I worship, my worship will be one of doubt and distrust, whenever it is at all sincere. If I do not seek all strange monstrous means of propitiating the unknown Being, it is only because I am altogether uncertain whether he is real enough for such services. And that uncertainty in some critical time, will for practical purposes disappear. I shall assuredly make the experiment. I shall see whether some sacrifice of my devising may not move Him, or may not remove the weight from my own breast. I may always have scorned superstition, and treated those as fools who yielded to it, but I shall find that the folly is one against which I have no security, and which is quite as ready to attack me as any other of my race.

All superstition, all priestcraft, in its worst and most evil sense—we cannot repeat this proposition too often, or put it in too many shapes—has its root in vague, indefinite religious apprehensions; not resting upon the knowledge and confession of a Being who is not our image, but who has declared Himself to us that we may receive His image. The teachers of the early Christian Church had a strong impression of this truth. It was forced upon them by all their experience. It went deeper than their experience. They were led by a higher wisdom than their own to feel that they had inherited the Revelation of God's Name, which was made to the Jewish fathers; that the greatest privilege they possessed was to know this Name fully, to be stamped and sealed with it. Their baptism into the Name of the Father, and of the Son, and of the Holy Ghost, they felt was a redemption from the worship of partial, divided powers; the fragments of the true, but conceived after men's own notions; the reflections, to a great extent, of their own feelings and passions. The Fathers used strong language respecting these Gods. They called them Devils. And assuredly very much of the worship they saw in the Roman Empire was devil-worship in the strictest sense. There was a faith in GOD lying beneath this worship; there were Heathens—how many none can tell—who strove to cultivate that faith in themselves and their fellows, and to use it against the other; but the tendency was more and more towards the adoration of beings whom it was not safe to leave unhonoured, because they were dangerous and hateful. How was a Reformation to be effected? How were men to be delivered from this most fearful of all abysses? The Christian Catechists taught their disciple the Name into which at baptism he would be received. We are not left to conjecture the nature of the instruction. The short treatise of St. Augustine, '*De Catechizandis rudibus,*' is at least a voucher for the African Church in the fifth century. From the severe opinions which we have heard imputed to that great man, and which unquestionably may be drawn out of his controversial writings, you would imagine that he especially might have been inclined to lay the foundation of his doctrine in some dark view of the Divine character, however he might afterwards introduce the consolations of the Gospel. A man who had felt sin so deeply might, one would have thought, have laboured first to awaken the sense of it in his Heathen converts before he proceeded to any other side of divinity. The great duty he conceives of the Catechist is to set forth the absolute eternal love and goodness of God. He is to declare *God the Father Almighty, Maker of Heaven and Earth.* Here was the first step in the divine revelation; that which laid the axe to the root of the devil-worship, divided worship, material worship; that which offered to the victims of each a high tower in which they might take refuge. No doubt they would often have a hard struggle in flying to it; the enemies would dog them continually; they would be asked how they knew that there was such a Being whom their senses told them nothing of. They would be called Atheists and self deceivers. Polytheists and Philosophical seekers after Unity would mock them equally. Their own hearts would repeat the scoffs which came from without. But are the words true or not? If not, men must of course go on in their delusions; there is no helping them; material worship, divided worship, devil-worship, must be left to degrade and rend in pieces the Universe. If the words are true, they will prove themselves true. The Father Almighty will prove himself to be a Father. They that know that Name will trust in it. They must. Their misery, their Atheism will drive them to it. And He will not fail those who seek Him.

But the question—How is He a Father, how do I know he is? cannot be evaded. The Church had no wish to evade it. She acknowledged that something more was implied in the Revelation of a Father than His name; that there must be some one to reveal Him. She proclaimed the Name of *His only-begotten Son, our Lord*. She says that He revealed Himself as the Son of God by being conceived of the Holy Ghost, our Lord, by being born of the Virgin Mary, by suffering our death, our burial, by going down into the Hell we tremble to think of; by facing all our enemies visible and invisible, all that we actually know we must meet, all that our imagination dreams of; that he rose again from the dead, and ascended into heaven, and sat down on the right hand of the Father, and will come again to judge the quick and dead. If God be absolute eternal love, as St. Augustine makes the Catechist affirm, how has He shown it? Has it come forth, or is it all hidden in his own nature? Has it come forth to some other creature, or to man? Has it met him where he needs to be met or somewhere else? Has it encountered the actual woes of mankind, or only those which affect a particular set of men? Has it been found mightier than these, or has it sunk under them? Has this love been cheerfully entertained, or did it encounter ingratitude? Was the ingratitude too strong for the love, or the love for the ingratitude? Is the victory for all times, or only for that time? Is He who you say is our Lord really our Lord? does he reign over us? Will he leave all things just as they are, or set them right at last? These questions have a claim to be answered; that is no Gospel to humanity which does not answer them; the Christian Church said, 'This is the answer.' Can you find another? Again we say it, if these words are false, men must be left to their delusions. They have not been redeemed yet, and none of you has told how a redemption out of human evils can take place except in this way. It has yet to be done, if it has not been done. And again, supposing the words be true, all we have to do is to proclaim them and live upon them. He who has sent us into the world for that end can prove them. Those that know his name will trust in Him, and so they will find that He has not deceived them.

Still there are inquiries which arise in our hearts that cannot be disposed of by these answers. Such as the following: 'Set this Divine Father before us as you will; affirm as you please that the Son has revealed Him to you, or to any number of men, yet the world is divided by a multitude of opinions, split into a multitude of parties. If you could bring a whole nation or age to your side, how could a sympathy be established between different nations and ages with their different habits, prejudices, and modes of thought? The sense of evil in men's minds is multiform. How can you prevent it from seeking infinite devices and a multitude of Gods for its relief? The body of each man does die, and is buried, say what you will about Christ's victory over death. The vision of the Divine Kingdom was bright in my mind yesterday, is dim to-day, say what you will about the perfect Revelation which there is in Christ.' The reply is, *I believe in the Holy Ghost.* I believe that there has come from the Father and the Son One who can reveal them to me and to all men; who does promise to dwell with us for ever, and to remove the corruptions that hinder us from receiving the Light which would enter in and fill us. I believe that He has brought men into a Unity which is not based upon different notions and opinions, but upon the Divine Name, a Church for all kindreds and nations. I believe that this body does not belong to space or time, but that those who dwelt on earth in past times, those who are dwelling on it now, those who shall dwell on it in ages to come, and those who never dwelt on it, the inhabitants of other worlds, created by the same Father, in the same Lord, are members of the same Communion of Saints, taught and filled by the same Spirit. I believe that this Spirit meets all those diversities in the sense and feeling of sins which divide individual consciences and send them to seek various medicines, nearly all unwholesome and poisonous, that he carries the same forgiveness of sins, the same witness of the Father's absolution, of the Son's conquest over sin, to the whole Church and each person in it. I believe that He who quickens our spirits will quicken also our mortal bodies, will deliver them out of the bondage of corruption, and make them like Christ's glorious body. I believe that we shall not always see truth in dim mirrors with winking and feeble eyes, but shall mount up on wings as eagles, and gaze upon the sun in its brightness, and enjoy that life everlasting, which is the knowledge and love of God.

I believe this. If it is not true, then I grant you there always must be strifes and divisions, and a perpetual repetition of past miseries, and a hopeless circle and endless retrogression; but I believe it is true, therefore I can tell you I believe it and invite you to believe it, and trust God to make all the experience of your lives the means of leading you to the fuller belief of it.

Yes! 'I believe.' In this form the Church taught its baptized member, if not its Catechumen, to speak. For she felt that the baptized man is not to lose hold of that which at such a cost has been won for him, but that he has need to be trusting every moment the Name that has been made known to him. And so this creed, this baptismal formulary, has become a Christendom possession, which all beggars and nobles, old men and children have a share and a right in. There is no charm in its words; they may have been varied at different times; new clauses may have been introduced into it to protect the rest from invasion. The worth of it is this especially, that it has so little to do with sounds, that it is so much a Creed of acts, that all the Divine Mystery comes forth in real manifestations meeting real necessities that are common to all.

It is a creed for the people which the schoolman cannot and dares not meddle with, and yet which he is obliged to confess says much more than he can say in hundreds of folios. It is a tradition—often it has been called *the* tradition of the Church. As such we receive it, and rejoice in it. But on this ground especially, that it is a continual protection against traditions, that when they try to force themselves upon us, we can always put this forward as a declaration that what we believe and trust in is not this or that notion, or theory, or scheme, or document; but that it is the Eternal Name into which we are baptized, and in which the whole Church and each member of the Church stands. As it has come down to us it must be a tradition. But it is a tradition which we cannot value for its own sake. Not the utterance, but that which is uttered; not the form, but the substance which is set forth is the object and the ground of our belief.

And, therefore, I say that the daily use of the Creed in our service, while it connects us with hundreds of thousands in all nations and ages, who have spoken these words in lonely cells, or on sick beds, despairing of life, and crushed with a sense of evil, realising their relation to God through all variations of opinion, through all confusion and ignorance which they had inherited from others, or into which they had fallen themselves, it does at the same time more effectually deliver us from Romish dogmatism, and all other dogmatism, than any form of words which it is possible for us to use. No protests against those substitutes for living faith in a living God, which have been introduced into any part of Christendom, can have anything like the force which there is in a distinct, personal, united assertion of that faith. And this especially because the Creed occurs in the midst of confessions, prayers, thanksgivings, which interpret its use. We do not put it forth to show what a different religion we have from other men. We say in whom we believe, because we are about to cast ourselves upon Him in utter helplessness, to ask help from Him for ourselves and all mankind, to beseech the Father, through the Son, to renew in us that Spirit of Holiness, and Fear, and Love, who can enable us to know His name, and to trust in it evermore.

SERMON XI.

EJACULATIONS AND COLLECTS.

Preached on Sexagesima Sunday, February 11, 1849.

> But when ye pray, use not vain repetitions, as the heathen do: for they think that they shall be heard for their much speaking. Be not ye therefore like unto them: for your Father knoweth what things ye have need of before ye ask him.—MATTHEW vi. 7, 8.

THESE words express the whole difference between Heathen and Christian prayers. Heathen prayers are attempts of man to climb up to God. Christian prayers are founded on the belief that God has looked down upon man. Heathen prayer rests on the hope that there is a deliverer somewhere. Christian prayer presumes that the Creator of man is one, and that He has wrought out a deliverance for us. Heathen prayer supposes that man may be related to some superior Being in as close a way as a child is related to its father. All Christian prayer is founded upon the actual manifestation of a father to his children. All heathen prayer supposes that a man knows his own wants, and that He whom he worships may attend to him when he makes them known with sufficient clearness and earnestness. Its strength therefore lies in much speaking. A number of arrows must be shot at different distant marks that there may be a chance of some hitting. All Christian prayer supposes that our Father knows what we have need of before we ask Him; that He makes us conscious of our needs, and leads us to declare them to Him; that He gives us all the clearness which we ever have in realising them, all the earnestness which we ever have in pouring them forth.

But the words 'Heathen' and 'Christian' may be easily abused to purposes of self-exaltation and self-delusion. Our Lord never taught his disciples that they would be exempt from any of the temptations or evil inclinations of other men. Neither the Old Covenant or the New, Circumcision or Baptism, Law or Gospel, Nation or Church, has the power to make us *in ourselves* a race of pure, holy beings. Were it so the just man would not live by faith, prayer would not be real or necessary.

The principle of the gospel is, that man is made a new creature in Christ, that God claims him as His spiritual child, that God gives him His Spirit to do His will. Such a gospel assumes that man apart from Christ is an evil creature, that in his flesh he cannot serve God, that he has a tendency not to do God's will, but to obey an evil will. These inclinations and tendencies come out not less, but more, under the new economy than under the old. The Christian is not less conscious of them than the Heathen, but infinitely more conscious. He may fall into them just as readily as the Heathen, and the fall will be accompanied with an immeasurably greater shock, with a more entire dislocation of his moral being. Every great position necessarily involves this possibility. The light must make the darkness more conspicuous. He who loves darkness rather than light must wrap himself in a thicker darkness than he who merely dwells in a darkness which the light has visited indeed but not penetrated. The Christian is such, so far as he does not trust in being a Christian, but trusts in Christ. The man who is made by Baptism a member of Christ, a child of God, an inheritor of the Kingdom of Heaven, takes up his rights by renouncing the world, and the flesh, and the devil, by telling them continually that they are not his masters. His privilege is to know the name into which he is baptized; to call upon the Father, as a member of His Son, in the Spirit which has been given him, for a renewal of that Spirit. Forgetting this calling, forfeiting that right, he will not cease to feel the need, but he will sink into the condition of those who send their arrows into the air, who pray to an unknown God, who think they shall be heard for their much speaking.

That this temptation will assail the Christian Church and each individual person in it, Scripture prepares us to expect. That it has assailed the Christian Church we know from history; that it does assail each one of ourselves we must have learnt, I should conceive, from experience. Do you find the mechanical repetition of Aves and Paternosters, or the invocation of Saints, or the most incoherent rhapsody which any Ranter ever poured forth, or the wildest ejaculation, half prayer, half curse, of a conscience-stricken dying man, or the torture of any Yogi, or the crying and cutting with stones of any Baal-worshipper in the old time, the least astonishing, the least meriting your scorn, or harsh judgment? Oh, beware! The thing is as evil as you describe it—more evil by far than your imagination can conceive it to be. But the root of it is in you—in you, though you have all the culture of modern Europe; though you believe you have cleared yourself of all earthly and all subterranean terrors; though you think you have sounded the depths of Nature, and know that there is nothing above Nature or beneath it; in you lies the capacity for all those fearful invocations to a dark power. A sudden change of circumstances; a sudden stroke of pain; the loss of something upon which you have set your heart; a sting of conscience altogether different from the dread of Hell, though likely enough, in spite of any charms you possess, to produce that dread, and to terminate in it; these may put you also upon shrieking aloud, in hope that some power will hear you for your much speaking. I do not say it will always be so; there are stout strong spirits which can bear up against much without making their voices heard; there are proud spirits which contract into themselves and defy all impressions that come from the world without, or from any hidden source. But I do not think any man who has much humanity, much care for his fellow-creatures, desires this state of mind; I think any one who fancied he was bringing it upon himself, and that he might become hopelessly fixed in it, would be greatly appalled. It seems, therefore, for one class as much as for another; for those who are tempted to direct superstition and false worship, as well as for those who are in danger of sinking into mere unbelief; and for that class, a very large one in our day, which is hovering between these two states of mind, often exhibiting symptoms of both—ready to plunge into Romanism one month, or week, scarcely a step removed from Pantheism the next, now eager to abandon all free exercise of thought and will, now eager to cast off all subjection—consistent in nothing but restlessness; it would seem desirable, I say, for all equally, that there should be some practical discipline which should be a warning against the Heathen notion of prayer, and an initiation into that Christian prayer described by our Lord as prayer to a Father 'who knows what we have need of before we ask.' Where such a discipline is to be had, if we are to look for it among individual priests, I know not; I do not believe that we can any of us be trusted so far. A judge who makes laws, instead of administering them, is not so dangerous a man as a priest who undertakes on his individual responsibility, or merely in general dependence upon the guidance of God's Spirit, to frame devotions for a number of people who happen to acknowledge him as their spiritual director. Not only his own temperament, but theirs, not only his prejudices and narrowness, but theirs, will come out in his utterances; more and more they will become utterances of personal feelings, less and less they will assume God's teaching as the real spring of these feelings— less and less, though there be a repeated reference in words to the divine Spirit, even though older forms be laid aside because the Spirit is to be his only guide. For there is surely no deeper error, no greater denial, than that which is implied in the notion that a sudden, momentary burst of passion comes from the divine afflatus, and that he who is emphatically the Spirit of

Order, of Peace, of continuous Life, is not the author of those acts which are preceded by deliberation and reflection. A true Church which confesses itself to be under the guidance of God's Spirit, which claims no power except in virtue of that guidance, and which desires that all her members should feel that it is meant for them—that if they submit to it, they will pray rightly—and act rightly—such a Church ought, I conceive, to provide us some common education, which may be useful in preparing our minds both for sudden emergencies and for steady exercises. Prayer has to do with the one as much as the other. It is likely to be perverted by the one as much as the other. Violent impulses may produce prayers that are selfish, and little better than curses. The reflections of the closet may be altogether divorced from the daily life; so that such monstrous contradictions will from time to time occur, as the one which a recent historian has brought before us, of a statesman laying a plot to draw his master into a violation of his marriage vow, and to make him the slave of an evil woman, on the very day he was writing a prayer (not intended for the public eye) that he might himself lead a more heavenly life. Such startling and awful facts should force every one to ask himself, whether prayer is to him a reality or not, and if not, how it may become so?

Now I believe that the Prayer Book has met the instincts of men in their modes of calling upon God for help. 1. By ejaculations. 2. By Collects. 3. By circumstantial petitions; such as those for the Royal Family, and all estates of men. 4. By a Litany. Of the last I hope to speak next Sunday. Of the former I will say a few words now.

EJACULATIONS AND COLLECTS.

1. The short prayers following the Creed, which are given to the Ministers and the Congregation alternately, are intended, I apprehend, as hints respecting what may be called our spontaneous thoughts. The expression is not exactly the right one. If the word 'spontaneous' is taken, as some in defiance of etymology and reason take it, to mean *involuntary*, none could be more unsuitable or unjustifiable. We are not at the mercy of our own thoughts, however rudely they may claim dominion over us. We have the power of saying to this, 'Go,' and it goeth, and to another, 'Come,' and it cometh. Every man knows that this prerogative belongs to him, and knows that he is guilty when he does not exercise it. But it is a gift which requires careful and incessant cultivation; it can be cultivated effectually only in one way. If each impulse from without be met by an impulse from within—if sudden impressions are sustained by prayers, as sudden, to the Lord of our Spirits, we may acquire a mastery over the subjects of our own spiritual kingdom, which will be otherwise always turbulent and refractory.

But there is a danger lest these acts, needful as they are for overcoming individual temptations, should become selfish, lest we should resort to these petitions only as helps against our special enemies. The thoughts concerning other people, which the daily events and accidents of life awaken, thoughts about our land and its rulers, kings and people, clergy and laity, the confusions of the world, the decay of morality in different classes—should not these, if they come forth in ordinary street-conversation, come forth also in petitions to God? A Church ought to suggest the events, ought to teach us in our public worship what a number of persons we have to do with in the common intercourse of life, and how solemn our relation to them all is, how certainly it has its ground in our common relation to God, and is only understood and acted on when we refer it to Him. The suffrages which follow the Creed and Lord's Prayer have, as I conceive, the object, and might have the blessed effect, of suggesting to Ministers and People what wishes they should be cherishing for each other, and for all men; what should be the habits of their minds, whether they are speaking or silent; what kind of aspirations the Heavenly Father, who knows their necessities before they ask, would be drawing forth from them.

2. But these sudden gushes of thought and feeling will be of a very poor earthly quality, they will not have any relish of that well of water which springeth up into everlasting life, if the spirit do not exercise itself in more orderly meditations. The right method of such meditations, it is, I believe, not easy to discover. Most who have desired to cultivate the habit have endured bitter mortifications—even cruel failures. How can I put myself in the right posture for thought? Where ought I to begin? What is the secret of realising the truths which I believe? What have thought and prayer to do with each other? What should I ask for when I pray? These are questions which are asked again and again; often I fear evaded rather than answered; sometimes replied to with a minuteness and precision which the conscience welcomes at first with exceeding thankfulness; afterwards complains of as burdensome and tormenting.

I know not what those may say who do not experience any of these difficulties, or who have mastered them, but to those who are conscious of great weakness and great tendency to incoherency in their own spiritual efforts, the Collects have afforded, and I believe will afford, unspeakable help. If you study the construction of them you will find that the principle, 'Our Father knoweth what things we have need of before we ask,' is assumed in all of them. Some strong satisfying view of the character of God, of His love to men, of what He has done for men, is the ground of the prayer; then follows the simple expression of some want of which the heart is conscious—some want which we feel, and yet which seems often to lie too deep for utterance; perhaps it is this very want of the power to tell, or even to know what one is wanting; the result is a petition that God, who desires us to have the good which we cannot grasp, will make His will effectual in spite of our inability, in spite even of our reluctance. This you will feel to be the form—the fixed form of the Collect—fixed in itself, but capable of expressing infinite varieties of feeling, of adapting itself with marvellous flexibility to the different conditions of the human spirit. To begin *from* God, and to consider how He meets His creatures, not to begin from some mere chance feeling of ours, and consider how we may work ourselves into a right state; this, I think, is the blessed and pregnant hint which the Collects supply us with as a guide in all our reflections upon ourselves or upon the world around us. And that hint, as it puts us into the posture for thought, so also explains most livingly the connection of thought and prayer; how one should interpret the other. We think because there is One near us who is prompting us to think and teaching us how to think. Our confession of His presence and of Him as the spring of every movement of our inner mind, is a prayer. Thought and prayer both come from a hidden source; they go forth to fight with foes and gain victory in the external world; they return to rest in Him who inspired them. Oh! how fresh and original will each of our lives become, what flatness will pass from society, what barrenness from conversation, what excitement and restlessness from our religious acts, when we understand these secrets!—when the morning prayer is really a prayer for grace, to one whose service is perfect freedom, in knowledge of whom is eternal life; when at evening we really ask One from whom all good thoughts, and holy desires, and just works proceed, for the peace which the world cannot give.

3. These Ejaculations and Collects have an ancient, if you like so to speak, a Catholic, origin; and are the best deliverances, as I conceive, from the idle repetitions and inflated rhapsodies of pseudo-Catholicism. The continuous circumstantial prayer, to which the Congregation does not respond, is more akin to the Puritan forms of devotion. In our State Services, which belong to the Puritan age, we have imitated its worst models, I am constrained to think, with great awkwardness. I know no compositions which are so perfectly contrasted in form and in tone with the prayers of our daily service, as the long, wordy, vituperative addresses to God—not free even from the vulgar aids of alliterations and puns—which are found in the services for the 5th of November, the 30th of

January, and the 29th of May. It is so infinitely desirable to recognise God in all our doings as the real King of the Nation, that I believe more good than harm has resulted, and even now results, from these acts of worship. I do not feel that the accident of their being called State Services, and wanting the authority of a body which was very imperfectly ecclesiastical, and which exercised the functions it did possess very little to the advantage of the country, or of the Church generally, should prevent us from submitting to the order which prescribes the use of them. But that they breathe not the earnestness of men struggling for a great truth, or a strong conviction, but the excitement and revenge of a triumphant party; that they confuse history; that they exhibit the English Church not in her high, noble character, as the reconciler of two principles, each of which is mischievous by separation from the other, but as the common enemy of those who maintained and perverted each of these principles, as eager to make the most of the wrongs which were committed by either, and to convict them of wrongs for which as religious bodies they were not responsible—this is too plain, and should be confessed with shame and sorrow.

But the Puritan type of prayer is not therefore to be rejected, as of no worth, because in this instance it has blended very ill with our other forms. It must have a truth of its own, or it could not have been adopted, so exclusively, by earnest and honest men. And it would be exceedingly dangerous that the Collect, the Litany, or any other mode of composition, merely as such, should be invested with an imaginary sacredness. The Prayer for all sorts and conditions of men, and the General Thanksgivings, though they bear marks of modern construction, have never, I think, been felt to be at variance with the petitions and songs which surround them. They are grounded upon an acknowledgment of God's fatherly love to all men; they ask that this love may be a bond of union between Him and all men. This is surely prayer in its highest power—that which our Father in Heaven who knoweth our necessities before we ask, and our ignorance in asking, Himself teaches, and Himself will answer.

SERMON XII.

THE LITANY.

Preached on Quinquagesima Sunday, February 18, 1849.

And above the firmament that was over their heads was the likeness
of a throne, as the appearance of a sapphire stone: and upon
the likeness of the throne was the likeness as the appearance of
a man above upon it.—EZEKIEL i. 26.

THE genius of Raphael has brought the vision of Ezekiel home to the imaginations, if not to the hearts, of a number of cultivated men in all parts of Europe who would not have cared to study the Prophet himself. His picture is certainly worth a great many commentaries. And it has this especial merit: it justifies his own art from a charge which Protestants are often inclined, and not without much plausibility, to bring against it. They complain that whenever it is applied to the highest subject of all, it must of necessity lower the idea of God, removing the thick cloud or the brightness into which no eye can look, and presenting some form which it is possible for us to apprehend and conceive. That there is this peril in sacred painting it would be folly to deny; that it may become the tool

M

of the senses, and of sensual worship, experience has proved. To know exactly when the limit has been passed, when the temptation has been yielded to, is not for us, but for the Judge who knoweth all things. But the moral sense which is exercised to discern good and evil, may be trusted to pronounce a safe general verdict; the conscience of each man may warn him to avoid that which does him mischief. There is, however, it must never be forgotten, another and as great a danger. We are as much tempted to become vague and abstract, as gross and carnal. The two errors succeed each other; the first is sometimes the parent, sometimes the offspring, of the last. It is a mistake to suppose that the Old Testament and the New exclusively denounce either. No doubt the Jewish Scripture is a continual protest against visible worship; against supposing God to be the likeness of anything in heaven above, or in the earth beneath, or in the waters under the earth, against bowing down to the works of men's hands. But the Ark of Testimony, the Mercy-seat, and the Cherubim which covered it, the Holy place and the Holiest of all, gave awful distinctness to the thoughts of the Jew respecting Him who was dwelling in the midst of his people. The vision of Isaiah was of one who is Holy, Holy, Holy; but it was of a king whose train filled the Temple. And this vision of Ezekiel, which carries us into so high and awful a region, is wound up with the words I have read to you. *And upon the likeness of the throne was the likeness as it were the appearance of a Man above upon it.* Assuredly the New Testament substantiates all the loftiest dreams of the former Dispensation. It carries us into that kingdom of heaven which

Kings and Prophets desired to see. The full uniting name is revealed to the Christian peasant, surrounds the Christian child, which Isaiah and Ezekiel were only contemplating on different sides through a glass darkly. But how comes it that this revelation is so much grander, deeper, more complete than the first? Because the King whose train filled the Temple is declared to be He who was crucified under Pontius Pilate, because the man above the throne is no more a dim likeness ('as it were an appearance'), but He who, when He had by Himself purged our sins, sat down for ever on the right hand of the Majesty on High. The painter, I think, may be a blessed help in connecting these truths together, just as he may be a means of weakening, by separating, them. He may give us a total impression of the Divine awfulness, of a glory which cannot be seen or uttered, and yet make us feel that a Man is in the midst of the throne, sustaining all things by the word of his power. The spirit which rests in that belief, and is kept by it from sinking, will not be satisfied with any outward image or picture. It will recognise an unfathomable depth below; but a depth which we can only see through and in the Man of sorrows, an abyss of love in which we can be content to be lost.

These remarks, I believe, have a close relation to the subject upon which I proposed to speak this afternoon. Of all parts of our Service the Litany is the one which lies most open to the charge of being anthropomorphic, and which has oftenest incurred it. The Son of Man is distinctly exhibited in all the petitions. His acts upon earth are put forward as the very ground of prayer to him. He is addressed as one who feels for all the common outward sufferings, and the bodily calamities, of his saints here on earth. Moreover, the Litany belongs to what may be called, without injustice, the anthropomorphic period of Church History. In all probability it was not composed within those first four centuries, which some English divines regard with such exclusive veneration. It may have been formed upon older models; but Gregory the Great would seem to have cast it into its present shape; Gregory, whose popedom is truly regarded as the commencement of the Middle Ages, and who partook so largely himself of the characteristics of the period which dates from him. The origin of the document is most suspiciously Latin; we may, if we please, consider it as a special badge of our own Latin slavery, seeing that Augustine and his brother monks probably entered our land chanting it, or some portion of it. And lastly, it cannot be denied that Litanies are closely connected in their form and use with Processions; some pressing local or national calamity suggested them; they were said and sung by priest and people as they moved along towards a church with rites that might be adopted from some Jewish or heathen ceremonial.

All to whom these facts are important, for one party reason or another, are fully entitled to the benefit of them; it is clearly dishonest to explain them away. They who think that we shall never be in a right state till we bring back the feelings, habits, forms, of Gregory's time, that what we chiefly want are outward tokens and emblems to assist devotion, that its spirit is departed, that to restore it we can do nothing better than revive periodical chants and processions, may make what use they can of our Litany and its history. Those who would show that the rags of Popery hang about our worship, and that they must be cast off or that it will penetrate into our inmost spirit, that the only way of producing a sound and earnest Protestantism is to enter the House of God with a determination that we will loathe and hate whatever reminds us of the centuries before the Reformation, should not be robbed of any evidence which may give such propositions greater strength and plausibility. I will not enter into any special pleading with either class. I appeal from both to those who have tried and do try to pray these prayers; who know what they are, not from books of antiquity, but from their own hearts. If there is a cure in earth or heaven for men who would turn prayer into a show, who would make it a part of the finery and ornament of life, not of its inner substance; who fancy we can train ourselves for devotion by putting on a dress or learning a tone, I should say this Litany must be the cure. What do you mean by saying it is so human but this: That it calls upon the Son of God as one who has actually entered into the depths of human sorrow; who has borne the agony and bloody sweat, the cross and passion, who has been dead, and buried, and has known the darkness of the unseen world? What do you mean by calling it human but this: That it speaks of the actual vulgar sorrows to which flesh is heir; that it supposes men to be praying who know them for themselves and for others, who are too much crushed by them to have any power except to lift up such a cry as this, "Good Lord, deliver us," "Lord, have mercy upon us"? It is in the press and tumult of life you learn the tones in which these prayers should be uttered; it is amidst the terrible realities of sickness and death, of conflict with flesh and blood and with principalities and powers, that you are taught with what kind of garlands, in what measures, you shall approach the divine altar. Surely you cannot be thinking of plays and baby-shows while you are crying out, "In the hour of death, in the day of judgment, deliver us." Or if you are— and who can say that the merest vanity and frivolity may not assault his mind at the most dreadful moment? —is not this one of the very temptations, the most tormenting, if not the most terrible, of all from which we come to seek deliverance? Are you not flying to Him who is all true, from your own follies and weaknesses and hypocrisies? Did you ever meet with words which expressed more distinctly, simply, passionately, the sense of that oppression and the hope of that refuge? From first to last the prayer supposes you to be surrounded with enemies; some visible, some invisible; both equally real; the secret pestilence no more than the drawn sword; the pride and malice and envy of our own hearts, no less than those of the persecutor and slanderer. Everything about this document is intensely practical. The man who utters it is alone in God's presence, yet he is speaking of evils that are common to thousands. He does not isolate himself from his fellows. Plagues and pestilences threaten the whole land; sin and death lay their hands on princes and beggars. You ask help for all nations, you beseech the Lord God to govern the whole Church in the right way. Not the less do you enter into every individual suffering and mode of suffering. For the transgression of which you accuse yourself may not be that which is pressing upon my conscience; if they are the same, our feeling of them may be quite different. A slanderous tongue may be more agonising to one man than the rack and fire to his neighbour. Each sorrow is entertained in a different chamber of imagery; strikes a different string of the heart. No wonder, therefore, people ask for special prayers, for prayers suited to their own cases. Their mistake is this—they suppose that it is possible for them to make, or for their priests to make, prayers which shall suit their cases and which shall not suit a multitude of cases besides. The individuality is not given by the words spoken, but by him who speaks them. You can make the expression of them wholly individual only by making them superficial and worthless. If they only touch the specialities of your suffering they will not tell what you are suffering; if they go down far enough into your experience to be adequate for that purpose, they will inevitably meet and represent the thoughts of people whose circumstances, education, temperament, are altogether unlike yours. The first simple idea of prayer, which is so apt to be lost in speculation about its qualities and conditions, that it is a call upon God who knoweth all things, is the true escape from these and almost all other perplexities.

You need not draw out minutely the particulars of your misery; you understand it very ill; you will describe it awkwardly and blunderingly; you want only to lay yourself, and all that is within you and around you, before Him who sees into the roots of your being, to whom past, present, and future are all open. The main thing in every prayer is that which we all see is the main thing in the Lord's Prayer.

The Being whom we worship should be set more clearly and directly before us than any of the occasions which lead us to seek him; then they will present themselves in their right method and succession. First of all, let a man feel that he has a real refuge and home to which he may betake himself; the avengers, who are pursuing him, will make him sufficiently conscious of *their* power. The obscure and unsatisfactory prayer comes from the uncertainty of the suppliant, whether he is betaking himself to a deliverer, or seeking to propitiate an enemy. As long as that doubt continues he must pray, at times with the vehemency, generally with the listlessness, of despair. He will make great irregular efforts to change the Divine mind; he will then sink into a half-Atheism, almost desiring it could be a whole Atheism, that so he might be freed from the presence of One who seems to delight only in punishing him. What a mighty witness does the Litany in its outset bear against this kind of worship! It is God the Father, of heaven, God the Son, the Redeemer of the world, God the Holy Ghost, proceeding from the Father and the Son—the holy, blessed, glorious Trinity, three Persons and one God—whom we beseech to have mercy upon us. Every distinct Name is a witness of care, deliverance, strength; the whole Name expresses the perfect charity, the absolute love; love in essence, in manifestation, in act; love forming, saving, indwelling. The mercy which we ask for is the nature and perfection of the Being from whom we ask it. The mercy has been most exercised towards those who ask for it. The righteousness of God has been set forth in the forgiveness of sin. 'Good and upright is the Lord, therefore will he teach sinners in the way;' miserable sinners, those who have wandered from His love, those who have lived out of the circle of it. Herein lies all their evil; their wretchedness has no other source. The next petition brings Him distinctly before us in whom the whole Godhead has dwelt bodily; who said, 'He that hath seen me hath seen my Father,' on whom the Spirit was bestowed without measure. We call upon Him who *has* redeemed us with His most precious blood. It is not an act to be accomplished hereafter. It has been accomplished. All our prayers assume it; they are unmeaning if this redemption is not a divine fact for us and for all mankind. Nevertheless we are sinners, we are miserable; there is no hiding that earthly fact, that fact of our own individual condition, to preserve a theory. With theories we have nothing to do. God's truths we know He can take care of and assert, and reconcile facts with them. That is what we ask Him to do. It is His anger to leave us in the condition to which we have brought ourselves by our ill-doings; we dread no other; the wrath of being left to ourselves, left to our sin, and to the crafts and assaults of the devil; to that damnation which it is not God's will that any should incur, but which means the loss of Him, the settled strife of our self-will against His loving will. From this we pray Him to deliver us, and therefore from all those habits and principles which are contrary to the nature of God, which make up the devil's nature, which constitute the curse and plague of our race—from pride, and malice, and envy, and hypocrisy, and uncharitableness. From those outward sins which corrupt and defile the world, and degrade God's image, and bring death upon the soul. From the plagues, pestilences, and famines, which are God's ministers for the punishment of wrong doings, and which He withholds when they have fulfilled their purpose. From the strifes and seditions which destroy the life of cities and nations. From the schisms and heresies which destroy the life of churches. From the contempt of God's Word and Commandment, which is the ruin of man. And this we ask for men, because there is a Man in the midst of the throne. Because He to whom we pray has not left us to fight by ourselves with these foes, and to be their victims and thralls, but has come down himself into the battle-field, has trod the winepress alone, and has come back with the stained garments of the Conqueror. By the Incarnation in which He made himself one with us; by the Nativity which shrouded His glory in human poverty and weakness; by the Circumcision which showed that he made himself obedient to the law for man; by the Baptism in which He was declared at once to be Son of God and Son of Man; by the Fasting in which He claimed that man should not live by bread alone, but by every word which proceedeth out of the mouth of God; by the Temptation in which He overcame the spirit of pride, and in human flesh asserted His filial relation to the Father, His filial dependence on the Father; by His agony and bloody sweat, in which He overcame self-will, and glorified His Father's will; by His cross and passion, in which He showed that malice, and hatred, and envy, and revenge, and hypocrisy, and all uncharitableness,

could not subdue love, but were subdued by it; by
His death and burial, in which He showed that there
was no dark anomalous condition into which sin had
brought those whom He called His brethren, which
He would shun; by His glorious resurrection and
ascension, in which He triumphed over death and the
grave, and hell, and space, and time, and established
a perfect union between the visible and the invisible
world, between God and His creatures on earth; by
the coming of the Holy Ghost, who proceeded from
the Father and the Son, to make us the sons of God
in Christ, to vanquish evil, and establish peace in
human hearts, to bind nations and churches in one:
by these acts and powers we adjure Him who lives for
ever and ever God and Man, to deliver us in all times
of tribulation and of wealth; in the hour when the
spirit leaves its case of death; in the day when the Son
of Man shall be seen in the glory of His Father and of
the holy angels. On this ground we rest our petitions for
blessings to the Church, blessings to our own nation, to
sovereign, priests, magistrates, to the nations of the
earth, to those who have erred and are out of the way,
to those who are sick and in travail, wanderers and
captives, to the fatherless and the widow, to all men.
No other ground is there for them; they are but
words thrown to the winds if there is not this way for
them to ascend into the Heaven of Heavens.

Brethren, is it by loud talking and railing against
Popish vestments and practices, is it by denouncing
all good and noble deeds which may unfortunately
have become stained with some childish affectations—
by exhibiting Protestantism not as it truly is and
ought to show itself, free, generous, comprehensive,

by narrow, snarling, exclusive, impatient of the minutest difference from its own standard and ritual —that you hope to prevent your children from relapsing into bygone errors, that you hope to make them true servants of the living God? Or is it by showing how they may be in sympathy with past ages and with those who lived in them, namely, by being men as they were, by entering into the woes of men as they did, by crying with real hearts to the Deliverer as they did? Are we ambitious of being like them? We cannot be like them except upon these terms. No costume will produce the resemblance. We shall only be mummies wrapped up in cerements which were once the clothing of actual men. Are we afraid of being like them? Do we dread their superstitions, or idolatries; the falsehoods into which they fell respecting the relations between God and man? The fear is legitimate; but how can we avoid a danger which is indeed close at hand? Their superstitions are ours, their falsehoods belong to our nature. No rules, cordons, schemes for preventing infection which you can devise, will keep them from us. The worship of the visible, the glorification of human gods or earthly gods, the trust in secondary or earthly mediators, may change its name and retain its nature; it may be exorcised under the title of Popery, and may use all its witchcrafts under titles which are approved and sanctioned and fashionable. Again and again it has proved so. The Middle Age habit of mind has been violently resisted; men have been afraid to acknowledge a Man in the midst of the throne. They have prayed hard prayers to a distant Being. The reaction has come with all its attendant evils. The humanity exalted above the divinity because the divine had been separated from the human; Christ regarded—strange and frightful delusion—as more benignant than the Father; his life on earth esteemed alone significant and precious; an opening made for the introduction of all Mariolatry, all saintly worship, all deification of men upon earth, as being nearer to the sinner and more capable of sympathising with him, than the perfect Lord.

To avoid these monstrous mischiefs, these dark superstitions, there is no course but to acknowledge and put forth prominently the truth which lies under them. God will never truly be worshipped except when man sees his own nature glorified at God's right hand. Man will never be delivered from the temptation to make God after his likeness till he fully sees and confesses that he is made after God's likeness, and that One who has his nature and continually sympathises with him, fully exhibits that image. The Middle Ages realised the conviction of Christ's humanity; they fell into all the corruptions and counterfeits of that conviction. But any sincere prayer which any man in those days offered to Him who had redeemed him by His cross and passion, was a prayer against his own infirmities, against his own propensity to glorify the creature more than the Creator. Such prayers were offered, and they were heard. We are receiving the blessing of them. God did open men's eyes to see wherein they had forgotten Him, and had set up themselves or creatures of their own kind in His place. He did teach them that only a Mediator who was one with Him and with them could satisfy their wants. He did break chains which they groaned under, and chains which they hugged. When we say this Litany we enter into communion with them; we pray against their falsehood and our own.

These petitions swell and expand with all our added experience as we pour them forth. 'Oh Lord,' we say, 'we have heard with our ears, and our fathers have told us, what Thou didst in their days, and in the old time before them.' 'We have heard how Thou didst break asunder the yoke of heathenism by which our land was bound, when monks from Rome came singing these Litanies to Thee. We have heard how Thou didst guide and govern our land in all the ages since, amidst the sins of the prophets, priests, and people, still keeping witnesses for Thyself, making their different partial views and imperfect confused efforts work out a great result. We have heard how Thou didst set us free from the service of a man who assumed a throne on earth, and hid from the eyes of Thy Church the Man who is on the throne above the firmament. We have heard how Thou didst teach our fathers to shake off idolatrous customs, which time had made sacred to them, and to worship the Father who is a Spirit, in spirit and in truth. Oh then, arise! help and deliver us for thy name's sake. From the sins of our rulers, and priests, and people; from the malice and pride and cruelty of our religious factions; from the coldness and hardness of our religious services; from the helplessness of our preaching; from the unreality of our sacraments; from the infidelity which our insincere profession is producing among rich and poor; from the stings of conscience and the dark despair which weaken our spirit, when we see multitudes without the bread that perisheth, or the bread of life; from our want of charity and sympathy with them, and with those who are troubled by doubts and despondency, and can find no helper; from our mammon-worship; from all the sins which we know, and from all which only thine eyes behold; by Thine agony and bloody sweat, by Thy cross and passion, by Thy glorious resurrection and ascension, and by the coming of the Holy Ghost, good Lord, deliver us.'

SERMON XIII.

THE COMMUNION SERVICE.

(1) THE COMMANDMENTS.

Preached on the First Sunday in Lent, February 25, 1849.

For this is the Covenant that I will make with the house of Israel after those days, saith the Lord; I will put my laws into their mind, and write them in their hearts: and I will be to them a God, and they shall be to me a people.—HEBREWS viii. 10.

THE Gospel has been often spoken of as a mild tolerant system, which was intended to mitigate the extreme rigour of the old Law. A number of passages could be quoted from Scripture which seemed to confirm this representation. The grace of Christ is continually opposed to the law of Moses. The one is said to declare death, as following from sin; the other to bring forgiveness of sin. Thunders and lightnings are the symbols of Sinai; a Father, a Saviour, a Comforter, are the characteristic words of the New Testament.

And yet any one who reads the Sermon on the Mount, where our Lord more formally than elsewhere sets forth the distinction between that which was spoken of old time and that which He came to effect, can hardly go away with the impression that He came to relax stringent rules, or to relieve the subjects of His kingdom from obligations which had been before imposed upon them. In every case the righteousness which the Scribes and Pharisees considered sufficient, He declares to be unsatisfactory. In every case the literal observance of God's own holy commandment falls short of the true obedience which He claims. He seeks not abstinence from murder, but from anger, wrath, contempt; not abstinence from adultery, but from inward lust. The permission of divorce is not to be used to set aside the sacred union of marriage. The solemn oath which is the end of strife, is to be no excuse for swearing in our ordinary communications, by the name of God, or by the great city. Evil is not to be resisted; the enemy is to be loved and prayed for. No wonder that many Christian teachers reading such language should have adopted precisely the opposite conclusion to that of which I just now spoke, and should have told their disciples that the demands of the New Covenant were altogether fuller, deeper, sterner than the Old.

In our own day, and in this country, the reaction against the first class of statements has been especially vehement; the others have been put forward with extreme rashness and recklessness. 'All our natural tendencies,' it has been said, 'are to sloth and self-indulgence. What possible danger is there in our setting before ourselves too high and severe a standard? All our most dangerous longings are for freedom; what can be worse than making religion a minister to those longings? If the state into which Baptism brings us is a higher one than that into which the Jews were brought by Circumcision, the demands upon us must be higher in the same proportion; the sentence upon the neglect of them more terrible. The obligations of gratitude, the returns of love for the death and satisfaction of the Son of God, must be immeasurably greater than any which could be looked for from a king or prophet of the ancient world.'

All these reasonings seem very plausible to those who utter them, just as the others did. Those who have listened to each and have confessed at different times, perhaps at the same time, the truth implied in both, become utterly bewildered. They feel as if they had no ground to stand upon; at all events as if Christianity and the Bible gave them none. They must ask help elsewhere; there may be oracles which return less ambiguous answers, which may not suggest one course of conduct to-day and the opposite to-morrow; which may not hold out the promise of liberty, and under pretence of fulfilling it, impose a more bitter bondage.

Before they quite adopt this resolution (shall I not say also, *after* they have adopted it and have found fresh disappointments, the responses of the priests and priestesses in the new temples and caves proving to be as little helpful for the actual work of life as those which they have rejected) will they not consider for a moment whether the Scriptures really adopt either of the theories which have been deduced from them, and why they seem to adopt both? In the verse which I have taken for my text this afternoon, we have a very distinct assertion of what the writer of this Epistle conceived to be the distinguishing glory of the New Covenant; in what sense he conceived it had overreached and set aside the Old. 'Behold,' he says, quoting from the Prophet Jeremiah, 'this is the Covenant which I will make with the house of Israel after these days: I will write my laws in their hearts, and in their minds will I write them, and they shall be to me a people, and I will be their God.' There is nothing here which would lead you to suppose that the New Covenant was a mitigation of certain penalties which had been denounced against transgression, by some elder code; there is nothing to warrant the inference, that it comes making exactions which that elder code had not made. The Apostle puts the relation between them in a different light altogether. A law had been proclaimed, a good law, a sufficient law. A new one was not wanted, either gentler or harsher. But this was wanted—that the law should be practically efficient; that it should not be at strife with the minds and hearts of those to whom it was proclaimed, that they should *be* such creatures as would *do* what it prescribes. Precisely this want, he says, the Gospel Covenant satisfies. It promises to bring the heart and mind of man into conformity with the heart and mind of God; it promises that there shall be a creature capable of acting out, willing to act out, the commands of the law. The more you consider it the more you will feel, I think, that this is precisely what those Scriptures are saying which seemed to be at variance with each other. Is the law of commandments represented as terrible, as causing Moses to fear and quake, as expressed in thunders and lightnings? How could it be otherwise if the law was received by a creature who felt that it was proclaiming war upon his acts or upon his inclinations? Is it said to be a curse? Must it not have been a curse if it made men conscious of a separation from God and from each other; of something in their own very selves which produced the separation? Is it said to be a law of death? And what is death but the sense of being utterly torpid and helpless, incapable of movement, crushed by a power which you cannot resist? In proportion as the law was confessed to be right, and the man knew himself to be wrong, it would be to him a law of death—a law declaring death, and actually fulfilling its own sentence. Is the Gospel spoken of as essential grace? Would it deserve that name if it were the mere abatement of the penalties decreed by the law, when it is the law itself—the feeling of its divine righteousness and of man's incapacity—which is so horrible? Is not the title justified if the Gospel is able to assert this righteousness and to set up faith as the very means of removing this incapacity? Is the Gospel said to be the deliverance from a curse? Must it not be so if it removes the consciousness of a separation between man and God, between man and man? Is the Gospel said to bring in life? Must it not do so if it shows that the very power which was felt to be crushing the creature is quickening and regenerating him? Is it strange if this was so that our Lord should require a higher righteousness than that of mere obedience to the letter of a law? Must not the conformity of the inner mind to its principle be something immeasurably higher? Is not the root of murder, wrath and contempt; of adultery, impurity; of swearing, want of reverence for God; of dislike for any creature—want of resemblance to Him who formed all and loves all? And would not the creation of a fellowship with God be the destruction of this root, the establishment of men upon another and opposite root; one of which gentleness, goodness, long-suffering, are the fruits?

There is, however, a difficulty of which we have need to clear our minds, and which is wont to recur again and again after we have seemed to be dispossessed of it. Can we suppose that men for so many generations were living merely under a curse, a penalty, a law of death, and that then at once a Gospel of blessing, of freedom, of life, was announced to them? Can we think that there is such an advantage as this notion would imply, in being born some centuries later into the world? Assuredly the Apostles and Evangelists exact no such belief of us, but discourage it. They assume that their forefathers had a Gospel as well as themselves. They are careful to note that Abraham their first father was not under a law. They do not, however, on that account, conclude that those who received the law entered into a lower condition than his, for the Lord God made Himself known to them as the Lord merciful and gracious, and slow to anger; all His acts towards them were the acts of a deliverer. He was proclaimed to be so at the opening of the Ten Commandments themselves. The Book of Deuteronomy is throughout declaring a gracious Covenant, an inward law, which men would obey while they trusted in the Lord God, and which would only be turned into a curse when they forgot Him. How that gracious Covenant would be carried out, how that inward law would be fulfilled, and in the meantime what comfort there was in meditating upon it, and in submitting to be governed by it, the Psalmist and Prophets are setting forth in every song, and prayer, and discourse. The law was a curse, a bondage, a death, only to those who looked to its letters; when they looked up to Him from whom it came, when they thought what He was, and what He had done for their fathers and them, when they hoped for a more complete revelation of Himself and of His relation to them, gloom, dread, weakness, disappeared: they felt that there was light near them, which would grow brighter and brighter, a forgiveness to which they might fly after every sin, a strength which could not fail them in any work or any sorrow. The revelation of Jesus Christ, so said the Apostles, was the discovery of Him in whom these holy men had trusted, and not been confounded; the Law had come by Moses, the grace and the truth of the Law had come by Him; Abraham had seen His day, and was glad. He had been with the people in the wilderness as they journeyed to the promised land, the Angel of the Covenant in whom God's name was, the Word of God who had spoken to the Prophets, and from whom their words came; He had now appeared in the likeness of sinful flesh, had been proclaimed the Son of God at His baptism, had been proved to be so by the resurrection of the dead, that he might make men sons of God in Him, that they might attain to that true estate of spiritual creatures, to which they had always felt they had a title, that they might be accepted in Him, forgiven, justified, that they might be baptized with the Spirit of the Father and Son, and be made after their likeness. The New Covenant, in this name, the New Covenant, of which the Spirit of God is the seal,

THE COMMUNION SERVICE.

and of which the promise is, 'I will write my laws in their hearts, and in their minds will I write them,' is the fruit of this revelation; the old vanishes away because its meaning has been fulfilled, because it only implies a light which has been manifested, because it does not recognise men as standing to God in the complete relation of sons, and as endued, quickened, regenerated by the Divine Spirit.

You will feel, I think, that a Gospel of this kind would of necessity present two aspects to persons who looked at it from different sides, and that those who were determined to consider it only in one of these aspects, would adopt one or other of the statements which I said had been so prevalent in the Church. The Gospel would be regarded as a provision against the discouraging disheartening threats of the Law. The Gospel would be regarded as carrying out the Law to its utmost extent, and to an extent *it* could not reach. Both statements are true; but see how by exaggerating each and making it exclusive, you reduce it into meagreness, barrenness, unreality, even for its own professed object. Is the Law stripped of its overwhelming killing quality by discovering a scheme for enabling men to live more at ease? Not at all. It is too true, too fixed, too perfectly in accordance with the witness of the conscience, for any such arrangements. He who has fallen into transgression—even the merely careless man—will find it invested again with its thunders and lightnings, not to be stilled by all his notions of a price having been paid for pardon, or of God's willingness to grant it when he asks for it. He will be tormented with the thought, how far the ransom applies to his case; he will find that he is not able to ask. Again, is the man able to lead that exalted life which he is told the Gospel demands of him, because he is frightened with the threat of tremendous consequences if he does not lead it? Can you make him grateful and loving, by reminding him how much gratitude and love he ought to show in return for the benefits that have been bestowed upon him? Can you make him right and true within by convincing him how many more outward services are demanded of him under the New Covenant, because it is perfect, than were required under the Old? Past history—the experience of every fresh day—answers No to all these questions. You multiply your threats; they produce alarm, some feeble efforts at reformation, then indifference, alienation, disgust. You talk of the obligation to love; he to whom you speak tries to love, feels how impossible the struggle is, and ends with becoming a hypocrite or an atheist. You impose new rules to protect the old, which were too weak to protect themselves; each one seems to carry your pupil further from his aim; to make the attainment of an inward life more hopeless, to throw him more upon visible things, to put him at a greater distance from God. If the Divine Law had not found out a better way of meeting man's wants than that which they dream of for themselves, if it had provided nothing better for us than alleviations, if it had not bestowed the power to do that which it asks of us, promised to originate the love which it wishes us to show forth, we should be indeed more miserable than Jews or heathens were or are.

But is this more excellent way one which we are

now for the first time discerning in the Scripture, a grand eclectical device for reconciling opposite notions which we in this nineteenth century have been privileged to strike out, and of which our forefathers knew nothing? That our forefathers were tempted into each of the views I have condemned, we have abundant proof; that the experience of the results to which each has led should give us an advantage which they did not possess; that if God's promises be not vain, and the Spirit be not withdrawn from the Church, we may attain to a simpler perception, of the meaning of Scripture, to a clearer unlerstanding of our own position than they enjoyed, I believe fully. But I believe also that this simpler perception, this clearer understanding, must be attained by their help, and not without it; by our using their knowledge and not despising it. I believe that in their highest thoughts, in their devotional acts especially, they were carried far above the partial notions which beset them when they were grovelling in the mud of controversy, and that the more we sympathise in these acts, the better we shall be preserved from their errors and our own. In this belief I have been speaking to you since the Sunday before Advent on the different parts of the Liturgy, especially for the purpose of showing how the faithful study, and far more the faithful use of them, would deliver us from a number of errors and superstitions incident to these times, and to all times, which we may naturally fall into and which are more fatal to our practice than even to our doctrine. On this First Sunday in Lent I have reached the most sacred portion of the Liturgy, that to which all the rest is pointing—The Service of Communion. This Service and various questions connected with the Eucharist, which arise out of it, will, if God permit, occupy us till Easter. To-day I wish to speak a few words on the part of the Communion Service which we read every Sunday to our ordinary Congregation, and especially about the way in which the Ten Commandments are introduced into it.

The prayer which we repeat at the end of each Commandment is obviously formed upon my text. 'In those days, saith the Lord, I will put my laws into their mind, and in their hearts will I write them.' 'Lord, have mercy upon us, and write all these thy laws in our hearts, we beseech thee.' The prayer after each Commandment is only a variation from this form, 'Lord, have mercy upon us, and incline our *hearts* to keep this law.' There can be no doubt then, I conceive, that those who enjoined the use of the Commandments in this place intended us especially to recollect what the Epistle to the Hebrews says of the promise which we pray may be fulfilled to us. He calls it the promise of the New Covenant. He sets it forth as emphatically *the* blessing which belongs to us as baptized men. Why it is so we have been considering to-day. We can ask for God's laws to be written in our hearts, because He has reconciled us to Himself in his Son, because He has established a communion between us and Himself through his Spirit. On the ground of that Communion all strength to do His will, all hope of participating in His character stands. Be ye holy, for I am holy; be ye perfect as your Father who is in heaven is perfect. There is to be no struggle after saintship; no wild efforts after perfection. It is God's will to sanctify us; we come to ask that He will do that will for us and in us.

Our first prayer here again, is the Lord's Prayer. 'Our Father' must be the ground of every petition that the promise of the Father may be accomplished in us, that the Comforter may work in us. The second is, that by the holy inspiration of that Comforter we may perfectly love God, and worthily magnify His holy name. What a help and deliverance it is to read the Ten Commandments after this Prayer! What a witness it bears that the curse of them is taken away, that we are not under the law, but under grace! that the power of an endless life is imparted to us, that we are subject to the royal law of liberty, to the law of the Spirit, the law of love! But what a witness it also bears that the Commandment is still that which we had from the beginning. It has not been changed or modified. It is in no degree made obsolete by the New Covenant, by the law, 'Thou shalt love God with all thy heart, and thy neighbour as thyself.' They have changed their places, but they stand side by side; that which is the law of God's Being, has been proved to be the law of Love; Christ the perfect image of the Father has shown it forth in His own person, in His life and death; every man has a right to put himself under it, to claim his place as a citizen of that Kingdom of Heaven which is subject to no law but this. Yet the old law still speaks on earth, still condemns the outward transgressions which are destroying the earth, still imprecates curses upon those transgressions, still threatens our flesh, our evil nature, which is prone to those transgressions, and ever ready to tempt us into them; still conjures us to throw ourselves upon the power of the Spirit, as the only adequate protector against the temptation. On the highest ground of the spiritual life we are still reminded of all the grossest outward offences which the sword of the magistrate punishes. We are not allowed to fancy ourselves of any different nature from highwaymen and assassins. We are not allowed to suppose that there are any treasures of mercy and love in which they may not become sharers with us. Those who are admitted to the communion of saints and angels, are carefully and continually to consider that they are also in communion with the earth, and the animals which move upon it; that if they are capable of perpetual growth, they are also as capable of perpetual degeneracy; that grace and love are no respecters of persons; that the law is no respecter of persons; that the former admit all sinners into their embrace, that the latter pronounces impartial sentence upon the sins into which the most seraphic person falls through self-confidence and spiritual pride. We are taught also that we are not less members of a nation bound together under a visible Sovereign, subject to local laws, because we have entered into a higher Kingdom. There is nothing which clashes in the two relations when they are seen in the light of these Prayers and these Commandments. He who is led by the Spirit of love will not commit the acts which subject him to the animadversion of human laws. He who is admitted into the Christian fellowship will faithfully honour, and humbly obey his earthly Sovereign in God, and for God; the obedience will be translated from the obedience of a slave or a parasite to that of a man; one who sees a Divine government in all the commonest doings of the world, controlling the counsels of princes, making them willingly and cheerfully, or else in spite of themselves, the ministers of His purposes to carry out His gracious ends for the well-being of His creatures.

And here then, brethren, we find once more the counteraction of two mighty and monstrous evils and superstitions which have been the plagues of churches and nations, by the reconciliation of two great and seemingly opposed tenets.

It is not because churchmen have taken too high a view of their own spiritual position, that they have been often bad citizens in national communities. They have had too mean a notion of their calling. They have made the Gospel another Law, the Church a rival State; so they have found their chief duties incompatible with their subordinate duties. Place the Gospel on its right ground, as that which brings men into communion with God, and there is no possible collision between it and the power which, for another purpose, testifies against the outward acts which destroy that communion. Regard the Church as indeed the communion of men as men, brethren in one Lord, children of one Father; and the State which requires men, and not animals, for its subjects, will feel that the Church, by conferring the highest freedom, is cultivating the only safe obedience. He who promises to write His laws in our hearts, will take care that our acts shall not be at variance with them. Every man who claims his citizenship in heaven, will work manfully and heartily on earth.

SERMON XIV.

THE COMMUNION SERVICE.

(2) THE EPISTLE AND GOSPEL, AND NICENE CREED.

Preached on the Second Sunday in Lent, March 4, 1849.

Built upon the foundation of the Apostles and Prophets, Jesus Christ himself being the chief Corner-stone.—EPHESIANS ii. 20.

IN the First Epistle to the Corinthians St. Paul uses language which seems to be at variance with this. He says: 'Other foundation can no man lay than that is laid, which is Christ Jesus.' There he appears to affirm that our Lord is the only groundwork of His Church and of Human Society; here he tells us that we are built upon the foundation of the Apostles and Prophets. The difficulty is not an imaginary one, or one which lies only in a particular form of words. It has been a grand question in all ages of the Church, a vital practical question, whether the Doctrine of great and divine men, or whether the Person of the Son of God and the Son of Man, be that upon which our fellowship rests. The question is coming before us in many forms, some of them very startling forms.* With it is involved the awful doubt, whether Society has any foundation at all—whether it is not a mere mass of atoms, held together by an external force, or the attraction of self-interest, ready to be dispersed whenever that force shall be removed, or that principle of attraction shall become, what naturally we should conclude it would always be, one of repulsion. If such a fate can be averted, will our belief in certain opinions, handed down by Apostles and Prophets, avert it? Or is it our belief in Christ himself, or is there yet something deeper than both? To such great and terrible questions, so nearly affecting ourselves, brought so home to us by the earthquakes in the world around us, does this subject point.

In the letter to the Corinthians, the Apostle was speaking of divisions and parties which had sprung up in their Church. One said he was of Paul, one of Apollos, one of Cephas: others used our Lord's own name as a symbol of faction. Paul was thought to have proclaimed a larger and freer Gospel than Peter; Peter to have maintained the dignity of the Old Covenant better than Paul; Apollos, the Alexandrian, to have sounded depths which neither of the others had reached. In the spirit of Greek partisanship these baptized men ranged themselves round a leader, inscribed his name upon a separate banner. This was the favourite doctor or sophist of one, that of another. The notions of each would be discussed, criticised, defended, refuted, skilfully or ignorantly, but in either case frivolously,

* In the Sermon on the New Testament Lesson, I have considered it in its relation to Theology; *here* in reference to the Constitution of the Church.

by men who were coming less and less to feel that the words of any one of the three really concerned their own lives, or were to govern their acts. Those who said that they preferred Christ to Paul, or Cephas, or Apollos, were probably as proud and contemptuous in their tone as any; they meant by Christ a teacher of certain notions which they had gathered out of his discourses. To one and all St. Paul makes the same answer: Were you baptized into my name, or the name of Peter, or the name of Apollos? If you were baptized into the name of Christ, did that mean into the name of the leader or head of a certain sect? Or is our Gospel this—That God has revealed His Son the Head of the whole family, in whom men were created, in whom alone they are united? If the news we brought was not this, it was nothing. We had no business to turn the world upside down by preaching it. You had better have kept your old forms of divided idolatry, and gone on wearying yourselves to death with arguing whether this or that School had the most satisfactory theory of the universe. If it was this, what are these parties and divisions? Do Apollos, Cephas, or I, saying that we are preachers of the one Christ, give you some notions of ours to build upon? Verily, they will all be burnt up, let them be as subtle and devout as they may. Other foundation can no man lay than that is laid, which is Jesus Christ. We declare Him, and not our theories about Him, to be the root upon which you and all creatures must grow. We declare you to be a Church or family only in Him. And all sects, parties, factions, held together by a man, or a notion, are just so many denials of this foundation, so many attempts to build on the sand houses which must be swept away.

Certainly this language would not prepare us to expect that St. Paul could anywhere assume the mere teaching of the greatest and most inspired man to be a pillar on which the Church stands. Let us hear whether his words to the Ephesians convey that meaning. 'Through Christ,' he says, 'Jews and Gentiles both have access by one Spirit to the Father. Now, therefore, ye are no more strangers and foreigners, but fellow-citizens with the saints, and of the household of God, and are built upon the foundation of the Apostles and Prophets, Jesus Christ himself being the chief corner-stone, in whom all the building fitly framed together, groweth unto an holy temple in the Lord; in whom ye also are builded together for an habitation of God through the Spirit.'

That there is something more in this passage than in the former one; that the Church is presented to us under a different aspect; that a principle which was only latent there, is unfolded here; this may be easily admitted. But that there is not the slightest contradiction; that mere notions have no honour given them in one place, which is denied them in another; that the Church is not said to stand on the foundation of Apostles and Prophets in any sense which even remotely touches the assertion that Christ is its one foundation, I think a very slight consideration of the words will abundantly prove. What the Apostle is giving thanks for, and exhorting the Ephesians to give thanks for, is this—that Gentiles who had been paying a divided broken worship to a multitude of objects, are now claimed as children of God in Him who had taken the nature not of Jews, but of Men. In him they both had access by one spirit to the Father. They were not strangers, but fellow-citizens with the saints, and of the household of God, standing on the same foundation upon which Apostles and Prophets stand; on the everlasting ground which the Prophets declared when they were opposing the idolatries of their own countrymen; which the Apostles proclaimed as a deliverance from the idolatries of the whole world. They might all feel themselves joined together by that corner-stone which keeps the fabric of humanity from falling to pieces. They were builded together for an habitation of God through the Spirit. The passage assumes the most perfect union and sympathy between the poorest member of the Ephesian Church and Isaiah and Paul, because they all stood on the same foundation, united in the same Lord, by whom all things were created, by whom all things consisted.

But I have said that there is a difference between the two passages. If we read through the Epistle to the Corinthians we shall see how much of it turns upon the truth that God had given His *Holy Spirit* to dwell in men; how he had endued them with gifts as the witnesses of His divine Presence and operations; how these gifts were to be used, not for self-exaltation, but for the good of the whole body; how each member of that body had its own ministry; how Love was that which must enable each to fulfil his ministry, and was the bond of the whole family, and would last when all prophecies and tongues failed. This idea, which is diffused through the letter to the Church of Corinth, but not prominently expressed in the words which I have quoted from it, is concentrated and set forth with remarkable fulness in the sentences of which my text is one. The gift of the One Spirit was the sign that the Gentiles were adopted into God's family. That Spirit makes them fellow-citizens with all saints. That Spirit would inhabit them so that they should become a holy Temple to the Lord. *Therefore* they were built upon the foundation of the Apostles and Prophets. The Prophets had not spoken out of their own narrow, partial, private imaginations. A Spirit had filled and possessed them which was not their own, and yet which called forth in them their individual feelings and energies. A Spirit had awakened them to meditate upon the past, the present, and the future. A Spirit had made them feel that they were Israelites; that they were not to think for themselves, feel for themselves, hope for themselves; but to think, feel, and hope for their country, to find their own blessedness and glory in its blessedness and glory. They knew when they poured forth song and discourse that they were under the guidance and teaching of One higher than themselves; they were not afraid to think so, or say so; they were afraid to think or to say otherwise; afraid of the pretensions and lies of those prophets who spake words out of their own hearts, who did not believe, and tremble as they believed, that they were sent to utter the words of Him who is Truth, and in whom is no lie. The prophets hated idolatry—hated all partial sensual worship—because this Uniting Spirit working in them made them feel the awfulness and reality of Him whom eye hath not seen, nor ear heard, made them know that He was near them, and was related to them. The Prophets were led by the Spirit to cry out for the full Revelation of his Being, and to believe that he would be fully revealed. The Prophets, because they were taught by the Spirit, could not but feel that their whole Commonwealth must have one divine Centre; even a person who was the perfect Image of God, who would be manifested to break in pieces all false images of Him, to reconcile all imperfect images of Him.

The Apostles were told by our Lord that when He had gone out of their sight, a Comforter should come to them who should testify of Him; and should enable them to testify of Him, who should lead them into all truth. On the Day of Pentecost they felt that this promise was fulfilled, or began to be fulfilled, to them. These narrow, ignorant, Galilean fishermen, with more than the prejudices of Jews, with the prejudices of the most obscure and despised province of the Holy Land, were raised into the sense of being more than citizens of the Universe; citizens of Heaven as well as earth; connected with ages past and to come; with the invisible as well as the visible world; sharers in all the glories of Creation; partakers of that love which dwelt in the heart of the Creator. They were sure that no Spirit but that of Him who had created them in his own likeness could have brought them into such a fellowship, or have given them such strange powers of utterance. Yet they were sure that it was the Spirit of the lowly Man who had walked with them in the streets of Jerusalem—had borne with their ignorance and sin—had died their death. The more this expansive Spirit carried them beyond the limitations of space and time, the more it brought them into sympathy with things known or unknown, with those who were before them, and those who should come after them; the more it directed them to Him; the more His Person became the object and centre of all their thoughts; the more sure they were that He was the corner-stone, who bound together all times, and places, and living beings.

They had been used to read the old Prophets with reverence, and had tried hard to spell out their dark letters; now they read them with wonder and awe, as sharing the same spirit with them. Enabled by that Spirit to see Him with open face whom the men of old had only beheld under a veil, they felt that they were built upon the same foundation as the Prophets, in that the same divine Person was sustaining and inspiring both. And therefore they could tell all men that this was *their* foundation, that the divine Spirit had come forth to adopt them as much as their teachers into the great family, that they could only profit by their teachers or understand what they said, by submitting to the Spirit which dwelt in them. That Spirit was the pledge of a perfect communion, which had been established between God and His Creatures. By that Spirit only they could enter into this Communion. It was for all generations; in all generations men might claim to stand upon the foundation of Apostles and Prophets. If they did they must claim likewise the Spirit which dwelt in Apostles and Prophets; He would teach them to confess Jesus Christ as the one Corner-stone.

My brethren, a Church cannot put forth any lower pretension for herself and her members than this. If she does not believe that the Spirit of God has really been bestowed upon human beings, that they may be sons of God, and brethren one of another, she does not acknowledge the charter of her own existence; the word 'Church' has no meaning; it is a mockery and falsehood, and should be cast aside. A Church which is afraid to say that the Spirit of God dwells in her—which is afraid to tell her members that the Spirit is with them, and that they are responsible for the gift, and that the very humblest man of them is a sharer of that blessing which Apostles and Prophets counted the greatest of all—will find that she has nothing to oppose to the enemies which will rise up on every side against her. What avails it to say, 'We have traditions.' They may be good, they may be indisputable; what then? Can you use them? Because they have been handed down are they yours? Not except you are such men as they were who handed them down. The armour may have been made for giants; those who inherit it may be dwarfs. Or it may have been made for uses which do not exist, to fight one set of enemies, while you have to fight another. What avails it to say, 'We have Prophets and Apostles?' You have them —Where? In a book? And how will you convert letters into life? How will you know what Prophets and Apostles meant? Will Commentators teach you? *Quis custodiet ipsos custodes?* Who will interpret the Interpreters? Which School will you follow? Under which Sophist or Doctor will you fraternise? The Corinthians were sinful because they would follow one Apostle in preference to another. You must adopt some puny distiller of their words in preference to them all. The experiment has been made; age after age men have made it; one discomfiture after another has been the result. Never did people feel the hopelessness of the trial more than now. Never were there so many cries, 'Give us an infallible authority to tell us what notions and opinions we shall stand upon;' or, 'You know there is not *that*, therefore leave each of us to stand by himself, and take his chance.' Or, 'Philosophy must give us that firm ground which Christianity cannot give.' Or, 'Let us cling to the outward realities which our senses tell us of, and leave the invisible world to the dreamers who think they know something of it.' Such utterances, vague, confused, contradictory, all leading to the same result, telling us plainly that our systems and conclusions offer no home to the wearied spirit, have been ringing in our ears, and will ring more and more loudly. God forbid that they should be silenced, or that we should be able to stop our ears to them; or that men who feel that they are interested for the sake of their worldly ease and prospects in keeping things quiet, should succeed in procuring a hollow and momentary adjustment of the great controversy! God forbid that we should find any escape or refuge but in falling back upon the old principle which is proclaimed in our forms, which our Bibles are testifying of in every page, that we stand not upon traditions, or upon men, or by men, though those men were Apostles and Prophets; but that we stand upon their foundation, that the Spirit in which they spake is given to us, to make us true men, to make us understand true words, and to make us speak true words ourselves; that this Spirit is meant to bind all kindreds and nations and tongues together; that so far as men have yielded to it they have been united in the confession of one living Lord as the object of their faith, the bond of their fellowship; that all parties and factions have been and are rebellious against Him; that they must come to naught, and perish; that the great battle will then be really, and will be understood to be, between those who are governed by the Spirit of Love and Unity, and those who are possessed by a Spirit of Selfishness, which draws all men apart; that the former will acknowledge Him who gave up Himself, and became of no reputation to be the Lord of all; that the others will fraternise in the acknowledgment of some selfish brute power. Which of these will at last prevail we shall believe just as we believe that a Good or Evil Being is the Author of Man and of the Universe.

If these things are so, it must be all-important for us to know whether the Church of which we are members does or does not bear witness for this principle. That she bears very poor and feeble witness for it, in the ordinary acts and words of her children, laymen or priests; that she is torn by parties as much as any Society ever was; that each one of these parties does most indistinctly, mutteringly, reluctantly declare, that the Spirit is really given to the Church, not of some former age, but of all ages; that each of these parties suggests the thought that our foundation is not the one that is laid, but some notion, opinion, and belief of ours, of some tradition of our fathers or the letters of a book, not He of whom the book speaks; this we are bound sorrowfully to confess. I do not excuse our practice, but ask whether we have anything among us which might have corrected our practice, which might have carried us into a higher region of thought, to a surer and simpler ground of life. This, in other cases, the Prayer-Book has furnished us with; the part of it which I have reached to-day, bears, I think, especially upon the point we have been considering.

Last Sunday I spoke of the use of the Commandments in the Communion Service. Oftentimes it has been deemed a return to the Old Dispensation. I showed you that the opening prayer in this Service, the prayer after each of the Commandments, and the prayer at the end of all, were framed upon those express words of the *new* Covenant, 'I will write my laws in their hearts, and in their minds will I write them.' Instead of being a witness that we are under the law, the Commandments, occupying that place, expressly remind us that we are under Grace; that we are expected and enabled to fulfil the Commandments, not in the oldness of the letter, but in the newness of the Spirit; while at the same time they stand out in all their old terrors, against actual wrong-doings.

The Prayer for our own Sovereign, connecting the Law of God with our national life, was a witness that we are just as much under the divine Government as the Jews were, only that our theocracy has been raised as the whole dispensation has been raised. The fuller revelation of the Name of God and of His relation to us, the knowledge that we are children and not servants merely, places each office and calling in God's Kingdom on a higher, more spiritual ground—its formal, legal aspect not being obsolete, but being secondary and subordinate to this. Then follow the Collect, the

Epistle, and the Gospel. It is of these last and of their connection that I wish to speak now.

You may often have wondered why their order is not that in which we find them in our Bible—why the Epistle takes precedence of the Gospel. It is, I believe, in strict accordance with the whole idea of this Communion Service that they should be in this relation to each other. The Epistle is the language of Apostles and Prophets, addressing themselves to a community of men, called to be saints, endowed with the Spirit. It is the witness to them of the nature and meaning of their position. It tells them that the Spirit has been given, and why He has been given, and what He is working in them to do. Turn to the Epistle for this day, and you will find an illustration, the first that occurs, of their general character. It is an exhortation to abstain from open and gross vices. That exhortation is grounded upon the assertion that such acts are 'grievous to the Spirit,' that we 'resist not man but God.' The assumption from first to last is that men of all kinds and degrees have this mighty Teacher, Helper, Indweller; that every temptation to evil, great or little, must be overcome in the strength of that recollection; that every right determination must be made, and every good act done, in the same belief, by the same inspiration.

But these Epistles are, I must repeat, addressed to men *in a Society*. They are assumed to be mixing together, to be holding continual intercourse; neither their virtues nor their vices to be solitary, or to terminate with themselves. And that Spirit, by help of which each man is to repel the closest and most secret suggestions of his own heart, is the Spirit which moves and quickens the whole body, which alone makes its different limbs act as parts of the body in their due relation to each other. It is not merely that this Epistle is addressed to us by a very high and divine authority, but that it is addressed to us as persons capable of listening, able to understand, what is said to us, because we are under the same conditions with the writer, endued with that Spirit from which all his utterances proceeded. Does this belief confuse our minds respecting the relation of different persons in the Church—respecting the Teacher and the pupil, the Minister and the people? Quite the contrary. It removes confusion. It sets all things in order. For the Spirit we believe in and confess is the Spirit of Order, the Spirit who bestows gifts, who leads men to apprehend what offices they are intended to fill, who keeps them from intruding into the offices of each other. The notion of such a Power existing in the world may be scouted, if you please; you may explain the facts of the world's history without it if you can. But, having admitted it, you admit also that obedience to such a Power is the secret of all free and quiet working in the different wheels of society; resistance to it, the secret of all disturbance, interruption, collision. Or does this view of a portion of the Bible destroy the distinction between it and other books? Quite the contrary. If the Bible is indeed to set forth God's Revelation to men, to set forth the relation in which we stand to Him and to each other, this Spirit explains our need of such a book, and wherein such a book must be unlike all others; what gives purpose and distinction to its several parts; what constitutes it a whole. At the same time the invisible Teacher shows us how vehemently the Bible itself disclaims the honour which some would put upon it when they exalt it into the place of God; with what continual effort it directs our thoughts from itself to Him, making us feel that the ground of our Communion is not in that which the Spirit has enabled men to utter—wonderful and divine as that is—but in the Spirit Himself. And this, while he shows us also how the Bible, instead of putting a slight on the thoughts and wisdom of the ages after it should be closed, is the justification and explanation of them.

The Epistle, then, speaks to us as men endued with a Divine Spirit, built upon the foundation of Apostles and Prophets. The Gospel speaks to us of Jesus Christ the Corner-stone. Given the one, we must have the other. The Spirit does not bear witness of itself, nor does He ever lead us to dwell upon ourselves and our acts. Nor does He permit us to contemplate the Church as an aggregate of ourselves, of our acts, or even as a body pure and spiritual and united *in itself*. He directs us to Christ, from whom He proceeds, in whom all the Divine life which he would produce in us is fully realised; to Christ as the only Person in whom we can safely contemplate ourselves, who is the end as well as the root of our acts, Christ, in whom alone the Church lives and moves and has its being, apart from whom it is not spiritual, not pure, not one, but a collection of sensual, corrupt, divided atoms.

The Epistle and the Gospel are followed by the Nicene Creed. I have spoken already upon the use of Creeds, and their relation to our prayers generally. I will only say a few words of the place which this Eastern Creed occupies in our Communion Service.

They will illustrate the whole subject, and will show from what special perils we need and may find deliverance. All false systems give us an organ of seeing in place of an object, or present an object to creatures who are incapable of beholding it. Romanism is altogether subjective at one moment, altogether objective the next; now leading its votaries to hopeless acts of self-consciousness and self-accusation, now compelling them to strain their minds in the contemplation of some Image wholly external to themselves. Both tendencies exist in human nature, both are working mightily among ourselves. We are continually tempted to make the Epistles mere records of our individual experiences, the Gospels a mere external history of one who was born at Bethlehem and died on Calvary. Then comes a vehement reaction against each habit: the Epistles are discarded, for we want some real Person to behold; the Gospels are thrown aside, for what call have we to believe a mere set of Facts which may be perhaps mere symbols of certain general human feelings, or of certain local notions? You may denounce the language in which these opposite tempers express themselves; you may scorn the rapidity with which men pass from one to the other; you may tell them that they can have no stedfastness unless they retain their reverence for the written Word, and for the Church's teaching. But what power lies in these denunciations, this scorn, these grave warnings? Have not you tried them all, and do not you know that they have effected nothing for those to whom they are addressed, that they very often exhibit nothing but your own superciliousness, hardness, want of sympathy with other men's temptations, ignorance of your own; nothing, in short, but your incapacity to communicate the mind of Christ to others because it is not in yourselves? Oh, surely there is a more excellent way! Let us be taught practically, continually, that there is a Divine Spirit to whom we may refer our spiritual acts; that there is a Son to whom that Spirit is leading us, that there is an eternal relation between them dependent upon the eternal relation of both to the Father; and self-contemplation will turn to adoring Faith, and the formal History will become connected with our own personal being, and with the being of our race. Let each one say when he closes the Gospel, I believe in Him who was born at Bethlehem and suffered at Calvary, as the Light of Light, the very God of very God, begotten, not made, of one substance with the Father, by whom all things were made, who for us men and for our salvation came down from heaven. Let each one say, I believe in the Holy Ghost, the Lord and Giver of Life, who proceedeth from the Father and the Son, who with the Father and Son together is worshipped and glorified, who spake by the Prophets. Epistle and Gospel are distinguished, united, transfigured, when they are thus referred to a ground in the being of God Himself, and in his relations to man. Yet they are nearer and closer to us than ever. They assure us that we, even we, are built upon the same foundation with Apostles and Prophets, Jesus Christ Himself being the Corner-stone of the one Communion to which we and they belong.

SERMON XV.

THE COMMUNION SERVICE.

(3) The Offertory, and Prayer for the Church Militant.

Preached on the Third Sunday in Lent, March 14, 1849.

Work out your own salvation with fear and trembling; for it is
God which worketh in you both to will and to do of his good
pleasure.—PHILLIPIANS ii. 12, 13.

THE two clauses of this sentence are sometimes regarded
as antithetical. 'Work out your own salvation,' that
is your *duty*. 'God is working in you,' that is your
faith. Or the second is supposed to explain how the
command in the first is possible. 'You can work out
your own salvation, *for* God is working with you.'
Both explanations are, no doubt, good; but they seem
to overlook or to regard as merely accessory, words
which I conceive express the very spirit of the exhortation. 'Work out your salvation with *fear and
trembling; for* it is God who is working in you.' This
thought is to make you tremble more than the thunders
of Sinai did the Jews. There is a power which is near
you at every moment, which is working in you mightily.

And that power is the power of God himself. If anything can inspire you with awe, will not that recollection do it?

By giving these two words their rightful force, I believe we discover a force in every other which the passage contains. The word '*Salvation,*' how apt it is to become a mere technical theological term! How quickly we forget that it meant originally, means now, and always ought to mean, deliverance, or safety from some mischief! In this very sentence how continually it is taken merely as an idle equivalent for the rewards of a future state! But surely personal experience may bring back the etymology. This hot lust, this strong passion, this habit of indolence and despair, has enslaved me. I feel myself a captive, bound with invisible but not the less galling and oppressive chains. Sometimes I seem to long for freedom, sometimes I seem to love my fetters, sometimes I make wild efforts which increase the sense of misery, sometimes I sleep heavily, but it is a sleep broken with painful nightmares and incoherent or terrific dreams. Strange contradiction! whence comes it? The solution is more wonderful than the problem, but there is no other. God is energising in thee to bring about thy deliverance, to break this yoke from off thy neck.

God is energising or working in thee. But for what? That *thou* mayest energise. He is stirring thy spirit when it is asleep, almost dead; bidding it live and move, and act. He is stirring up the powers within thee, all the faculties of thy mind, all the limbs of thy body, to do what thy spirit determines and aims at. He is working for thee both the spiritual act and the outward act, both the willing and the doing.

THE COMMUNION SERVICE.

And what then wilt thou do? Wilt thou struggle hard to obtain salvation from some power which is refusing it thee? Wilt thou say many prayers, perform many penances, to get back the good-will of some distant unknown being whose nature thou guessest from thine own? Or, on the other hand, wilt thou lie still, saying, 'It will come, if it will come; I have nothing to do with it; God can send it me if He likes.' There is fear and trembling, no doubt, in those who pursue the first course, but fear and trembling which alternate with recklessness and indifference, which are accompanied with an habitual want of awe; for you can have no holy awe of a being whom you think you can persuade and cajole into compliance with your wishes, nor of one whom you contemplate merely as a fulfiller of those wishes. The other course, with all its seeming contentment, includes also much fear and trembling. A man cannot give up working altogether, though he pretends to do it, though his theory leads him to it. He cannot give over hoping something from his exertions, though he says all is arranged for him, and depends upon circumstances, or upon necessity, or upon what he calls *God*; there will be fearful struggles, quiverings at the thought of what he is, and of what he may be. But the fear will not be reverence, the trembling will not be the confession of one purer, and holier, and more loving than himself; a confession of his own impurity, unholiness, unlovingness; that only comes from the belief, God is working in me, and therefore I may work. He is working in me *to will*, and therefore I must feel how awful all my voluntary acts are, how wonderful, how blessed. He is working in me *to do*, and therefore I must feel how sacred all my outward acts are, how earnest I ought to be in the very least of them. He is working out my *salvation*, therefore how must I tremble when I give way to the tyranny of any thought or desire within, or of any influence exerted upon me from without, which is contrary to His mind. Must I not tremble at the readiness which I feel in myself to court slavery and to become a slave? Must I not work earnestly, awfully, for emancipation, knowing what the will of this Being who is nigh to me, is concerning me, knowing what power is prompting my sluggish will, and is ready to work with it.

But in a really careful consideration of this text we cannot forget the plural, 'Work out *your* own salvation.' All that I have said is there. Each individual man may hold these colloquies with himself, must hold them if he believes St. Paul's assertion. But St. Paul, as I said last Sunday, is always writing to a *body* of men. He is addressing a Church—a Church each individual of which is a distinct being, and would remain so if the whole human race were to fall into ruins about him; but a Church which is a living whole made up of distinct living parts, or, in the much better and more definite language of Scripture, a body with many members, a body filled with a spirit by which every joint is quickened. When therefore the Apostle says, 'Work out *your* own salvation, it is God that worketh in *you*,' he surely means us to understand that the work which each is carrying on is not a solitary one, that numbers are affected by it besides himself, that all true workmen are taking part in it. The temptations of men are various in their outward forms; this evil tendency is more predominant in one man than in another: but the slavery into which they bring us is the same, and the salvation from it must be the same. The slavery is the dominion of self; the man who is overcome by lust, by vanity, by anger, alike separates himself from his kind, and becomes shut up in himself. Therefore the Scripture is wont to describe all evil under the name of 'covetousness,' the desire of things for our own sakes, whatever those things may be. All superstition, all that kind of working which I spoke of just now, working in order to escape some punishment or to secure some individual reward, keeps alive their covetousness—even invests it with a holy character. That lazy expectation of interference from Angels, or from God, to do that for men which they will not do for themselves, is a form of this selfish slavery; it is abetted by a host of religious theories. But a Church lives only so far as she resists this covetousness—so far as she encourages her members to feel that they are striving together for a common object which God wills that all should possess together; so far as she teaches them that He is working with us to save us from the selfishness which makes the pursuit of this common object and the attainment of it impossible.

I have spoken of our Communion as setting forth with great clearness the One Spirit which worketh in all the members of the Church, and the One Divine Lord whom He teaches them all to contemplate. The Epistle and the Gospel, considered in their relation to each other, seemed to unfold this double mystery; the Nicene Creed to show how it was grounded on the Name of the Absolute God, the Father: how upon it rested the One holy Catholic Church, the One Baptism for the remission of sins, and the life of the world to come.

Of the sermon which follows the Creed it is not my purpose to speak, seeing that my subject is the Prayer-Book. But this I must say; the Sermon is interposed between the Creed and the Offertory; it is to be a bond between them. The words, 'Let your light so shine before men that they may see your good works, and glorify your Father which is in heaven,' should be the application of the Sermon, as they most remarkably explain the purpose of the Epistle and Gospel, and show what responsibilities the Creed has laid upon us, and what the whole idea of Communion implies. As this text is put first among those which introduce the Offertory, and is a key to the rest, I will say a few words upon it.

Our Lord had said to those who were about Him on the mount, 'Ye are the lights of the world.' He added: 'Men do not light a candle and then put it under a bushel; but they put it in a candlestick, and it shines on all those in the house.' Evidently he assumes that another than themselves had kindled the light which was in them. That Father of whom he is speaking throughout this Discourse, who had created the world, and had formed men in His image that they might show him forth to all creatures; this Father was the original fountain of Light. He in whom it was perfectly reflected, the Light of Light, the Only-begotten of the Father, had come forth that men might see the Light which had been lighting all who came into the world, though the world had not known it, but had shrunk from it, and had loved darkness. As many as had received Him had been partakers of His light; to them He gave power to become the sons of God. And now He was calling all men to repent and turn to this Light, and now He was appointing messengers who would invite all to own this Father and to become brethren in Him. They were to be lights of the world, shining by His light, not their own; they were to be cities set on a hill, that men might see there was a light in the world, and might know whence it came. Therefore He says, 'So let your light shine before men that they may see your good works, and glorify your Father which is in heaven.' The light is there: there is no doubt of that; it is within you; but it dwells in a strange ungenial atmosphere. Not only when it comes out will it meet this atmosphere; within, in the vessel which contains it, there will be always that which threatens to put it out. Above all, beware of *this* stifling air—the thought, 'It is mine; the light comes from me; I kindled it.' Then instead of letting it shine forth, you will be fancying that you can make it shine; and you will be seeking to make yourself shine; you will be saying, 'What good and great works can I do that men may admire, and that God may pay me for?' Oh! be sure that the flashes of light which will come forth from you when this is the thought of your heart, will be startling and bewildering for a moment, but that the light itself will be waning and dying in the socket. Oh! remember that the light comes from above, and must be received by you from above, and that all you have to do is to remove whatever in yourself dulls it. And remember that when it goes forth freest and clearest it will not bring you glory. 'Men will see your good works, and will glorify your Father which is in heaven.'

So spake the Son of God on earth to the future Ministers of His kingdom, and through them to all who should hear their words. So speaks he now to the Ministers of His kingdom, and through them to all who shall hear their words. The teacher may easily preach the doctrine that there can be no good work but that which proceeds from the operation of God's Spirit. The members of his congregation may repeat his phrases, and vehemently denounce all who fancy they can do anything right of themselves, or who in any measure sanction the doctrine of human merit. But the priest is every moment apt to forget that the words he speaks are not his own words, that the acts which he does, if they are prompted by some external impulse, by desire for the applause of men or by the force of opinion and example, are scattered sparks which do not proceed from the source of Light, and can impart no steady light to those who behold them. And you are equally liable to forget that the same Father in heaven whom the minister should wish to glorify is desiring to show forth His light through you, and that by everyone of your words and deeds you may either be quenching this light or diffusing it. If you come to church, if especially you listen to the Communion Service, you will be reminded that something else is required of you than to repeat watchwords and denounce men of different opinions from your own. Have we learnt the Article by heart, that acts done without faith and divine inspiration are not meritorious, but have the nature of sin? Have we used that Article to convict some one else of Romanism or heresy? Proud

Protestant dogmatist! insolent professor! Let us see whether thou understandest thy own language, whether thou meanest what thou art saying. If thou dost, thou wilt fear and tremble. For verily God is working in thee to will and to do of His good pleasure. Art thou then willing and doing it, or art thou doing thine own acts, and seeking thine own pleasure? The Light is seeking to penetrate thee. Does it penetrate thee and exhibit itself through thee? Do men see your good works, and glorify, not you, but your Father which is in heaven?

Brethren, this is a very solemn question which is proposed to each one of us at that altar, and which I think each one of us must fear and tremble when he attempts to answer. The Offertory brings it before us in what we may regard as the simplest form of all, that of mere almsgiving. But is that a simple form? Do you find it so? Is it easy to do the commonest acts —the very commonest—as if they were not our own, as if we were to carry out in them the mind and will of another? Is it easy to know how these common acts ought to be done, so that they shall bring blessings and not misery, light and not darkness, to our fellow-men? If we are honest, we shall not talk so proudly and contemptuously about *mere* duties, and the great principle of faith. 'Show me thy faith without thy works,' cries St. James. You talk much about it; I want to see it. Where is it? What if your works not only do not prove its presence, but bear clear testimony to its absence?

If the Apostle asked us that question, what should we answer? 'See our subscription lists, what we raise at public meetings, at bazaars, at feasts! See what competition does in calling forth the zeal of this man; how another is actuated by shame; a third by the excitement of numbers, a fourth by a moving speech. These are our works. Perhaps they will not bear the examination of St. James. But he was legal. If St. Paul, the Apostle of faith, were with us, he might judge differently.' Hearken then to what he would say. 'God worketh in you to will.' Was the will which proceeded from this competition, this shame, this melting discourse, that which He wrought? God worketh in you to do. Are these doings like His doings? Is there any earnest, continuous, self-sacrificing loving-kindness in them, which evince Him to be their author?

It cannot be concealed, that of all the arguments in favour of a return to Romanism which have been urged in our day, none have been so effectual as those which are derived from these specimens of Protestant philanthropy. Again and again they have been set, now in serious, now in ludicrous, opposition to such acts as those which are recorded of Francis of Assisi, of Carlo Borromeo, and of a multitude more, whose names are preserved in the histories or legends of the different countries which acknowledge the dominion of Rome. We should not shrink from the severity of the denunciation, or the bitterness of the scorn. Both are richly deserved. Then comes the question, What is the remedy? 'You can do nothing without the belief that acts of charity have a merit in them, without the notion that by them men may be delivered from punishment hereafter, may obtain God's grace of congruity. These are the influences which we command, and which you have thrown off!' Oh! that we could throw them off more entirely, the principle of them as well as the form! But it is not so. The craving for distant rewards in a future state is found inoperative, so we help it out with the immediate reward of popular approbation. The chance of deliverance from the misery of another world is found inefficient, therefore the disagreeableness and discredit of being considered uncharitable takes its place. The change shows, perhaps, that we have less imagination than our fathers; but if they had no other motives than these, we are in all essentials like them. In wealth and prosperity they might have felt much as we do; a sudden calamity may revive their vague terrors and expectations in us. But these were *not* the inspirations which produced any righteous or loving deed among them; no one who reads the records of such deeds, as they are recorded by Romish writers, can believe that it was. An overpowering sense of the sympathy of the Saviour with every poor man, an intense participation in that sympathy, this made Francis a beggar, this gave him and his order all the moral strength which they have ever possessed; to the grossness, and materialism, and vanity which mixed with their divine impulses, we owe their Mariolatry, their heresies, their fanaticism, their tyranny. The holiness of their will had this origin, God wrought in them to will. The effectiveness of their acts had this origin, God wrought in them to do. If we would be like them in anything but that which was weak and inconsistent, that which they must hate when they see things in God's clear light, we must act upon the truth of these words, and cast all notions of earning heaven or escaping hell by our charity, to the winds. It is not a bad thing for us to have discovered that we want more direct influences than the hope or fear of some distant result. For there is a power nearer to us not only than these, but than all the motives of present selfishness, which we have invented as substitutes for them.

I do not wonder that some excellent men, seeing the confusion of our practice in respect of charity, and seeing what a beautiful simplicity there is in the language and the idea of the Communion Service, should have urged a return to what they call the old practice of the Sacramental Offertory, believing that there is in it a deliverance not only from the almsgiving which is made under the influence of popular excitement, but from that which is enforced by State decrees. But I must think that they are beginning the reform which they desire at the wrong end. There is no charm in money put into a church-plate more than in money given at the door of a crowded hall or to a collector of rates. One may be bestowed from as wrong a principle, and have as little of the meaning of charity in it, as the other. If ungodly influences and habits are diffused through society, are tolerated by ourselves, are recognised as parts of our religion, we shall assuredly not leave them at the church-door; we shall take them with us into our solemnest acts; those acts will be the fruits of them. If you encourage the notion in any men's minds that by changing their plan or the mode of their proceeding, they are commencing a reform, you make their old feelings more inveterate, you give a sop to their consciences, you teach them to ascribe a sacredness, and probably a merit, to acts that are indifferent, and in their root are evil.

If we would profit by the Communion Service, we must seek a principle in it to govern our conduct at all times and in all circumstances, a principle quite independent of any external arrangement, though one which will eventually mould external arrangements rightly. And we shall find such a principle. We shall find embodied in the Offertory the grand truth—not that money must be put into Communion-plates, but that wherever it is put, it must be an offering to God from His children, who are to do as their Father in heaven does, who are to bestow their gifts as He bestows His, upon the just and the unjust, upon the good and the evil; and to bestow them as He does, from an internal spring and principle of love; and bestow them as He does, with wisdom and providence, adapting them to the condition of those who receive them, studying their moral health and well-being. A man who really believes that God is working in him will do this act as all others with fear and trembling, knowing that it is a solemn act, one which must have issues that he cannot foresee. He will be therefore quite ready to consider all objections which economists offer to one or another scheme of charity; he will not repulse them with any pleas of sentiment or resolution to do as others have done before him. He will weigh and deliberate, ready to give up any scheme, new or old, any favourite of his own, any error into which he has fallen through routine, if it is shown to be mischievous to those whom it professes to benefit. He will most attentively and respectfully, and with a certain moral prepossession in favour of the conclusion, listen to any evidence which shows that gifts which do not contain in them an impulse to work, bodily or spiritual, are in the vast majority of cases hurtful. God worketh in him to will and to *do*; he must seek to work on others for the same end. The mere name of giving, the mere notion of this act being one in which there is more show of self-sacrifice than that, will never determine him in its favour. The all-seeing eye is upon him, God is working in him; he must not, dare not, prefer a plausible act to a true one.

A man really feeling himself the steward of God's gifts will be in a condition to meet the different perplexing questions of our day honestly, earnestly, hopefully—ready to receive all hints respecting the best means of doing that which he knows he is bound to do—never dreaming that the means which were fittest for one time must be fittest for another, or that there is any sense in merely following the most admirable precedents. Nor will all objections in the universe convince him that *some* course is not the right one, or that he is not to take the best he knows, hoping to be taught a better, if it be by his own blunders. But the internal law is absolute and universal, and admits of no changes. Nobody is bound to do as Francis of Assisi did; any one in our day who imitated him would probably prove that he had *not* the spirit by which he was actuated. But those who, to comfort us in our bad ways, say that he loved the poor too well, or had a larger sympathy with human beings than can be felt in our time, utter a damnable heresy, which we are bound to anathematise in our practice. Nor can we stop here. Charity, which starts from a divine source, which finds its expression in gifts considerate and adapted to its objects, must take innumerable forms, and spread itself in countless directions. Our habits of thinking about all people, our words, our tones of voice, must be moulded by it. God, who worketh in us to will and to do of His good pleasure, must assuredly, if we yield ourselves to Him, bring our whole lives and character into conformity with His own, so that they shall be manifestations and expressions of what He is. The light, if we did not hinder it, would shine forth upon all; and how many withered and broken hearts would learn from us that they have a Father in heaven, and would glorify Him.

Yes, brethren, let us consider it well. This, and nothing less than this, is implied in our Church-life, and our acts of Communion. We are actually taken to be members of Christ, children of God. The words are simple, but, oh what a depth is in them, what an infinite reproach to every one of us! 'The Bible,' we are told sometimes, 'gives us such a beautiful picture of what we should be.' Nonsense! it gives us no picture at all. It reveals to us a fact; it tells us what we actually are: it says, This is the form in which God created you, to which He has restored you: this is the work which the Eternal God, the God of truth and love, is continually carrying on within you. Brethren, do we fear and tremble as we hear it? Let us keep our fear for the reality. Not the Minister's words, but God's presence so near us, is what should make us tremble.

But it should make us rejoice too; for it is this which redeems us from slavery to the world's law and the opinion of men. God is with us, the shout of a King is in the midst of us; let us fear Him and give Him glory: then we shall be able to resist all in earth and all in hell which is striving against Him.

In the strength of this assurance we can kneel down and pray for the whole state of Christ's Church militant here on earth. A hard warfare it is against principalities and powers, against the rulers of the darkness of this world; a hard warfare for kings and priests and people. But the Helper and Conqueror is near; God Himself has commanded us to make prayers and supplications, and to give thanks for *all* men. He is on our side and on theirs, whoever may be against us. The secret battle in the closet, the open conflict with the tormentors and destroyers of the earth is all present to Him. He is engaged in it. He is working in us to will and to do of His good pleasure, though ten thousand foes in us and around us may be urging us to disobedience. And there is an invisible company about us in whom His mighty love has worked effectually, who have departed this life in His faith and fear, and are showing forth all that light which they borrow from Him, as suns and stars in glory.

SERMON XVI.

THE COMMUNION SERVICE.

(4) THE EXHORTATION AND CONFESSION.

Preached on the Fourth Sunday in Lent, March 18, 1849.

Then Paul and Barnabas waxed bold, and said, It was necessary that the word of God should first have been spoken to you : but seeing ye put it from you, and judge yourselves unworthy of everlasting life, lo, we turn to the Gentiles.—ACTS xiii. 46.

'COUNT yourselves unworthy of eternal life!' And were they not unworthy of eternal life? And was it not the business of St. Paul and Barnabas to tell them that they were? They were speaking in the synagogue of Antioch in Pisidia, to an assembly of Jews, men characteristically self-righteous, self-glorifying. They had said in plain language, that the countrymen of these Jews had crucified the Lord of life, and that they themselves were in danger of becoming despisers, and of perishing. Should they not have endeavoured to lower the pretensions of these proud men? Should they not have made these despisers feel that they had need of mercy to escape the doom which was threatening them? What could they mean by encouraging such people to think themselves worthy of eternal life—by even complaining of them that they did not?

Assuredly, as St. Luke says, the Apostles must have 'waxed very bold' before they could have ventured on such an utterance. It required a mighty inspiration, carrying them far above the level of their ordinary understandings, to give them courage for it. And yet these words were words of truth and soberness. They could not have used any so entirely suitable to the characters and circumstances of the men they were addressing; so proper to convince them of their sin and their weakness, and to humble them.

These men *did* think very highly of themselves. They thought they were altogether different from the Heathens round about them. They knew who the true God was; they despised idols, they had the Law and the Covenants. The Jew dwelling in Jerusalem cherished the sense of his superiority by looking at the Temple with its goodly stones and tokens of a Divine Presence. The Jew in the provinces of the Empire was reminded of it by the sight of all the abominations of Gentile worship; by the habits which he saw it had engendered in the worshippers. A conceit of his own privileges was quite as likely to arise in the heart of one as of the other. Nor could this be merely a claim for his nation. It was a claim for himself. Every Jew was disposed to think that he individually was in a better position than another man. He might not be what he ought to be—but he had a better prospect of averting the punishment of his sins, and of obtaining any benefits that God might design for His creatures

THE COMMUNION SERVICE.

hereafter, than the Romans who were his masters, or the Greeks who were so much his superiors in external earthly cultivation. In proportion as he had taken pains to avert these punishments, or secure these rewards, his prospect would seem to be improved. And then lastly, he had the deepest ground for his convictions, seeing he referred them all to the will of the Supreme Being. God had chosen his nation. Jews were his favourites. This belief did not rest upon surmise, but upon revelation. He had told them they were the objects of His care and affection.

For these reasons the Jew was always disposed to be what we see the Pharisee actually was from the intercourse he held with our Lord, 'One who counted himself righteous, and despised others.' But did he then consider himself 'worthy of eternal life'? What did the Apostles mean by 'eternal life'? They had the definition from the highest authority of all. Our Lord had said, 'This is life eternal, that they may know Thee the only true God, and Jesus Christ, whom Thou hast sent.' Now surely the Jews had a warrant for thinking that this gift was intended for them. Why was Abraham called out of his father's house? Was it not that he might know the only true God? Why was the Covenant given to him and to his seed after him? Was it not that they might live under the guidance and teaching of the only true God? Why were they brought out of Egypt? Why was the Law given them? Was it not that they might know Him to be the righteous Being, the Lord God, merciful and gracious, slow to anger and of great mercy, forgiving transgression and sin, but not sparing the guilty? What was all their after discipline for, but that they might know this only true God better, and might not confound Him, as they were always prone to do, with the works of *their* hands, and with the works of *His* hands—that they might worship Him with circumcised hearts? Why did all the Prophets come to them, if it was not to announce some day of the Lord, some revelation of this only true God, which would show more clearly what He was and what He was doing on the earth? Why did all the Prophets speak of some King who was to reign over them, 'who was to be a hiding-place from the heat, and a refuge from the storm'? Why, but because each step of their experience had shown them that they needed to see the true image of God set forth before them, in opposition to all the images they had formed of Him? Why, but because the very first chapter of Genesis, and every subsequent page of the Divine Records, and every testimony of their own hearts, made it clear that this image must be in a Man? that in a Man only they could know God; that in a Man, and not in any part of the Universe, or in the whole of it, He could reveal himself? To expect a Man, therefore, who should be one with the only true God, who should fully manifest Him, who should entirely sympathise with them, was involved in the first belief; if they were the chosen people of God, if they had any privilege at all above other people, they were bound to claim the fulfilment of both God's promises; the promise that they should know Him; the promise that One should be sent in whom they might know Him.

Now precisely the charge which the Apostles brought against their countrymen was this: You have not believed these promises; you have not cared to know the only true God; you have not known, and do not know, what His character is, what His relation to men is, what kind of feelings He has to them. You have proved this to be the case by refusing Jesus Christ whom He has sent. You refused him because He had the image of God. He came to publicans and sinners, meeting them in their degradation and sin, and you said, He was Himself evil. He came delivering men from plagues of body and spirit, and you said, He had a devil. Why? Because the image which he presented to you was one altogether unlike that which you had made for yourselves. You were worshipping a being with a character like your own, cruel, hardhearted, selfish. You did not like to be confronted with one altogether opposite to this. Again, when He said, 'I and my Father are one,' you said, 'He blasphemeth.' You did not like to feel that there was so near a relation between the Lord of all and yourselves. You wished that He should be at a greater distance, afar off in the clouds, an unapproachable essence with whom you might terrify other men, but who might be half imaginary to yourselves. He said, 'The Kingdom of God is at hand.' An actual King is near you, claiming dominion over your hearts and spirits, willing to mould and fashion them according to His own mind, and to use them as His servants; and you said, 'We do not desire this man to reign over us; we have no king but Cæsar.' You did not wish to be the servants and friends of a true and loving master; you would rather be the slaves of a tyrant.

Now might not all these charges be summed up in

the one: 'You count yourselves unworthy of eternal life'? You will not have these privileges which God has been in all ages bestowing upon you, and promising to you. You talk of the Covenant, but you will not have the Covenant. The Covenant is, 'I will reveal Myself to you; I will show you Him in whom I have created you, and in whose image you are formed. I will mould you after that image; I will redeem you from the power of the visible tyrant, to whom men naturally bow down, and will bring you under a loving gracious yoke; I will make you willing in the day of my power;' and you say, No—we are not worthy of such blessings as these; we are glad to be Jews; glad to scorn other people, glad to think that we have the true Book, and the holy Temple, and that all people shall some day pay homage to us. But the higher things you speak of, the knowledge of God, the beholding of His likeness, conformity to it, being used as the ministers of His love and blessings to mankind, we ask not for; we never supposed ourselves good enough for such gifts as these.

The case then stood thus. These Jews were proud, and self-exalting, and contemptuous, precisely for this reason, that they had taken no adequate measure of the kind of mercy which God had designed for them, and for their race, and which they and their race had need of. The only way to humble them effectually, was to raise them to a higher point of view. Let them continue to fancy that God had promised them something, and would pay them something for their work, and they would continue to be religious hucksters, counting up how much they had done, how much they were entitled to for what they had done, how much more they had done than others. Let them once feel, 'That which God, who cannot lie, has promised to us is eternal life,' and they would be obliged to give up all such calculations; to cast themselves simply upon Him; to acknowledge that they were not better than the meanest of their brother-men; to feel that they were worse in proportion to the capacities of knowledge with which they had been endowed, to the mercy which had been surrounding them, and offering itself to them. Let them once understand that God by sending His Son into the world, made of a woman, had declared that He counts men worthy to be His sons, that He counts men worthy of that Divine life which is in His Son; and they must arise and go to their father, must say, 'We have sinned against heaven and before Thee,' must give up boasting, must be content henceforth through all ages to come to be mere receivers of His love, that they might manifest it to the universe.

With this charge, then, against a portion of the Jewish people—and it was in fact a charge against the great body of them—were connected the bold words and the bold act of the Apostles, 'Lo, we turn to the Gentiles.' We have told you what the promise is, which was made to your fathers, and how God has accomplished it for you. We have told you the meaning of your Calling and your Covenant, and how you may receive the full blessing of them. Now to carry out the purpose of that promise, that calling, that covenant, we are about to speak these good tidings to the men whom you have despised. We shall tell these worshippers of wood and stone, The everlasting God counts you worthy to be His children;

He has sent His son to claim you as His children. We shall say to men who are given up to furious lusts and passions, The holy and loving God counts you worthy of eternal life; worthy to be delivered from bondage to these tyrants, worthy to be endued with His own gracious Spirit. We shall address this language to them, simply because they are men, bearing the same nature which our Lord bore, under the same curse of death to which He submitted. We shall ask no other proofs or tokens but this, that they are intended to hear the Gospel of God's love, that they are capable of all the blessings whereof it declares men to be the heirs. We shall invite these men, when they have understood our message, to receive the seal of God's new Covenant, the filial baptism; the witness that they are adopted into the Divine family. We shall bid them claim a portion in it for their children also; for God has not made them fathers and mothers that they should bring up sons for the evil spirit, but for Him. We shall tell them that they are Sons of God, and therefore members of another, and that they have God's good Spirit to enable them to act out both these characters. We shall tell them that a living and perpetual communion has been established between God and man; between earth and heaven; between all spiritual creatures: that the bond of this communion is that body and blood which the Son of God and the Son of Man offered up to His Father, in fulfilment of His Will, in manifestation of His love; that God is as careful to nourish their spirits as their bodies; that as He provides bread and wine for the strength and life of the one, so in this body and blood of His Son is the strength of the other; the Sacrament of His continual presence with His universal family; the witness to each man of his own place in that family, and of his share in all its blessings; the pledge and spring of a renewed life; the assurance that that life is his own eternal life.

This was surely a Gospel to the nations. And first one, then another, of the nations received it; and Churches were formed; and the kingdom spread from East to West; and a Christendom grew and fashioned itself out of the wreck of the old Roman world; and men believed—not always clearly, amidst many perplexities, contradictions, infusions of old heathenism, but they did believe—that this Christendom was a reality, and that the testimony which their baptism bore was not a lie; and that they were meant to be sons of God, and that they could call new kindreds and tongues into the same fellowship, and that there was no opposition of race in the spiritual family; that it had the same Father who was over all; the same eternal King and Priest; the same indwelling Spirit; that the commonest earthly symbols were those which God chose to express the deepest spiritual gifts He had to bestow; because these were really as common as the other, not intended for one here or there, but for humanity and for all who would claim it, that is, for all who did not count themselves unworthy of eternal life; who were willing to receive it of God, not to earn it for themselves. I say, brethren, this faith is implied in the very existence of a Christendom; it is the mystery which lies beneath the history of our modern world, and interprets it, just as the *expectation* of this gift of eternal life, the longing for a manifestation of God, is the mystery which lies beneath the history of the ancient world, and interprets it. One is embodied in the ordinances of the Christian Church, as the other was embodied in the ordinances of the Jewish nation. And the presence of these Christian ordinances, and their diffusion over so many countries, composed of the most various races, and opposing tempers and diverse opinions, are witnesses what a great word the Apostles spoke in the synagogue of Pisidia, when they waxed bold and said, 'Because you count yourselves unworthy of eternal life, lo! we turn to the Gentiles.'

But we cannot forget, if we would, that we are in all respects like those men of the older dispensation, though our blessings are so much greater; though the warnings they have left us constitute such a volume of rich and terrible experience. Supposing St. Paul and Barnabas in a church of English Christians of these days, would they not find all and more than all the same arrogant notions of superiority to the outlying nations, and to individual unbelievers; all the same self-righteous conceits in the minds of their hearers respecting their superiority to their own fellow-Christians; all the same dreams of some indefinite blessings to be won, some punishment to be avoided hereafter in virtue of that difference—on the strength of their believing more, or doing more than others, or merely on the strength of their having the Christian name—all the same fears, and suspicions, and uncertainties, arising from the feebleness of this security; all the same coldness of heart towards men, and want of confidence in God; all the same thoughts of them as rivals, and of Him as a jealous and suspicious tyrant—which worked in the hearts of those Jews in Antioch?

And would not the Apostles refer all these evil fruits to the same root? You count yourself unworthy of eternal life! You are not really understanding what the blessing is which God has promised you, and how freely it is given, and how simply you must be receivers of it. You are not really convinced that He is a Being of absolute infinite love, that He is your Father, that He has sent forth His Son to claim you as His children, and His Spirit to move and quicken you, and give you the eternal life, which is the knowledge of Him and of His Son. You speak of your baptism, and dispute about it; but you do not believe your baptism, for you do not think that it has sealed you members of Christ, and sons of God, and inheritors of the Kingdom of Heaven, and that God is ever with you to make this inheritance actually yours. You talk of the other Sacrament, and have endless disputes about the nature and properties of the elements in which you receive it; but you do not believe that it is the Sacrament of Christ's presence, the assurance that He is with us even to the end of the world, the witness of an eternal communion with God and His children; the assurance that He communicates his own life to them, and teaches them to communicate that life of love to all creation. You do not believe this. You count yourselves unworthy of this eternal life. And therefore are there those endless strifes and infinite contradictions among you, which set at naught the idea of a Church, and betoken that a day may be near at hand when God will take your candlestick out of its place, and will once more impart to the world those blessings which you have contemned.

These are awful warnings, but they are those which

the Church addresses to us here Sunday after Sunday. Have you never wondered at the language in which we are invited to join in the feast which God has provided for us at the altar? Have you never contrasted the freeness, earnestness, and indiscriminateness of these invitations, with the stern warnings respecting the danger we are in of eating and drinking damnation to ourselves? Has it never seemed to you that those who wrote these two documents were strangely at variance with each other; that those who adopted both were at variance with themselves, and mocking you? 'Come at your peril, stay away at your peril. How can you be so mad as to refuse! How can you be so mad as to partake?'

Or, perhaps, you had a sense of these contrasts once; now you have dismissed it. The thing is altogether so unreal, the very notion of a Sacrament so incomprehensible, the importance attached to a particular act so preposterous, that you do not care any longer to investigate the reasons of an apparent inconsistency, which is only one instance of the general superstition of those who fell into it.

I do not wonder that any should arrive at these conclusions; I cannot cast stones at them. We are most to blame—we who do continue to believe that these words of the Church are true words, we who still partake of her ordinances. For, oh brethren, we ought to have understood this language which she so solemnly speaks in our ears; we ought to know whence it comes that the graciousness and fulness of this gift are commensurate with its awfulness. How can it be otherwise than awful, that God himself should be

THE COMMUNION SERVICE.

with us; should be offering to come to us, and hold converse with us? How can it be otherwise than the very blessedness which a spiritual creature asks for, and cannot bear to want? Is it not perilous to shut the door of the heart to such a visitant? Is it not perilous to seem to spurn it, and to forget whom we are receiving?

But is it all a delusion? Are we investing bread and wine with some magical properties? Are we supposing that they admit us into a presence which but for them would be far off from us? Do they not rather bear witness by their simplicity, by their universality, that it is always near to us, near to everyone? Do they not say: Will you live, move, have your being in God, and yet be practically at a distance from Him because you will not let Him approach you, enter into converse with you, subdue you? Shall all this love be about us day by day, and shall we be living shut out from its power and influence, in a region of ice?

Do you answer: But may not many have enjoyed this presence, may not many enjoy it now, who do not taste the elements? Believe, and give thanks that it is so. Acknowledge with hearty delight every fruit of God's Spirit which you see in any person who rejects every Christian ordinance. Canvass it not, try not to make out that it is unreal, or less than it seems to be, lest you blaspheme the Holy Ghost. Prize this Sacrament as the witness, the deepest, truest, simplest witness that God is with men, that all good things are from Him, that nothing can be true in us but what is the reflection of His truth. Do not *you* discard it because it is so childlike, because it carries such a whisper of love to each individual heart, because it puts you on a level with hundreds who you fancy may know less or feel less, may know nothing or feel nothing. Oh! think of God's love and not of your neighbour's sins, or your own advancement. The Church invites you to come with the most profound confession of sins which can be put into language. Let no one persuade you that your heavier sins are those which you share with the general congregation, that being communicants you have only venial sins to cast off and be delivered from. May God put this horrible and accursed pride far from us! The communicant should feel the exceeding sinfulness of sin as none other does. He should feel sin not as that which may bring a punishment after it, but as that which is itself the intolerable burden. He should regard it not as something to be weighed in human scales, but as the contradiction of God's own nature, the resistance to His love. The nearer his contact with the perfect light, the greater must be the sense of the darkness which will not comprehend it, the more certain must he be that this darkness is in himself. If we suffer the Church to lead our hearts in these confessions, and surely we feel more the want of a guide now than ever, we shall apprehend what infinite mercy is about us and the whole universe; we shall be appalled at the selfishness by which we have kept that mercy at a distance, we shall tremble as we consider what our state must be if that selfishness should become fixed, triumphant, unresisted; we shall cast ourselves and all upon that love which is a deep below all other deeps; in lowliness of heart we shall ask that the eternal life, of which we have counted ourselves unworthy, may be granted us for His worthiness, who went through death, the grave, and hell, that he might obtain it for us.

SERMON XVII.

THE COMMUNION SERVICE.

(5) THE ABSOLUTION, AND SENTENCES, AND TRISAGION.

Preached on the Fifth Sunday in Lent, March 25, 1849.
(The Annunciation.)

Come unto me, all ye that labour and are heavy laden, and I will give you rest. Take my yoke upon you, and learn of me; for I am meek and lowly in heart: and ye shall find rest to your souls.—MATTHEW xi. 28, 29.

MOST of us, perhaps, at some moment or other of our lives, have been greatly struck with these words. They have seemed to us full of sweetness and power, such as in hours of heart sickness, when the sense of death was upon us, we should delight to think of. When those hours actually came, when we did despair of life, was the charm in them found as effectual as we expected it would be? Let us not deceive ourselves or lie for God. I think in most cases, I am sure in some, it does not prove so. The words are repeated by some minister at the bedside of an oppressed conscience-stricken man. The answer is a look of languid helplessness, which says, without any need of the voice to articulate the sounds, 'Come; and what is coming? I am weary and heavy laden truly, *therefore* I can make no efforts. Rest is indeed what I want; but if I am to go in search of it, I must die without it. And will death bring it? I have no reason to think so. If it be a sleep, will it not be as the poet has said, a sleep full of horrible dream?' Does the friend or the priest who reads in the countenance, or hears from the lips, such language as this, turn away half in anger, half in despair, proclaiming the sufferer to be a hardened infidel whom nothing can move? Alas! he has yet something to learn about himself; he must yet feel—let him thank God if he is made to feel—that he is of the same nature with the object of his pity or displeasure, that there is in himself an infidelity quite as fearful, quite as deep. He too may know one day that there are in him holds and fortresses through which Christ's own words merely read out of a book, or uttered by a man's lips, will not penetrate.

Some such experience, I believe, is necessary to make the meaning of these words intelligible to us. For if they did say that by some great effort we are to break loose from the chains of habit and evil, and to bring ourselves into a Christian and divine state of mind, they would assuredly be words of discouragement, and not of comfort. The music might be pleasant at a distance; the nearer it approached, the less soothing and harmonious would it become. We are restless and feverish already, tossing about in hopes of ease from this posture or that. How strange to say, Be more restless still! Make yet a harder struggle for peace! then you will obtain what your souls sigh for. Do not our consciences and hearts witness,—' The merciful and gracious and true Lord did not intend to tell us this; He does not speak to mock us?'

No! if we believed *He* was speaking, the case would be changed altogether. If we did not think that we were listening to the sounds of certain letters printed on paper, if we did not think that a long line of human teachers, and a different language, and thousands of miles in space, and eighteen centuries in time, separated us from Him who said, Come unto me—in that hour when He rebuked the cities where most of His mighty works were done, and wherein He thanked His Father, the Lord of heaven and earth, who had hid these things from the wise and prudent, and had revealed them unto babes—if we did believe that He, even He, is addressing that speech to ourselves, for that He is as near to us as He was to those who sat with Him in the synagogue, who heard Him out of the ship, that He is the Lord of our spirits as He was of theirs,—then indeed the weary and heavy-laden man might feel that the invitation was all the more gracious and helpful, because it took the form of a command. 'Come unto me,' would then not signify, Go down into the deep, that you may bring Christ up from the dead; or ascend into heaven, that you may bring Christ from thence. But it would mean, 'Why kick against the pricks? why try to be separate from Him with whom thou art created to be one? why not confess Him to be thy Lord from whom thou art receiving the very strength which helps thee to strive for independence? Give up

THE COMMUNION SERVICE.

that strife, seeing you find it so wearisome and destructive. Do not try to be what you have discovered you cannot be—without a master. Do not resolutely choose a hard and evil master. Submit to one who showed Himself meek and lowly of heart when He was walking on earth in your flesh, and who seeks to make you meek and lowly like Himself. Take his yoke upon you—be content to work under Him, so will you find rest to your souls.'

It is in this way that these words have actually interpreted themselves to poor bed-ridden women, and sin-oppressed men; it is thus that they have acquired present deliverance, and a hope full of immortality. And, brethren, the time is come when divines must interpret in that way the records of Scripture to all people whatsoever, or must prepare themselves for—why need I say prepare themselves? they meet it already—utter indifference, listlessness, unbelief. The course which has been too much followed is this. People in general have been spoken to as if the Bible was a mere book of other days, which might be ingeniously applied to our use. A few have heard a different language, and have been pampered with the notion that *they* possessed the right and privilege of regarding it in a mysterious, esoteric sense, that *they* might receive it as the revelation of truths directly appertaining to their own inner life and experience. The first are growing weary of the husks which they have fed on. They know that they want something else than these; if we cannot supply it, they will seek it elsewhere. They say, 'You call upon us to believe one thing

R

and another, and tell us that it is wicked not to believe; yet, so far as we can see, what we are to believe has no concern with our lives; it is a story of events that happened in other ages to people in circumstances and with notions most unlike our own.' And this impression is deepened and confirmed by what they see of the other class, of those who boast that they have broken the exterior shell of theology, and are in possession of the kernel. If that kernel be, as our Lord seems to say it is, meekness and lowliness of heart and thence rest to the soul, all external indications would seem to show that it is not in their keeping. Nowhere more than in such persons do we find pride, exclusiveness, restlessness. And therefore the mountains and hills of religious profession in our time will surely be made low; or, in the words which belong to this day especially, the mighty will be put down from their seat, the rich will be sent empty away! But may we not trust and believe also that the hungry will be filled with good things; that numbers who have been treated by others, and have learnt to look on themselves, almost as outcasts from the fold of Christ, may find that He has never forgotten them, and that they stand in the nearest and closest relation to Him! It is not in a book they hear first of Him. It is not only with those who can read the book, or are possessed of it, or believe in it, that He holds converse. A thousand whispers have been heard in the heart and conscience of each living man. He knows that someone must have uttered them, that they were not the echoes of his own thoughts; that they came forth to reprove those thoughts, to reprove *him*. Yet not to reprove only, but to give him hope; to assure him that he may rise above himself, that he may be what he tries to be. But *whence* came those mysterious sounds so strangely blending with the cries of his own spirit; so distinct from them? If the Bible does not tell me this, it is not the book I need; if it does tell me this, I shall lay hold of it, I must have it, though all the wise men in the world proclaim to me that they have given it up, and find no more use in it; and though all the religious men in the world proclaim that it has quite another sense than this, or that this sense is for them, and not for me. Unless, brethren, I could say with the deepest, most inward conviction, 'This is the message with which we are intrusted; we can declare to you what the Son of Man is saying to you; it is here,—it is this, Come unto me;' I should think we were bound in plain honesty to be silent, and not to pretend that we had any good news for our fellows. And having this conviction, I contend that we can speak that which is good for all men to hear; are permitted to announce a treasure which is meant for all, and which is within the reach of all.

I spoke last week of an apparent contradiction in our Communion Service. A divine feast is announced, all are invited to come and partake of it; all are told that it is a sin to refuse the blessing. And yet it is represented as an awful act to join in the feast; men are warned how they come to it; they are told that they may eat and drink damnation to themselves if they consider not what they are doing. I traced this seeming inconsistency to a very different view of the nature of sin from that which commonly prevails amongst us—even amongst those, who, judging from their words, you would suppose had the most dreadful apprehensions of its heinousness. They look upon sin as the violation of the decrees of an omnipotent Being who has affixed an infinite penalty to the commission of it. The Bible and the Church look upon sin as the contradiction of the Divine nature, as a separation from a Being of perfect love, who has formed us in His image—as the determination to have another image than His. The first of these views has a look of far greater awfulness; it is immeasurably more *dreadful*, because there is no refuge from the dark object which it sets before our imagination. Hell is on one side; the Creator of Hell on the other. He merely exempts a few from that which He has Himself devised as the curse of the race. There is indeed no home for the spirit to flee to when it is surrounded by such a realm of darkness beneath, around, above. But it must find a home, or make one. It cannot acquiesce in such a sentence. Gleams of forgiveness, peace, hope, will shoot athwart the gloom. By degrees men become used to it, the vision does not appal them, for they have convinced themselves that it must be only a vision. And yet they cannot get rid of agonising recollections, and consciousness of present evil, and vague presentiments respecting the future, which seem to substantiate it and make them willing still to try methods for relieving the pain and propitiating the unknown power. Oh! that it should be so in the nineteenth century of the Christian Church. Oh! that at such a time we should have to learn the alphabet of the Gospel again; to be told once more that 'God is Light, and in Him is no darkness at all;' and that the pit of darkness which we have to dread is not that into which Christ went down, and from which He ascended again; but that it is the pit of selfishness, of hatred, of despair, upon the edge of which we are continually playing—gathering flowers while the grim tyrant is watching us and marking us for his prize—and from which only One mightier than the Prince of this world and the Prince of darkness can deliver us.

Now, brethren, those who are possessed with this idea cannot surely be less earnest in their language than others—language of expostulation and entreaty with men not to yield themselves to evil—not to admit it to parley with their hearts and understandings—not to tolerate its dominion. They should be much more earnest—it is a shame if they are not—just because their hope is so much stronger; because they are so sure that there is a Deliverer at hand, and that men are refusing that Deliverer, are choosing darkness rather than light, when they go in crooked courses. But their language must sound contradictory if it is merely listened to with the outward ear, if there is no other ear opened to take it in. They must at the same moment speak of an Infinite Love which is embracing us round, claiming us for its own, refusing to part with us; and of a self-will which is resisting that love, trying to do without it, and which may carry on the war for ever. They must tell men what the hardening of the heart consists in, how easily it increases in one and all of us, in spite of much knowledge, high professions, holy duties, holy ministries committed to us, in spite of the experience of sorrow, the sense of vanity in visible things, the consciousness of wrong, the sight of excellence in others and the admiration of it, the remembrance of dying beds and of those who have shown us love and done us good. With all things about us seemingly biassing us to good, that mind may be forming in us which formed itself in Judas while he was walking and listening to the Son of God, and preaching His kingdom to men. By proud thoughts; contempt of others; indignation at their contempt of us; self-pleasing, self-seeking, in common or in holy acts; thus, without flagrant immoralities or any loss of respect from our fellow-creatures, nay, most perhaps while we are most studying to keep it, we may be contracting a character which defies the impressions of love, which leads us to turn from the Holy One of Israel, and to wish that He should cease from us. You have heard of holy and wise men on their dying beds being appalled by a sense of moral evil, and of that evil as their own, which they had never experienced before. Do not suppose they were haunted with thoughts of punishments which God had appointed for them; such thoughts may present themselves in the form of material devils to the awakened hypocrite; they are part of the delusions which a long course of lying has made natural and inevitable to him; but it is not thus that these true-hearted men have been terrified. An unloving act or thought has seemed to them in that hour more terrible than all penalties which the most cruel imagination ever devised or inflicted. Selfishness has stood out before them as the real essence of the Devil nature, and the thought how near it had been to them, how they had succumbed to it, has given them an unspeakable shudder when the hope of awaking up after God's likeness and being satisfied was becoming brightest. Such discoveries are made to them, partly perhaps that they may be cured of the false notions of sin with which the heathenism of the world and of their own hearts had, in spite of faith and prayer, infected them, chiefly that their knowledge of the divine love might be deeper, fuller, more awful. And that same effect, I believe, the warnings which the Church addresses to those who will come to Christ's table, and the Confession which we make when we approach it, are intended to produce. I said that there, instead of coming to throw off the weight of certain venial sins, we should feel the weight of sin itself in its inmost nature and essence. What we are in ourselves, what *self* is, is shown to us if we consider what He is whose love is there set before us. The conflict between the two convictions, the sense of an eternal opposition between the powers of selfishness and of love, of evil and of good, which are wrestling with us and for us, will keep us indeed from all overstrained excited language —which betokens unreality of mind, a desire to lash ourselves into feeling—but it will lead us to cast the burden, as far too heavy for us to bear, before Him who knows what it is.

The answer which the Priest makes is, 'Almighty God, our heavenly Father, who of His great mercy hath promised forgiveness of sins to all them that with hearty repentance and true faith turn to Him, have mercy upon you, pardon and deliver you from all your sins; confirm and strengthen you in all goodness, and bring you to everlasting life, through Jesus Christ our Lord.' The Priest may say to a sick man confessing some load which is lying heavy upon his heart at that moment, '*I* pardon and absolve thee.' The man asks for that help, and it is the Priest's commission to be an absolver; he has no calling at all if he may not be the instrument of loosing heavy burdens, and bidding the oppressed go free. But when he is before the whole congregation, he asserts more distinctly the ground of his commission. He uses what is really higher language. He points to God as the Absolver; he is only the agent and mouthpiece. He speaks with perfect assurance. He has the whole Gospel of God revealed in His Son to stand upon. It is certain that he may bid those who have confessed God and desire to worship, rise up with cleansed consciences and pure hearts, and ask Him to open their lips that they may praise Him. *Now* he has to deal with a more inward and radical sense of evil, dwelling in the whole Congregation and in each man, a sense of collision with the mind of God. Therefore he casts them upon Him. They are come to seek communion with him. He has bid them come. May He himself direct the will which has been striving against Him; may he pardon and deliver you from all your sins, which are destroying the personal life of each of you and your existence as a Church.

The first Absolution was our baptismal Absolution, renewed each time we draw nigh to God as his sons. This is our Eucharistic Absolution, which is fully realised only when we cease altogether from ourselves and are content to abide in Christ, acknowledging Him as our righteousness and hope. We ask God to grant us, one and all, this resignation and this trust. It is resigning a delusion, it is living in our true and simple state; still He only can make us reasonable

XVII.]   THE COMMUNION SERVICE.   249

beings. Then follow the words of my text, 'Come unto me, all ye that are weary and heavy laden, and I will give you rest.' They *are* comfortable words in this connection; for Christ himself speaks them to us. They are not distant sounds coming from a far country; they tell us of home, of that which is nearer to us than all the most familiar objects and images, and which does not depend, as those do, upon the vividness of our memories, or our capacity of enjoyment. 'Come unto me, all that are weary,' does not mean, all whose affections are alive, who are full of sympathy and gladness. It means, you whose affections are blighted; you who are sensible in yourselves of coldness and dreariness; you who look out upon Nature, and 'see, not feel, how beautiful she is;' you who bring not life with you, but death, not peace, but confusion. Life and rest are for you, but you must confess they are not yours before you can possess them. This is a Sacrament; it is binding ourselves to another, and finding that in Him which answers to a blank and hollow in us. But these words are connected with others which go farther down. 'God so loved the world, that He gave his only-begotten Son, that whosoever believeth on Him should not perish, but have everlasting life.' That love is the original ground of all things, of ourselves, of our acts, of our creation, of our redemption. 'He gave his only-begotten Son, that in Him we might believe and have life.' He gives His Spirit, that we may have power to believe and possess this life. Then these words of Christ himself are taken as interpreting and giving a new significance to the words of St. Paul and St. John. They are not, any more than those of the Gospels, mere book-words. They are words of Communion, sacramental words. They come to us from Him. They come to us ever fresh and new. They speak to us as members of a Church and family: 'Jesus Christ came into the world to save sinners;' 'Jesus Christ is an Advocate and High Priest.' This language especially reminds us, that there is One in whom the whole Church is presented as a chaste bride to the Father, in whom it is holy, in spite of all the corruptions and abominations which its members commit when they forget their calling and live as if they were separate creatures. Their unbelief cannot destroy the reality and perfection which it has in God's eyes; which it does not derive from itself, but from Him; which it only understands when it turns from itself to him. Here therefore is the ground for the highest act of praise and devotion. 'It is very meet, right, and our bounden duty, at all times, and in all places, to give thanks unto Thee, O Lord, Holy Father, Almighty, Everlasting God.' There is no ecstasy or rapture in this language. It is our *duty*. Very cold, some will say. Very cold indeed, if duty is cold. But duty is grounded upon a truth; and truth lifts us above incidents of feeling and moods of mind. God does not cease to be the Holy Father, the Almighty, the Everlasting God, because we are low or sad, and feel physically or morally unfit to sympathise in the utterances of exulting spirits. He is, and abides; and if Christ has made us meek and lowly of heart, we understand that our privilege and glory consist in confessing God and His love, not in feeling very happy in ourselves. We have found out the great paradox and mystery of our humanity; how it is strongest when it is most weak; how it appreciates its own excellence only in God's. And therefore we say, 'It is our duty;' the function and business of our existence, at all times; in times of tribulation as in times of wealth; in all places; not here in church merely, but by the common hearth, in the law-court, in the shop, to give thanks unto Thee who art always and everywhere, the Holy Father, the Everlasting God.

This, I think, is a high act of devotion. And such the Church deems it. For she says, 'Therefore with Angels and Archangels, and with all the company of heaven, we laud and magnify thy holy Name, evermore praising thee, and saying, Holy, holy, holy, Lord God of hosts, heaven and earth are full of thy glory.' This she believes to be the worship of Angels and Archangels. They do not think of their own holiness, or think of themselves at all. Thoughts of self turn an Angel into a devil. Getting rid of the worship of self, men are fitted for the fellowship of Angels. Therefore we know that the meek upon earth, those who heard these words, 'Come unto me,' and obeyed them, and entered into Christ's rest, must be admitted into that company; must be sharing their unceasing work, their perfect rest; must be doing God's commandments, hearkening to the voice of His words; must be enjoying the contemplation of His goodness, and feeding upon the sacrifice of His son; must be able to help the meanest of those whom they cared for on earth with greater power, with more perfect love, because they are more like Him who gave Himself for us all.

SERMON XVIII.

THE COMMUNION SERVICE.

(6) THE CONSECRATION PRAYER.

Preached on Palm Sunday, April 1, 1849.

Therefore doth my Father love me, because I lay down my life, that
I might take it again. . . . I have power to lay it down, and I
have power to take it again. This commandment have I received
of my Father.—JOHN x. 17, 18.

THE contrast between our Lord's expressions in the last two clauses of this verse can scarcely fail to strike any reader of it: 'I have *power* to lay down my life, and have power to take it again. This *commandment* have I received of my Father.' The first words seem to assert inherent strength, and a dominion over the laws of Nature; the last speak of submission and absolute obedience. To regard these ideas as hostile, as necessarily excluding each other, is the impulse of us all; one which shows itself forth every day in our commonest acts and language; one which has fixed itself in a multitude of social theories; one which is at the root of the subtlest heresies.

The connection is most intimate between the different expressions of this tendency. Freedom or self-ruling power is proclaimed by one set of politicians as the great condition of our civil existence; entire obedience to some outward authority, by another. Freedom of the Will is the watchword of a whole class of moral philosophers; Necessity, of another. In the highest region of Theology all great controversies have turned upon phrases in Scripture which assign to our Lord a distinctly Divine character, and those which seem to represent Him as having no independent Will, as doing what He seeth the Father do.

Men in all ages have been striving after a reconciliation of these contraries. It has not been an idle passion to solve difficulties which lie wholly out of their sphere; they have felt that their homely duties, their daily lives, were interested in the result. Again and again learned men have returned from these inquiries, discomfited, and saying, 'There is no settlement of this endless debate;' again and again rulers in State and Church have interfered to put down disputes which, as they said, produced infinite heart-burnings and dangerous disturbances of the peace, and turned away their subjects from that which concerned them most. Such experiences and such decrees have been in vain. The heart has affirmed that it *must* find some way out of this labyrinth, whether the Understanding can furnish the clue or not, and the Understanding has again set to work elaborating some new scheme with the same vigour, hope, and success as before.

Here there is no attempt to disguise the opposition. Neither is there any attempt to treat it as one which must be put aside and banished from our thoughts. It is brought clearly, palpably before us, by the beloved disciple, in language which he says was uttered by our Lord concerning Himself. However divines may have spoken of Him, He at one and the same moment claims the freedom, and confesses the subjection. He has power over His life; for He has received a command. My brethren, Christianity is either destroyed by this contradiction, or is the solution of it; not for one case, or one fragment of our existence, but for all cases, and for the whole of our existence. Christianity, I say, meaning not a system, but that which over-reaches systems and shows their inadequacy, and exhibits the different sides of them distinct, alive, harmonious; Christianity, as another name for the manifestation of Christ, the perfect Image of God, one with the Father, one with us.

I have spoken of the last words of the text first. But our Lord had given the clue before He led us into the labyrinth. 'Therefore doth my Father *love* me, because I lay down my life, that I may take it again.' Here is the great ground of reconciliation. Here it is that the Free-will meets the Command. 'I am under no stern law of Necessity, binding me to a certain act which it is physically impossible for me to leave undone. I am under a law of obedience; I cannot break that law without self-destruction. And why? Because I am under the law of a Son to a Father, under a law of eternal Love. Here is the secret of my freedom, of my inherent power; here is the secret of my perfect, entire subjection. I could not be free except I were bound by this fetter; there is no freedom without it. I could not be obedient except I had the power of not being obedient. I should not be submitting to the

control of love, but of something else over which I
am entirely master. My Father loves me, because I
lay down my life. That perfect internal delight which
He has in me expresses itself in this act, binds me to
this act. It would be suspended, there would be a
clashing and contradiction in the eternal Unity of our
Being, if I did not lay down my life. The perfect
fulfilment and unfolding of that Unity is in my giving
up of myself. The love of the Father sees itself,
realises itself in this act, and is satisfied. Here is the
manifestation of that love; here it shines forth full
upon you; here you must see it, confess it, submit
to it.'

My brethren, this is unquestionably a depth
which a man on earth or a saint in heaven may
tremble and wonder to look into; which the second
must regard with more awe and amazement than the
first. But have not we the strongest assurance in
ourselves that it is a depth which men must look into
for the sake of their ordinary pursuits; that their
deeds and thoughts may not be in endless strife? We
must be taught what lies at the foundation of things,
whether it is a hard power, a hopeless compulsion;
whether it is nothingness; whether it is something
which we have projected out of our own minds; or
whether it is this truth of a Father united with a Son
in an eternal Spirit of Love; which Love is the ground
of his Nature, which Love has been ever coming forth
to us in acts of Creation and Redemption, which Love
was consummated and fully embodied in the act of
sacrifice that Passion-Week sets before us. Beggars
have felt that they had a right in this week, that it
belonged to them as much as to princes; to princes

only if they would become beggars. It has established itself in the very heart of our yearly life; it comes round to us always with the same witness: 'God of His tender love to mankind has given His only Son to take our nature upon Him, and to suffer death upon the Cross, that all mankind should follow the example of His great humility.' 'Therefore doth my Father love me, because I lay down my life that I may take it again.'

You have heard much of the Christian doctrine of Satisfaction. In your hearts you, perhaps, shrunk back from it, regarding it as something fictitious, inexplicable, even cruel. You submitted to it, for you were told it was true, and divines probably know best. But you put it as far from you as possible; it was a theory to be held or not denied—and forgotten. Did you ever consider what the Christian doctrine of Satisfaction is; and whether you may not unconsciously have been bringing with you, in your own minds, certain heathen notions of satisfaction which mingled with it, and destroyed its nature? Here our Lord is stating it Himself. You can have no higher words. I do not think you will find any clearer words. Let them be taken as the interpreters of our notions, not our notions as the interpreters of them. 'Therefore doth my Father love me, because I lay down my life.' Is not this Satisfaction? The entire complacency which the Father feels in the entire surrender and sacrifice of the Son? Is not that Sacrifice the expression of the Original Fatherly love which none save the Only-begotten could express? Have you some fancy about Satisfaction which is inconsistent with this; some notion which supposes that the Son did an act which was *not* the image of the Father's mind and character; that by this act He changed the Father's mind and character? If you have, it is not wonderful. Such notions are natural to us. They are just what we should all fall into if the contrary were not revealed to us. They are those which gave Heathen sacrifices their malignant character. Do not hastily say that you have got these views from divines; perhaps they meant no such thing; perhaps they meant this, and something much better than this, at the same time. Perhaps their language was too much drawn from the maxims and types and associations of the world; and you made it worse by the worldly habits which you brought to the consideration of it. But be that as it may, whether the fault was theirs or yours, be assured that just so far as you or they denied the eternal essential unity of the Father and the Son, just so far as you or they supposed the Son to be the ground of the acts and purposes of the Father's mind, and not the fulfiller and manifester of them, just so far you departed from the Spirit and the language of our Creeds. And be assured, that in that language lies the direct and formal (though we must look elsewhere, as I shall show presently, for the full practical) correction of those hard theories which have darkened the truth of God, and set at naught His loving purposes towards men.

The expression in our second Article, that the Son of God reconciled the Father to us, has pained many who have seen the immeasurable importance of recognising all love as proceeding from the Father, and having its root in Him. I do not wonder at their distress; and if the phrase was inconsistent with the assertion in the text, or with the principle of this week's Collect, I believe it ought, at all hazards, to be got rid of. I fear greatly that in many minds it is held in a way which *is* inconsistent with our prayers and our Lord's words, and therefore with the express doctrine of the Creed. But I fancy they bring their own doctrine to explain the Article, and read themselves into it. If the idea of satisfaction as the fruit of Love, as the image of Love in the Son, answering to the archetype of it in the Father, were filling our minds, there could be no difficulty in admitting the assertion that the Son reconciled the Father to us. He presented that perfect reflex of His own character to the Father with which alone He could be satisfied. In Him only could He see Humanity as He had formed it, with all its powers in full exercise, free and glorious—free and glorious, because entirely submissive to love; exercising dominion over all Nature, because surrendered to its true unseen Lord. Christ alone offered Himself a complete Sacrifice, not to necessity, not to the tyranny of Death, but to Love. He had power to lay down His life. He gave it up. Wherein had all creatures failed? Simply in this: they had not trusted God. They had not yielded themselves to Him, relying on His love, casting themselves unreservedly upon it; certain that in suffering and anguish, He was there and was the same, and that in death He would not leave them. The poison of distrust entered into our first parents. God awakened faith in them after they had fallen. He was ever calling forth this faith in their descendants, making them feel by practical discipline how reasonable it was. But none had fully, absolutely believed. And therefore their practice was confused and irregular. They did not yield themselves to God that they might execute His gracious will towards men. They were not brave, cheerful, confiding in their transactions with each other. There was a leaven of suspicion in all their thoughts and acts. They could not fully confess an Invisible Power above them; therefore they must do some homage to the things beneath them. Self divided their hearts with love, sometimes wholly vanquished it. I speak of the best, of those who were trusting God in the main, who were regarding their offices as trusts from Him, who were showing forth something of His character. None ever showed forth His whole character; none ever sympathised with the whole human kind, and with each member of it; none ever felt towards their brethren as the Father of all felt to them. Therefore none of them could destroy the separation between God and His creation. None could present such a mirror of His own infinite charity as He could look into and be satisfied. Only the Son could reconcile the Father to men; could make humanity wholly acceptable to a wholly loving Being. But was this reconciliation a change of His mind? Did it make His character other than it was before, or His feelings towards our race more gracious? No! for the very complacency of God was for this, that His character could now first be seen in One who bore our nature; that His purposes of grace to us could now first be accomplished in One who called us brethren.

I should be grieved indeed if I led you into theological controversies on such a day as this. My object is to lead you out of them. These incompatible thoughts about the meaning of Satisfaction and the nature and end of Sacrifice, are likely to confuse us all through this week, when we wish to think simply of our Lord's Passion, and of its relation to us, if we do not find some guidance in the consideration of them. If once the hint is given us, I believe the events which this week brings before us are themselves the best expounders of it. We often make a great and painful effort to realise, as we call it, our Lord's Sufferings, to think how transcendently great they must have been, hoping in that way to kindle our sorrow and devotion. The result, I think, is generally disappointment. We rarely work ourselves up to the point we wish; if we do, there comes a strong reaction afterwards. The Church teaches us to avoid such carnal struggles. It is humility we want, not exaltation. It is in submission to love, not in striving to understand it, and to measure its workings, that we enter into our Lord's mind, and follow His example. The person who most simply confesses his own want of charity, and desires to rest himself and all upon the infinite Charity of God, that he and they may be filled with it, will see most into the divine meaning of the Passion. And there is no clashing between that and its human meaning. The divine Charity reveals itself in suffering; can reveal itself perfectly to us only in suffering. We are suffering ourselves; see suffering all about us; if God had not met us and held converse with us in suffering, we must be strangers to Him. The Passion does not want theoretical explanations. It explains itself to the hungry man by his hunger, to the sick man by his sickness, to the man who is suffering from the unkindness of others, by that bitterness; to him whose past is crowded with fearful images, by his recollections; to him who trembles at the future, by his dread; to him who grieves over the sins and divisions of the Church, by that appalling vision; to him whom the accumulated sorrows of humanity are crushing, by the death-anguish which he has to bear. Every one feels that the Son of Man is entering into his grief—knowing the inward source of it—penetrated by the sense of it, as he never can be. All that we feel weakly, imperfectly—all that we wish to feel and do not, we are sure was part of His sympathy and agony. What in us is mixed so consciously with selfish retrospections, indignations, apprehensions, we are sure was in Him the perfect sorrow of Love; possessing the most exquisite intenseness, just because it had no alloy; because it found no compensation or relief in hard or vengeful thoughts of any creature. He bore the burden alone.

The passages which we read from the Evangelists do not enter into this secret grief, they only hint at it; leaving us to learn it from what passes in ourselves. The blessing of these passages consists in their perfect outward reality. We feel sure that such a Person actually went into the hall of Caiaphas, and before Pilate's judgment-seat; that it is no phantom-record; no history of sufferings that seemed to be endured by a man, but were not. And yet the more we read, the more we become aware how unreal this most real story becomes, if He who is the subject of it is not directly related to us, to each one of us, to the whole human family—if He who bears the grief of every man, is not the same who awakens that man's individual conscience, and all his yearnings for sympathy with other men. If we do not believe that Christ is in us, the Lord of our hearts and spirits, the story of that which He did and suffered soon becomes the dream of a shadow. *That* makes it the most substantial of all verities.

And, therefore, brethren, the Creeds and Passion-Week, and these Evangelical Histories themselves, lose their significance, if we do not connect them with the Sacrament of Christ's Presence with us— of Christ's death for each of us. By its help, if we use it simply and faithfully, we may overcome that fearful tendency to reduce the laws of the divine Love under the notions and conceptions of our own minds, of which I have spoken, and that as fatal tendency to separate Christ from the Father, Christ's life from our life, and the life of each member of His body from that of the rest. The Sacrament of His Body and Blood is the great witness against all these destructive habits of mind—a witness by this very fact, that whenever we have begun to notionalise about it, and to disconnect it with the belief of the absolute Love of God, the perfect Sacrifice of Christ, the privilege which we possess of presenting our own bodies as sacrifices to Him, its character has perished; it has become an expression of our division from God, instead of our reconciliation with Him; of our quarrels with each other, instead of our fellowship; of our carnal tendencies, not of our spiritual capacities. We have proof enough in its history that no charm lies in it—considered by itself, apart from God—to preserve us from the most fatal confusion, the deepest moral death; but equal proof that when it is taken as God's method of communicating with His creatures of unfolding the relation in which He stands to them

—when He is believed really to be present in it, and they come really trusting in Him, and yielding themselves to Him,—it is the very most wonderful means of translating words into life, and of reconciling truths which, when they are offered as propositions to the intellect, must be contradictory. I would speak to-day not of the feast itself—that I reserve for Easter Day—but of that part in our Service which especially concerns Sacrifice, The Consecration Prayer. This Prayer is introduced by an act of humiliation: 'We do not presume to come to this thy Table, trusting in our own Righteousness,'—words which express, very simply and very completely, our sense of being in a Presence in which it is the highest blessedness to dwell, and which it is impossible that we should enter into, unless God vouchsafed Himself to remove the veil from our eyes, and, above all, to take away the self-righteousness and self-glory, which hinder us from beholding the true Righteousness, and the true Glory.

Then follows the act of Consecration. I would earnestly ask you to think of it this week. You will find, I believe, that it embodies in a very remarkable way the principles I have been elucidating; those which I discovered in the words, 'Therefore doth my Father love me, because I lay down my life that I may take it again.' You will find it declared that, 'Almighty God, of His tender mercy, gave His only Son to suffer death upon the Cross for our Redemption.' You will see it affirmed, that 'by the one oblation of Himself once offered, He made a full, perfect, and sufficient sacrifice, oblation, and satisfaction, for the sins of the whole world.' Here is the Christian idea of Satisfaction clearly set forth.

Not the satisfaction to a tyrant, who wishes the death of his creatures, and must be persuaded to deal kindly with them; but satisfaction to a Being of tender mercy, of absolute charity, who could be satisfied with nothing but such an act as that of dying on the Cross; who could not behold His creatures redeemed, raised, glorified, partakers of His own likeness, except in one who rendered this perfect oblation. Next, the prayer assumes and affirms that the oblation which has been made for all is accepted—that God does look upon His creatures well-pleased. He asks nothing of them but to come into His presence—to believe that they are reconciled in His Son—to believe that He has come who has presented to Him that image in which He rests with perfect complacency, and in which we may rest with perfect complacency, He beholding us, we beholding Him, in his Son. Next, the Sacrifice is said to be not for the sins of a few picked persons—not for the sins of the Church—but for the sins of the whole world. Humanity is redeemed by Christ's death. The Redemption is free and universal. What remains? To take the cup of thanksgiving, and call upon the name of the Lord. To enter into God's presence believing that a living way is consecrated for us through the veil, that is, His flesh. And here are the sure tokens that the Sacrifice has been offered; here is God himself inviting us to come and partake of the Sacrifice. Christ did offer up Himself once for all. But he offered Himself that His creatures might draw nigh continually to God. They draw nigh when they present His finished Sacrifice to the Father—when they claim the privilege of being His reconciled and accepted children.

A priest offers up this Consecration Prayer—only a priest may offer it. Does it seem to you a dangerous privilege, one which is likely to make a mere feeble man feel that there is a mysterious and exclusive sanctity attached to his person; that he has an access to God which others cannot have? Consider, I beseech you, what the words are which he speaks—what makes his office divine. He speaks of Christ having died, that all men may be admitted to behold God's face and live; his right is to present that complete Sacrifice which God and not man has provided, and with which God is satisfied. There is no gorgeous ceremonial, no veiling of the face. The awfulness of the priest's duty consists in its simplicity, in his own nothingness, in the witness which he bears that the Mediation of Christ is a living, effectual, perpetual Mediation for the whole body, and for its most sinful member.

And do we not want such a testimony? Can you deliver men from actual superstitions and idolatries by introducing a true *notion* about our Lord's Atonement? If men are required to come with clear notions to God, oh, what a barrier do you interpose between Him and those whom He has reconciled to Himself! The Atonement is a fact, not a notion. May we feel it to be so, dear brethren, this week and every week. In hours of brightness and in hours of obscurity may He who alway did those things which pleased His Father, He who was to feel forsaken of His Father, still sustain us. Here in Church while we kneel at that altar, when we are alone in our closets, may His Spirit enable us still to draw nigh to the Father in the strength of His perfect Sacrifice; still to present ourselves as sacrifices well-pleasing to Him.

SERMON XIX.

THE COMMUNION SERVICE.

(7) THE EUCHARIST.

Preached on Easter Day, April 8, 1849.

And so it is written, The first man Adam was made a living soul; the last Adam was made a quickening spirit.—1 CORINTHIANS xv. 45.

SOME members of the Corinthian Church, St. Paul says, denied that there was any future resurrection. It is not probable that they belonged to the Judaising party which professed to follow St. Peter. That class, if we may judge by the intimations in the Epistles, had more of the Pharisaic than of the Sadducean leaven. They probably brought the doctrine of a resurrection both of the just and unjust with them from the rabbinical school, and incorporated it with their faith in our Lord. It is more natural to suppose that those who adopted the notion which the Apostle of the Gentiles refuted in this chapter, fancied that they had derived it from himself. He had said, that in one most important sense, the resurrection *was* past already. He had taught them that they were risen together with Christ; that their baptism was the pledge to them that they possessed a new and risen life. If the Jewish converts imported from their doctors a hard and carnal notion of future rewards and punishments, and imputed it to that apostle who speaks of 'the God and Father of our Lord Jesus Christ, having begotten us to a lively hope by the resurrection of Jesus Christ from the dead, to an inheritance incorruptible and undefiled,' those who had been educated in the Porch, or the new Academy, might just as easily connect opinions which they had received there with this language of St. Paul. To exalt the soul above the body was the very business of philosophy. Whether it was immortal or not, might be a ·question for debate; but that the thinking, judging part of man is to be honoured above that which eats and drinks and sleeps, was practically asserted even by the disciples of Epicurus. For how were they able to trample upon popular prejudices, to overcome the fear of divine powers which tormented vulgar men, otherwise than by the exercise of a faculty which the merely sentient multitude did not exercise? A Greek indeed could hardly dispossess himself of this feeling. It was a national belief as much as a school-tenet. He had been told, and he was convinced, that he had a right to rule over barbarians by strength or craft; if not by the word and sword of the freeman, then by the wit and cunning of the slave; and this because they were merely animal, and he had a soul. The belief that Christ by rising from the dead had asserted the dominion of the soul over the body—had proclaimed that the death which overtook and mastered the one could be cast off by the might of the other—

was a natural graft upon this previous persuasion. No doubt it was not this belief which the young convert welcomed when the Gospel first came to him as a message of peace, and deliverance, and joy. No doubt it had to struggle with very great and obvious difficulties; with *this* startling difficulty—that our Lord's death had not been apparently a victorious one for the intellectual part, but one of humiliation, sorrow, almost despair; and with *this*, that if his resurrection was a fact, he brought back from the grave that body which was supposed to be the soul's cage and prison-house. But there is a stage in human experience when simple faith departs and gives place to some theory, and when the mind is not yet awakened to the contradictions of that theory. Afterwards, as we know from ecclesiastical history, innumerable schemes were resorted to for removing the perplexity which the understanding had created for itself. 'The sufferings of Christ,' it was said, 'were imaginary; His body itself was not real: the spiritual part was accidentally or phantastically associated with the visible.' Such notions were in their seed in the Apostles' time; elsewhere they are distinctly hinted at and resisted. Here St. Paul only alludes to a crude undeveloped form of heresy, but, that crude and undeveloped form, one of wide-spreading influence, and certain to appear in every after age. 'The Resurrection,' so spoke these proud Paulicians, 'is past, not future. The soul rises when it attains higher perceptions, a new sense of its own destiny. Christ has given this higher privilege to those who believe in Him. For this they are to be most thankful. They need no longer be merely creatures of the earth, as men generally are. They can look up boldly to heaven, as we are meant to do. Is not this enough? What more do we want? All your faith, poor Judaisers, is in something that is to be or that may be. We *receive* our blessing. As our great teacher has told us, We *are* risen to newness of life.'

There might be many who could see that this interpretation of the Apostle's language put great dishonour upon the *body*. There might be some who felt that it led to great intellectual pride and self-glorification. Experience might prove that the seeming contempt of the body, in many cases at least, led to the indulgence of its most degrading appetites. Experience might prove equally that the soul, when it began to worship itself, lost its capacity of acquiring further light, and could only revolve in the narrow circle of its present acquisitions. St. Paul was aware of all these perils to which his disciples were exposed; these, and many more, are hinted at in his letter. But he saw another and a worse danger which was at the root of all these. He held man, merely considered in himself, to be a miserable creature; an utter absolute contradiction, an eye without an object, an image without an archetype. The curse and misery of man he believed to consist in this, that he had tried to be something in himself. He had refused to confess Him in whom he lived, and moved, and had his being; he had determined to be an independent creature; therefore he became the most dependent of all creatures—the slave of the things which he might have ruled. This was his infinite fall and degradation. It *involved* assuredly the victory of the body, of the mere sensitive nature over the intellectual; it involved the victory of the Earth, that is, of the objects which appeal to this sensitive nature, over it. But the *source* of the evil was in the separation of a being which could only realise its own truth, and life, and blessedness of another, from that other. Suppose then Christ had come down upon earth, and had taken man's nature, and had died, and had risen, to give your souls a victory over your bodies, to enable you to feel yourselves greater and more exalted creatures than you were before, what would He have accomplished? Would He really have solved the great riddle of the prostrate condition of humanity, or have raised it, and replaced it upon the ground on which it feels that it ought to stand? No! He would but have given it a dream of glory, from which it must presently awake to the sense of a deeper degradation. 'Man being in this honour would not abide in it, but would become like the beasts that perish.' He would fret his little hour in the pride of being a living soul, and would use his living soul to make his animal instincts more fierce, more grovelling, more penal.

But supposing He came from Heaven to bring men the news of a Father: to tell them that He would not permit them to be separated from Him, but was claiming them as His children. Supposing that He who brought this message was indeed the Son of God, and that He became endowed with a human soul and human body, such as each one of us has; and that in every acting of this soul and body He kept up a continual dependence upon His Father, and was possessed and quickened by His Spirit; supposing that by that Spirit He offered up His body and soul to death, a most real actual death, a death which showed what death is; and supposing that He brought back this soul and body from the grave, and said to His disciples, 'My Father is your Father, and my God is your God, go testify to all nations of my Resurrection, and my Spirit shall testify of it with you and in them;' would these be the same cold, dreary, ineffectual tidings as the other? would they contain no better assurance of good things bestowed, and of good things to come? Would they not say, 'The dream of man, that there is something near to him which is mightier than he knows, or can grasp, is not a dream, but a reality. The vague fear of man, that what is near him may be not a thing but a Person, is a verity. The vague hope of man, that this Person may be gracious and not malignant, the source of all the good which he beholds, or believes, or imagines, and not of any of the evil, is established. The sense in every human heart that it must have one to lean upon who is higher than itself, and to whom it may give up itself, from whom it may be every moment a receiver, is shown not to be a delusion. The conviction that He to whom the heart looks is stronger than all the enemies which are crushing it now, and threatening it hereafter, than death, than the grave, than the formless abyss, is ratified by Him who first inspired it. See The Source of Life is himself renewing it in one who was dead. The Spirit which he commended to His Father has quickened His body and soul. The Father has raised up the Son, and in raising Him up has raised us up, whose nature He took. He has declared to us that the Life which is in Him is capable of quickening, and shall quicken, our souls and our bodies; that we are restored in Him to our rightful state of union with God, of dependence upon God; that no power, visible or invisible, can break that union which He has established between Himself and His creatures, in the body and blood of His Son.'

I have very unwillingly used my own poor and confused language, rather than the high, and clear, and glorious language of St. Paul's Epistles, that you may not lose the reality of the things in the familiarity of the expressions. But I do entreat you to consider the passages in which our Lord's Resurrection is spoken of, and to see whether they do not all point the same way; whether the idea which my text embodies is not the key-note to them all. 'The first Adam was, as the Old Scriptures affirm, made a living soul. But the second Adam was made a quickening Spirit.' In these words St. Paul abundantly justified his own previous teaching, while he removed the false inferences that had been drawn from it. The Son of God has come to be the quickener, and restorer, and regenerator of our race. In His Resurrection God declared that death had no power over Him, because He was united by an eternal bond to Himself. In His Resurrection He declared that death had no power over us, because we are united to Him in the Well-beloved. Our Baptism proclaims this truth. God acknowledges us in that simple act as members of Him who died for us and rose again. We give ourselves to Him to be quickened with His Spirit. He does quicken us with that spirit. In the strength of it, in entire dependence upon Him, we are to live day by day, hour by hour. This is the fruit of the Resurrection—of that restoration of the Universe which He fulfilled when He broke from the tomb, and declared that Man was under a law of life, and not of death; the child of a living and loving Father, not the bondsman of Nature. But because the Resurrection is past, because we may claim the blessing at once, because we have claimed it, and have tasted of its power and freedom, is it therefore not future? Can we receive it at all without receiving it as the pledge of an infinite treasure for which we are to hope? Has Christ died and risen again to give a few proud Philosophers or ascetical Pharisees some high notion about the powers of the soul, and the meanness of the body? Has He not entered into the state of the lowest beggar, of the poorest, stupidest, wickedest wretch whom that Philosopher or that Pharisee can trample upon? Has He not come to redeem the humanity which Philosophers, Pharisees, beggars, harlots share together? Has He not come to tell each man, 'There is no life for thee in thyself; there is perfect life for thee in God, and it is a restorative life, which can work in thee, at the very root of thy being, and make thee a new and holy creature?' Is there any limit to the feebleness of either body or soul in themselves? Was Christ's death only a bodily agony? Did not His Soul sink into a deeper weakness—a more awful desertion? Is there any limit to the Restoration which is effected in man when the Divine Power acts upon him? Did Christ's Resurrection only show that His *mind* was still the same as it was before the nails pierced His hands and feet? Did He not say, 'Handle me and see; for a spirit hath not flesh and bones, as you see me have.' If we claim some high glory and inherent immortality for the soul, we come inevitably—men always have

T

come—to think that this wonderful frame of the body, this glorious sense of sight, with all that it has apprehended and may apprehend, this mystery of sound, this power of touch, and taste, and smell, the capacity of motion, even the organs of speech, are all to be cast aside, and become the prey of death. Some fine particle, some pure essence of this which I call myself, is to survive: all that has been most intimately and dearly associated with me, that has been the instrument of my communion with the bright world around me, and with brethren of my own race, all this living machine, the mystery of which it has required six thousand years very imperfectly to penetrate, must be extinguished utterly for each man after threescore years and ten, during which it has been maintained through sorrow and strife, endured rather than enjoyed. Oh, strange and cruel faith, to come forth from those who so eagerly and passionately proclaim the dignity and glory of the species! Faith which they do not hold, or how could they admire men who devote themselves with honest zeal to the investigation of the truths of science, and of those laws of art, which concern the relation of our senses with the external world? Those truths, those laws bear witness, as the mythology of every civilised and savage people does, the dream of every Elysium and Walhalla, that men do look, must look, for a redemption of their bodies. That they are bound down to earth, tormented with plagues and diseases innumerable, unknown. That this bondage, these plagues and diseases, express their true state, their proper meaning, no man in his senses can really believe. Yet it requires nothing less than the faith that God is the restorer and regenerator of Humanity, and that He has commenced the restoration and regeneration of it from its root, to justify the witness of our reasons and consciences, and to persuade ourselves that the charnel-house does not interpret the law of the Universe. 'If the Spirit of Him who raised up Christ from the dead dwell in us, He shall quicken also our mortal bodies;' this is the answer, the one answer to that horrible and crushing, but most natural supposition. We must mount higher than the soul, if we would descend lower. We must believe that a man is not merely made a living soul, but that he is joined to One who has been made to him, and to the whole body of which he is a member, a quickening Spirit.

And thus, my brethren, has the Resurrection become so inseparably connected with the Christian Passover, the eating of Christ's flesh, and the drinking of His blood. Apart from the belief of Christ, as the risen Head of humanity, the source and spring of life to it and to each man, that festival is the most idle and unmeaning of mockeries; grounded upon that belief, it is the profoundest and most comfortable of all verities. How fearful to say, 'The Body of our Lord Jesus Christ which was given for thee, preserve thy body and soul unto Everlasting Life,' if we do not think that the body of our Lord was actually given for that man to whom we speak, if we do not believe that it is God's good pleasure that his soul and body both should attain an everlasting life; if we do not think that he has a right to trust God, that he ought to trust God for all that He has promised. How good is it to say such words, if we have felt the utter impotence of our own; if we feel that no quickening power dwells in us; but that we are meant to be the utterers of God's will, to be the bestowers of God's gifts to the world which He loves, and for which He has given His only-begotten Son. What a rest there is in the thought, He can communicate to you that which our lips cannot tell. You are His; He has redeemed you to Himself. He has raised you up by His Son Jesus Christ. And though there are powers of death ever at work upon your souls and bodies both, threatening the destruction of both, there is a mightier power which is sustaining, preserving, quickening both; a power to which we cannot commit ourselves and you in too childlike dependence and trust. Is there a man or woman of whom we dare not say, Christ died for thee? And if not, is there a man or woman to whom we may not proclaim, 'The Spirit of Him who raised up Christ from the dead is seeking to raise thee out of this natural death, to quicken all the energies of thy soul, all the energies of thy body, to make thee a new creature with a soul like His soul, with a body like His glorious body.' To each man we say this, 'Christ died for thee.' Each man has need to hear it for himself, to believe it for himself. But the language which speaks to him as an individual claims him as the member of a family. He is eating the one bread which is to sustain all as well as himself; he is drinking of the divine universal life; He has no property in Christ which all around him have not, which all who have the same flesh and blood, the same death, have not equally. The Father who raised Him from the dead has in Him quickened the whole race. Though we receive each for himself, the gift contains a promise and a prophecy for the whole Church and for mankind.

Therefore so soon as we have received this bread and wine, we say, 'Our Father.' And we bless God that we who have duly received these holy mysteries have been fed with the precious body and blood of His Son, and are owned as very members incorporate in His mystical body, which is the company of all faithful people; that we are heirs through hope of a wider, an enduring inheritance—the inheritance of mankind. And as we say, 'Glory to God in the Highest, Peace on earth, good will to men;' as we glorify God for His great glory; as we invoke the Lamb of God, who takes away the sins of the world; as we declare that He only is holy, He only is the Lord, who with the Holy Spirit is most high in the glory of God the Father, we confess a Unity which lies beneath all other Unity; a deep eternal mystery of Reconciliation and Peace, which shall overcome the mystery of Division and Evil once and for ever.

Yes, brethren, the Eucharist is a pledge of that great and final victory, the mightiest pledge which God himself has given us. It is a pledge that all the dark and carnal thoughts of men, which have gathered about it, and tried to draw it down to their own level, all those corruptions of it which have changed it into a minister of sense and an instrument of idolatry, shall be scattered altogether. They will not fly before any other charm than that which is contained in itself; before any other witness than this, that Christ is the quickener of humanity, and therefore of the body and soul of each man. They will not fly before dogmas or controversies, or ridicule; they will wax stronger the more you set at naught the meaning and power of Sacraments, the more you refuse to recognise them as witnesses of a Present God, of a Living Helper. For this has been their real origin, as it is the origin of all the schemes and systems which in past days or in our own have excluded the light that would shine forth upon men, which have driven poor people into confusion, and earnest hearts into doubt and despair. The connection between God and man has been lost out of Theology; a notion has been substituted for a Living Being; a power working in past time for one that is acting upon us now. When the evil becomes felt, when a deep groan proclaims how hard the bondage is to the spirits of men, they seek all devices for deliverance. They fancy that the evil lies in the reverence for that which is old: in the acknowledgment of a Divine Revelation; in forms which speak of an invisible world, as related to ours; in the dream that a Divine Presence is still ruling amongst us. They seek to break these bonds asunder, and cast away these cords from them. They know not that in them lies the secret of their emancipation from the fetters which human systems have fastened on them. They know not—though they may learn by sad experience—how they are riveting all those chains of iron by their zeal to shake off these silken chains. If anyone ventures—not in harshness, but in deep sympathy, with a consciousness of all their temptations, and an inward sense of the truth of their complaints against the sins which he and his brethren have committed—to tell them so, he must look for pity and scorn from them, as well as indignation from those whom they denounce. But if it be the truth, it will prove itself truth to some hearts here and there. There will be old men fainting and weary, there will be young men utterly failing, who will hear the testimony which comes to them from words that they loved in their childhood; who will learn from them that God is still with us of a truth, that He has raised up His Son Jesus Christ, and us in Him, and that He does quicken us anew day by day with His Spirit. They will wait upon Him, and renew their strength, and at last mount up on wings as eagles, and run and not be weary, and walk and not faint.

And those who are sighing over the condition of the Church, and have tried scheme after scheme for reforming it and bringing back its unity, and have found only fresh disappointments and despondency, will learn that they may go back to the one source of reformation and restoration—to Him who is the same yesterday, to-day, and for ever. As they think upon the stones of Zion, and it pitieth them to see her in the dust, a voice will come to them from the innermost shrine of mercy, and they will know that it is the voice of Him who spoke of old to His prophets. It will come to them like the full melody of an Easter Hymn, answering to the low Miserere of Passion Week. 'Thy dead men shall live, together with my dead body shall they arise. Awake and sing, thou that dwellest in dust, for thy dew is as the dew of herbs.' 'The Spirit shall be poured upon us from on high, and the wilderness shall become a fruitful field, and the fruitful field shall be counted for a forest. And the work of Righteousness shall be peace, and the effect of Righteousness quietness and assurance for ever.'

THE LORD'S PRAYER.

ADVERTISEMENT.

I WISHED in these Sermons to connect the Lord's Prayer with the thoughts which are most likely to be occupying us at this time. If they lead any to ask themselves how their study of passing occurrences may be made more serious, and their worship more real, my purpose in publishing them will be answered.

LONDON; *May* 25, 1848.

THE LORD'S PRAYER.

SERMON I.

Sixth Sunday after the Epiphany, February 13, 1848.

After this manner therefore pray ye: Our Father which art in Heaven.—MATTHEW vi. 9.

'AFTER *this* manner,' and therefore any manner but this is a wrong manner; a prayer which has any other principle or method than this, is not the Lord's Prayer.

The remark may seem superfluous, but it is not so. The Paternoster is not, as some fancy, the easiest, most natural, of all devout utterances. It may be committed to memory quickly, but it is slowly learnt by heart. Men may repeat it over ten times in an hour, but to use it when it is most needed, to know what it means, to believe it, yea, not to contradict it in the very act of praying it, not to construct our prayers upon a model the most unlike it possible, this is hard; this is one of the highest gifts which God can bestow upon us; nor can we look to receive it without others that we may wish for less—sharp suffering, a sense of wanting a home, a despair of ourselves.

At certain periods in the history of the Church,

especially when some reformation was at hand, men have exhibited a weariness of their ordinary theological teaching. It seemed to them that they needed something less common, more refined than that which they possessed. As the light broke in upon them, they perceived that they needed what was less refined, more common. The Creed, the Ten Commandments, the Lord's Prayer, were found to contain the treasures for which they were seeking. The signs of such a period are surely to be seen in our day. We can scarcely think that we require reformation less than our fathers. I believe, if we are to obtain it, we too must turn to these simple documents; we must inquire whether there is not a wisdom hidden in them which we do not meet with elsewhere; whether they cannot interpret the dream of our lives better than all the soothsayers whom we have consulted about it hitherto.

I. Much of the practical difficulty of the prayer lies assuredly in the first word of it. How can we look round upon the people whom we habitually feel to be separated from us by almost impassable barriers; who are above us so that we cannot reach them, or so far beneath us, that the slightest recognition of them is an act of gracious condescension; upon the people of an opposite faction to our own, whom we denounce as utterly evil; upon men whom we have reason to despise; upon the actual wrong-doers of society, those who have made themselves vile, and are helping to make it vile—and then teach ourselves to think that in the very highest exercise of our lives these are associated with us; that when we pray, we are praying for them and with them; that we cannot speak for ourselves without speaking for them; that if we do not carry their sins to the throne of God's grace, we do not carry our own; that all the good we hope to obtain there, belongs to them just as much as to us, and that our claim to it is sure of being rejected, if it is not one which is valid for them also? Yet all this is included in the word 'Our': till we have learnt so much, we are but spelling at it; we have not learnt to pronounce it. And what man of us—the aptest scholar of all— will venture to say that he has yet truly pronounced it; that his clearest utterance of it has not been broken and stammering? Think how many causes are at work every hour of our lives to make this opening word of the prayer a nullity and a falsehood. How many petty disagreements are there between friends and kinsfolk, people dwelling in the same house—so petty that there is no fear of giving way to them, and yet great enough to cause bitterness and estrangement, great enough to make this 'Our Father' a contradiction. How often does my vanity come into collision with another man's vanity, and then, though there be no palpable opposition of interests between us, though we do not stand in the way of each other's advancement, what a sense of separation, of inward hostility, follows! As the mere legal, formal distinctions of caste become less marked, how apt are men to indemnify themselves for that loss by drawing lines of their own as deep, and more arbitrary! As persecution in its ruder shapes becomes impossible, what revenge does the disputatious heart take under this deprivation, by bitter manifestations of contempt for an adversary, by identifying him more completely with his opinions, by condemning him, if not for them, then for the vehemence and bigotry with which he supports them! How many pretexts have the most tolerant amongst us for intolerance! How skilful are the most religious in finding ways for explaining away the awful command, 'Judge not, that ye be not judged!'

II. But when we say 'Father,' are we more in earnest? Do we mean that He whom we call upon is a Father actually, not in some imaginary metaphorical sense? Alas! in stumbling at the first word, 'Our,' we do I fear destroy the next also. For though all countries and nations had a dim vision of this name; though men, in whom the reverence for fathers had any strength, were taught by a higher wisdom than their own, to connect that reverence with their thoughts of the unseen world, and of One who ruled it; though the sense of this connection was a balance to the tendency which they felt to idolise the powers of Nature, and yet kept them from a mere abstract, formal notion of the Divinity; though by it they learnt to realise, in a measure, their own spiritual existence; yet the revelation which fulfils the heathen expectation, which turns the dream of a Father into substance, is that which is expressed in the words, 'He hath sent forth His Son, made of a woman, made under the law, that we might receive the adoption of sons,' and in those which are inseparable from them, 'Because ye are sons, He hath sent the Spirit of His Son into your hearts, crying, Abba, Father.' Now this revelation is grounded upon an act done on behalf of Humanity—an act in which all men have a like interest; for if Christ did not take the nature of every rebel and outcast, he did not take the nature of Paul and John. Therefore the first sign that

the Church was established upon earth in the name of
the Father, and the Son, and the Spirit, was one which
showed that it was to consist of men of every tongue
and nation; the baptized community was literally to
represent mankind. If it be so, the name Father loses
its significance for us individually, when we will not
use it as the members of a family. No doubt it is a
true name; it expresses an actual relation; and therefore, if we attain by ever so unfair a process, through
ever so narrow a chink, to the perception of it, we may
be thankful. But the possession is an insecure one: if
some feelings or apprehensions give us a title to it, the
title will become uncertain with every variety of our
feelings and apprehensions. We shall regard the Unchangeable as a Father to-day, and not to-morrow.
And then what becomes of the Lord's Prayer as a fixed
manner or model for all prayer ? What becomes of it
as a resource in times of tribulation, when our feelings
and apprehensions are in the lowest, most miserable,
state ? What is its worth when we are tempted by
suggestions addressed to these very feelings and apprehensions—suggestions which overmaster them, and
get possession of them? Does any one answer, that
God is called the Father of our spirits, that He is said
to beget us to a new life, that as natural men we are
not His *children*, though we are His creatures ? All
this is true and most important; and it is precisely
what we assert, when we say that God has redeemed
mankind in Christ. We mean that He has not left us
to be fleshly creatures, to be animals, as we are naturally
inclined to be, and would be altogether, if He were
not upholding us; we mean that He has owned us as
spiritual creatures, has claimed us in that character to

be His servants and children, has given us His Spirit. We say that when a man arises and goes to his Father, he renounces his vile, selfish, exclusive life, and takes up that human privilege which God has given him in Christ; he enters upon his state as a man when he confesses God as his Father. If, instead of doing this, he will stand upon certain feelings and apprehensions of his, which separate him from his kind, he is not a penitent; he is still a self-exalting, self-glorying man; he has not been brought to feel that he is nothing; he has not been forced to cast himself wholly and absolutely upon the love and mercy of God in Christ. And, surely, such dependence, such self-renunciation, such willingness to take up a common position as portions of a family, is very difficult for creatures proud as we are, eager to have something of our own, always hoping to make out for ourselves special pleas of exemption from the laws of the universe. Only by discoveries often forgotten, often repeated, that we cannot establish any such pleas, that they must prove trumpery and preposterous, when they are urged before the Judge of the whole earth, only through the dreary conviction that our faith and hope and love, as well as our deeds, are shallow and insincere, are we drawn to real trust in Him who is faithful and loving, who is the God of all hope; who can impart to us the power of believing, of hoping, of loving, of doing what is right; who is willing to impart it because He is our Father, and has promised all good things to them that ask Him.

III. It might seem, till we know a little of ourselves, that the next words, 'which art,' had nothing in them to cause us offence or perplexity. But they too are hard words. The greatest temptation, perhaps, of this age, is to think of the Most High rather as one about whom we read in a book, than as the Living God, the name by which the book always speaks of Him. It is a fearful tendency; but if you search your hearts, you will find it there. Nay, there is not need of much searching, the habit is so natural. In all ages, a disposition has been apparent, not in irreligious minds, but in those which are specially serious and reverential, to turn their devotion towards that which has been, rather than to that which is, towards images and relics, towards whatever carries with it the sign and reminiscence of personality, but is not personal. The modern English form of it which makes words rather than visible objects the substitutes for the unseen realities, is externally so unlike the other that we are not easily persuaded of their essential identity. It is the effort of prayer which brings the evil fully before us. What a dim shadow, thrown it would seem from our own minds, has often been before us when we were kneeling to the Majesty of Heaven. What a strange self-congratulation, that we were performing an act of worship, good and desirable, to *some* Being; but to *what* Being we hardly dared to ask ourselves! Oh! surely even in such hours there have been flashes upon the conscience, wonderful assurances that the place was a dreadful one; that God was there, though we had not known it. These are admonitions that the Father of all lives, though our spirits be ever so dead. But they are also admonitions that we should stir ourselves to the recollection of Him who is always near our spirits, who can both restore life to them, and keep them alive. And if, at any time, He has taught us to feel that the universe would be a horrible blank without Him; that His absence would be infinitely more to us than to all creatures beside; that if He is not, or we cannot find Him, consciousness, memory, expectation, existence, must be curses unbearable; but that when the burden of the world and of self is most crushing, we may take refuge from both in Him—if at any time such convictions have dawned upon us, let us not hope to keep the blessing of them by our own skill and watchfulness. Let us say, 'Our Father which art, when we least remember Thee, fix the thought of Thy Being deeper than all other thoughts within us; and may we, Thy children, dwell in it, and find our home and rest in it, now and for ever.'

IV. Once more: the words '*In Heaven,*' as they are closely united with those which went before in meaning, so too, like them, come into collision with some of our strongest evil tendencies. The impulse of ordinary polytheists was to bring God down to earth; to make Him like themselves. Against this impulse the philosopher protested, representing the Divine Nature as wholly inactive, self-concentrated, removed from mundane interests. The Gospel justifies the truth which was implied in the error of the first; Christ, taking flesh, and dwelling among men, declares that Heaven has stooped to earth. But here a great many would stop; they would bring back Paganism through Christianity. The Son of God, they say, has become incarnate; now fleshly things are again divine; earth is overshadowed by Heaven; it is no longer sin to worship that which He has glorified. In the manger of Bethlehem they sink the Resurrection and Ascension:

they will only look at one part of the great Redemption, not at the whole of it; at the condescension to our vileness, not at the deliverance from that vileness, which the Son accomplished when he sat down at the right hand of the Father. But He does not sanction this partial and grovelling view. 'After this manner,' he taught his disciples, even while he was upon earth, 'pray ye, Our Father which art in Heaven.' As if he had said, Do not think that I am come to make your thoughts of God less awful than those of Moses were, when he put his shoes off his feet and durst not behold; than Solomon's were, when he said, 'He is in Heaven and thou upon earth, therefore let thy words be few.' The revelation of the divine mystery in me is not given that you may entertain it better in your low carnal hearts, that you may mingle it more with the things which you see and handle; that each of you may have a warrant for the form of idolatry which is dear to him. This revelation is given that the mystery may be no longer one of darkness, but of perfect light: light which you will enter into more and more as your eyes are purged; but which, if it colour the mists of earth for a moment, will at last scatter them altogether.

'*Our Father*:' there lies the expression of that fixed eternal relation which Christ's birth and death have established between the littleness of the creature and the Majesty of the Creator; the one great practical answer to the philosopher who would make heaven clear by making it cold; would assert the dignity of the Divine Essence, by emptying it of its love, and reducing it into nothingness. Our Father, *which art in Heaven*: there lies the answer to all the miserable substitutes for faith, by which the invisible has been lowered to the visible; which have insulted the understanding and cheated the heart; which have made united worship impossible, because that can only be when there is One Being, eternal, immortal, invisible, to whom all may look up together, into whose presence a way is opened for all, whose presence is a refuge from the confusions, perplexities, and divisions of this world; that home which the spirits of men were ever seeking, and could not find, till He who had borne their sorrows and died their death, entered within the veil, having obtained eternal redemption for them, till He bade them sit with Him in heavenly places.

What I have said may have seemed to prove that this simple prayer is too high and too deep for creatures such as we are. Would you have it otherwise? Would you have a prayer which you can comprehend and fathom? I am sure the conscience and reason would reject such a prayer as a delusion, an evident self-contradiction. I have said nothing to show that this prayer is unsuitable to the wants and ignorance of any beggar in our streets. I have shown only, that the wisest man, who will not use it as that beggar does, who will try it by his own narrow methods and measures, will find that he has never entered into the sense of it, that he is condemning himself in the repetition of it. And if, brethren, we all know that we have been guilty of this mockery again and again, how clearly do our consciences witness, that it is after this manner, and no other, we must make our confession. What despair we should be in, if our unbelief were indeed truth, and not a lie! If the word 'Our' did *not* express the truth, that we participate in the blessings, as well as the curses, of the whole race; if the word 'Father' were a word merely, and not the expression of an eternal truth; if we might think of Him as not nigh, but afar off; in a book, not as one in whom we are living and having our being; if He were subject to the changes of earth, not for ever fixed in Heaven, whither could we turn under the overpowering sense of our own sinfulness and heartlessness? It is the full conviction that our misery has proceeded from ourselves, from our maintaining a resolute war with facts and reality, which can alone give us encouragement. For we know there is One who is willing to teach us how to pray this prayer in spirit and in truth; we know that there is One who is praying it. He who died for us and for all mankind, He who is ascended into Heaven, He, who is true and in whom is no lie, did when He was here clothed with our mortality, does now in his glorified humanity say, in the full meaning of the words, for us and for his whole family above and below, 'Our Father which art in Heaven.'

SERMON II.

Septuagesima Sunday, February 20, 1848.

Hallowed be Thy name.—MATTHEW vi. 9.

I SAID last Sunday that in this Prayer our Lord taught us the method, as well as the principle, of all prayer. It is, indeed, impossible to separate one from the other. The principle of a prayer which asks first for bread or forgiveness, must be wholly different from the principle of one which begins with 'Hallowed be thy Name.' The conception of Prayers which you would derive from them are unlike, nay, they are opposed.

I think there can be little doubt which form men would most readily adopt. 'Let us have bread enough, bread to satisfy all bodily appetites: bread, if you will, that shall meet our intellectual, our spiritual desires— what other petition can possibly take precedence of this? If an earthly ruler could send us this blessing, should we not implore him for it before all things? If we are hearty in believing that the Heavenly Ruler is willing to send it, shall we not take the same course when we call upon Him? Shall we strain ourselves to introduce needless, artificial preliminaries, when this is what He knows we are craving for?' So men are likely to reason till they painfully discover that there is something they need more than bread, till a certain inward gnawing in lonely hours, on a sickbed, suggests that sin has need to be pardoned, as well as hunger to be appeased. Is it not still more monstrous to interpose any check to the utterance of this cry? What can be so desirable as that it should be poured forth with all the agony and intensity of a spirit which has learnt that such a boon would be cheaply purchased by the sacrifice of all things else?

Language of this kind would seem to be religious as well as natural, proceeding from sympathy with human needs, and a belief that there is a divine provision for them. And yet our Lord says, 'After this manner pray ye: Our Father which art in Heaven, hallowed be thy Name.' He recognises the desires of which I have spoken as reasonable and true, but he postpones them; and this, too, when he is warning us against babbling in prayer, against all vain idle formulas; when he is directing us especially to ask for the things we have need of.

Brethren, in this difference lies, I believe, the great contrast between those systems of theological doctrine and practice, which have been shaped out by the subtlety of divines in accordance with the cravings of disciples, and that teaching which begins from God, which never lowers itself to the base and selfish thoughts of men, and which, therefore, is able to satisfy all that is real in man as nothing else can. Ask the systematiser what that Revelation is which the Bible records; he will tell you, that it is the announcement of the duty which man owes to his Maker for the good things he enjoys upon earth; and of a scheme of redemption by which he may obtain pardon for his sins, and higher blessings hereafter. Ask the Apostles, or our Lord Himself, what that Revelation is, and they say it is the revelation of a Father whom men were feeling after and could not find, and who at length declared Himself to them in His well-beloved Son. If the first statement be accepted as the truest and simplest, the prayers, 'Give us bread,' 'Forgive us our sins,' are all that we have any concern with; we should rush into them at once; by them we grasp all the good which creation and redemption have in store for us. If we are led by any process to feel that the news concerning a father is really *the* good news, apart from which the promise of food or pardon would signify nothing, we shall feel that 'Hallowed be thy Name' is the first and most necessary and most blessed prayer for the whole human race and for every one of its members.

For every gross and cruel superstition has this origin and definition: it springs from ignorance of the name of God; it consists in and by that ignorance. It mixes Him with His creatures; first with what is highest in them, next with what is mean, then with what is basest; finally it identifies Him with the Evil Spirit. What is darkest and most hateful; what a man flies from most and would desire should not exist; this becomes the object of his worship. He has within him a witness that there is a Being whom he ought to love with his heart and soul and strength. That which he conceives of as this Being, that which his fancy and his conscience represent to him is one whom he inwardly hates, and from whom he would be delivered.

But these horrors belong, it will be said, to the ages of priestcraft; civilisation puts an end to them. Let us understand ourselves clearly on this point, that we may not deny what is right in the assertion, nor be deluded by mere phrases. The classes which have been brought within the reach and sway of civilisation have, no doubt, learnt that the inventions of superstition are false and mischievous; they have seen that a dark notion of the divinity is at the root of them; they have made strenuous efforts to rid themselves of what they believe to be a phantom. In place of it they have substituted a being answering to their own habits of mind, good-natured, indifferent, tolerant of evil. To such a being they have paid a homage which they have almost felt to be fictitious, a homage justifying itself chiefly on the plea that the dependence of inferiors— the general order of society—could hardly be maintained without it. The humbler men, partly perceiving why this decent devotion was thought desirable, partly observing that it only lasted during summer-days, and was often changed for another and more vulgar sort in calamity; but above all, conscious that it was of a nature altogether unsuited to them, either cherish amid the glare and glitter of civilised life the dark thoughts of another age, or change them for a more resolute and courageous atheism, or lastly, learn that God is a refuge in time of trouble, a deliverer from the horrors of conscience, not an enemy who must be persuaded to forego his hatred of them, or a mere phantom of benevolence, who leaves His creatures undisturbed in their wickedness and misery. Upon our thoughts of God it will depend, in one time or another, whether we rise higher or sink lower as societies and as individuals.

The civility or intelligence of a people may seem to have grown up, and to be growing, under the influence of a multitude of adventitious circumstances. But if you search well, you will find that whatever there is in it not false, whatever has not the sentence of speedy death written upon it, has had a deeper and more mysterious origin. It has been the fruit of struggles, carried on in solitary chambers by men whom the world has not known, or has despised; struggles which were to decide what power they were meant to obey, and to what power they would yield themselves; struggles to know the name of Him who was wrestling with them; to know whether He was one who cared for them, or who hated them or despised them; whether they had a real or an imaginary Master; whether God is a presence floating in the air, or a Person who can be loved, feared, trusted; whether they and the universe were separated by a thin plank of opinion and sentiment from a bottomless pit of Atheism, into which both must sink at last; or whether they were resting upon a rock which could not pass away, though not earth only should be shaken, but also heaven. But for these questions, which those who were exercised by them knew were not propounded by any human doctor, do not fancy that there could have been any thought or energy or hope in the world. Luxury and comfort do not confer these; there is no exorcism in them to cast out the demons of indolence and despair. No: men have learnt to say this prayer, 'Hallowed be Thy Name;' and to say it before all others. They have found that the prayer for bread might mean anything, from an Eleusinian mystery to the cry of a Genoveva in the desert for milk to nourish her babe; that a prayer for forgiveness might mean anything, from the words, 'Thou desirest truth in the inward parts; Thou canst wash me with hyssop, and I shall be clean; Thou canst wash me, and I shall be whiter than snow;' to the sacrifice of a virgin, that the wrath of the gods might be averted, and a favourable breeze granted to a fleet. One petition as much as the other, these sufferers perceived, must derive its worth from that which went before. What is the name of Him to whom we pray? All the meaning of prayer of human existence turns upon the answer which we make to this demand.

II. But is it not quite certain what answer we shall make to it? How *can* we hallow the Name of God, if by *hallowing* is meant, keeping it separate from all other names; preserving it as the special treasure of our spirits; not suffering the idea of absolute holiness, purity, goodness, to be soiled by any defilements from without or from within? Suppose I could shut myself out from the world, drawing round me some charmed circle which should exclude not only its direct assaults but its secret plague influences, should I not still have to ask myself whether I was a safe steward of the divine treasure; whether my pride in the trust might not destroy it; whether the Name might not pass into a shadow, while I was thinking of it as most substantial; whether it might not be acquiring from the imaginations of my heart all the same mixtures which it had contracted among the tribes of men?

Experience authorises these inquiries; it scarcely authorises us in giving more than one answer to them. Solitude is no security for the hallowing of God's Name; recluses have dealt as irreverently with it as men in the world's bustle. For us, however, this point is of no great practical importance, except to preserve us from desiring a state which is evidently not intended for us. We know that our thoughts of God, as well as our other thoughts, are, and will be continually, affected by speech, by books, by the movement and attrition of society. We know how various these thoughts have been : earnest yesterday, indifferent to-day; the Name now so little heeded, that we could trifle with it in the most ordinary conversation, in the most vulgar adjurations; now so terrible, that we dared not entertain the thought of it; now looking so beautiful at a distance that we were content it should always remain at a distance; now approaching into awful nearness; now making us fear that it would ever be a shadow to us, and nothing more; now inviting us to take refuge in it from a hopeless Atheism. To hallow God's Name—habitually to hallow it—amidst such countless variations of the external atmosphere, such colds and heats in ourselves—how is it possible ? Must not we give up the attempt ?

III. Certainly it is better that we should; then we shall begin to pray, 'Hallowed be thy Name.' We cannot hallow it; we cannot keep it from contact with our folly, baseness, corruption; the world cannot keep it; the Church cannot. But Thou canst. Thou canst make the darkness of the world a foil to thy clear untroubled light, a means to its manifestation. Thou canst make the intricacies, falsehoods, contradictions of our hearts into reasons for our seeking and apprehending Thy simplicity and truth. That which would be in us, left to ourselves—terror of thy power—Thou canst make awe of Thy holiness; what would be presumption of Thy indifference, Thou canst make into hope of Thy mercy; what would be defiance of Thy judgment, Thou canst make trust in Thy righteousness. Thus will Thy image be restored in man, because he will be able to behold Thee the Archetype.

Such a prayer is not one which men could have dreamed of themselves, but it is one which God himself has taught them. He led His saints in the old time to pray that He would declare His great Name; to thank Him for all His past revelations of it; to flee to it as a strong tower, in which they were safe from their enemies. Every new act of His judgment and his mercy was an answer to the cry; in every such act the prophet saw the witness and pledge of a fuller manifestation. The petition then was no new one. The disciples had often heard it before that day when our Lord was alone praying, and when they said, 'Teach us as John taught his disciples.' But they knew that He had stamped it with a new impression; for though they understood but imperfectly why He had come, and who He was, their hearts testified that He had certainly come to do that which He bade them ask for. If He brought gifts to men, if He proclaimed forgiveness to men, this was His first gift, this was the ground of His forgiveness, He hallowed the Name of God. He showed forth the Father who dwelt in Him full of grace and truth. Men could see Him, after whose likeness they had been created, in a pure untroubled mirror. They were not obliged to measure the Eternal Mind by the partial distorted forms of truth and goodness which they found each in himself. Here was goodness and truth in its primitive form, in its entire fulness. They needed not to reduce goodness and truth into abstractions; here they were exhibited in actual human life; the perfect man reflecting the perfect God. They need not dream of qualities which the shock of the Fall had separated in their minds— mercy and justice, freedom and obedience—as having a corresponding conflict in the Eternal Mind; here they were seen working harmoniously in every word and deed.

Thus God's Name was hallowed for them, thus it has been hallowed for us. This revelation is for all ages: if one has more need of it than another, ours is the one.

We are in danger alike from the invasion of all old superstitions, and of a fanatical Atheism; for they have a common ground. All superstition, all idolatry has its root in the belief that God is made in our image, and not we in His: the most prevalent assumption of the modern as of the ancient sophist is, that man is the measure of all things; that there is nothing great or holy which is not his creation. Do not wonder, then, at any combinations you may see in our day between parties seemingly the most hostile—at any apparently sudden transitions from one camp to the other. There is no real inconsistency, no abandonment of principle. Do not let us be hasty in urging that charge or any charge. But let us be very careful in understanding the temptation of the age, because it is certainly our own. Let us not think we escape it by doing just the opposite of those who seem to us to have fallen into it; by cultivating all opinions and notions which they reject; by fearing a truth when they speak it. We may find that their practical conclusions meet us at the point which we thought the furthest from them, and that we have turned away from the very principle with

HALLOWED BE THY NAME.

which we might have strengthened ourselves, if not have done some good to them. Still less let us refuse to have our own loose and incoherent notions brought to trial, lest in losing them we should lose the eternal truths of God's Word. Depend upon it they are in the greatest peril from every insincere habit of mind we tolerate in ourselves; they will come out with a brightness we have never dreamed of when we are made simple and honest. Therefore let us pray this prayer, 'Hallowed be Thy Name,' believing that it has been answered, and being confident that it will be answered. It was answered in the old time by God's covenant; by the calling of every holy man; by the Divine law; by all the ordinances of family and national life; by every prophet and teacher whom God sent; by every witness which He bore to one people or another, in their consciences, in the discipline of their lives, through nature, through death, of His own character. It was answered by the whole life and death of the only-begotten Son, the firstborn of many brethren, the Prince of all the kings of the earth. It was answered by the gift of the Holy Spirit to abide with the Church for ever, for this end, that He might teach men of the Father and the Son. It is answered by our baptism into the holy and blessed Name, the Father, the Son, and the Holy Ghost. It is answered by confirmation and prayers, and holy communions, by individual trials, by visitations to nations, by the gift of new life to churches, by the conversion of sinners, by dying beds. It will be answered when we all yield ourselves up in deed and truth to the Spirit of God, that we like our Lord may glorify His Name upon the earth, and may accomplish the work which He has given us to do.

SERMON III.

Sexagesima Sunday, February 27, 1848.

Thy kingdom come.—MATTHEW vi. 10.

WE have reached this petition of the Lord's Prayer at a time which would seem to give it special emphasis and significancy. I suppose few have repeated it this week without a kind of impression, however vague, that it bore upon events which were occupying themselves and the world. The words, '*Thy* Kingdom,' must have suggested to most a contrast between a Kingdom which cannot be moved, and kingdoms which appeared firm one day, and have been shaken to the ground the next.

But this general reflection will have taken different forms according to the previous habits, convictions, associations, of those who entertained it. The first and most natural form is surely an expectation that there will be some time or other a better order in all our relations to each other, and in all the circumstances which affect us here on this planet. Upon what ground soever this expectation rests, it lasts with wonderful vitality through fair and foul weather, through killing heats and frosts. No one who has once cherished it entirely loses it; or if he loses it he loses himself with it. Disappointments, desertions, mockeries, may change its shape, or drive it further within, but they do not destroy it. If it fades away for a while it bursts out more vigorously when you least look for it. Many who have expected from one civil movement after another that which they have not found, believe that a better ecclesiastical organisation, or a freer working of that which exists, would remedy all confusions; others find refuge in the promise of a universal education; not a few, who have convinced themselves that no human rulers of one kind or another, in Church or State, no systems of government or instruction, will avail for the removal of evil and the establishment of good, cling more strongly to the belief that One who is above all human rulers and systems will soon claim the earth as His rightful possession; that all convulsions in the existing order of things are the trumpets by which He announces that the city He has accursed is about to fall down. All these convictions, different as they are, belong to the same habit of mind. Those who entertain them mean when they pray, 'Thy kingdom come,' 'Let the earth be governed wisely and truly, not as it has been, by the help of folly, insincerity, crime.'

Such a prayer will call up some echo in the hearts of all. But in many good men only a feeble echo; for the wish which it expresses is, in them, swallowed up by a stronger one. They never knew where to find or how to make for themselves a position upon earth; it never cheered them or soothed them. Now and then they have had sudden revelations of beauty in hill or valley, at sunrise or sunset, but these spoke, as they appeared and vanished, of some region to which the eye could not reach. Now and then they have met faces which smiled on them, but they seem to have descended from a distant home to which they soon returned. Even the narrow circle in which these pilgrims dwell confuses them by the various interests and opposing sentiments of those who belong to it; the larger circles of society, with their manifold complications, altogether bewilder them. It seems to them a weary maze, without a plan; men are running a race with each other, of which a few withered leaves are the prize; they are beginning a tale which must be broken off in the middle; death makes all plots imperfect; only that state to which he introduces us can unravel them. There in that state must lie all that we dream of and hope for. Their vision of the land that is very far off may be not as clear as they wish, but it is more clear than their vision of anything which lies about them; without it all would be shadow and darkness. When such persons think of tumults and revolutions, they feel more keenly what it is they would escape from. When they pray, 'Thy Kingdom come,' they ask that the Great Shepherd will lead them and their brethren out of a land of pits, a thirsty wilderness, a valley of the shadow of death, to a peaceable habitation, and a sure dwelling-place.

But there are also men who feel strongly that the kingdoms of this world are of a weak and perishable material, and yet who cannot be satisfied with the mere anticipation of a better inheritance after death. They require what is different in kind from anything which their eyes see, not merely *that* in an improved and perfected form. They desire a blessing which by its very nature cannot be more for one time than another, cannot be less needful for men here than hereafter. They have spirits which are haunted with the sense of a beauty and righteousness and truth which may be imaged in the world around them, but of which the source must lie much nearer to themselves. Some of them would say that it is *in* themselves: if men were but great and noble, and disengaged from the impressions of sense and the notions of society, they would perceive it. Others affirm, that when they exalt themselves this secret is hidden from them; that they enter into it only when they are humbled.

The first would say, not indeed in a prayer, but in their professions, their daily acts, their processes of self-discipline, 'My Kingdom come;' let my spirit be lightened of the outward impediments which prevent it from being right, wise, free; let it be lifted to its proper throne, from which it may look upon all beneath and around it, and if there be aught above it, as its own possession. The other says, 'Thy Kingdom come;' let the eyes of my understanding be cleared of their native mists, that they may see Thy wisdom; let me be purged of my inward pride and self-seeking, that I may know Thy truth; let me be set free from my exceeding sinfulness, that I may confess Thy righteousness, and be clothed with it. And that this may come to pass, do Thou take the government of all that is within me, of conscience, affection, reason, will, that they may do Thy work and not their own, and be directed to the great ends for which Thou hast designed them, not to those meaner ends which they would invent for themselves.

We have found then, at least, three distinct interpretations of this prayer, leading to practical conclusions, apparently very remote from each other. It is surely important to know whether they are incompatible; if they are, which is the right one; if they are not, how they are reconciled. I think you will agree with me that there is but one authority which can decide these questions. He who taught His disciples the prayer, can alone tell them what the nature of that Kingdom is, which He bids them desire.

I. You will remember, that when our Lord began to preach, saying, Repent, for the Kingdom of Heaven is at hand, the expectation of a coming kingdom was strong in the minds of at least a large body of the Jewish people. Those who felt the Herodian family to be cruel oppressors and foreigners likewise, those who were tormented by the recollection of a still more shameful servitude, which the sight of every Roman soldier, of every tax-gatherer, brought before them, believed that the Divine Kingdom, the Kingdom of God, was to be the deliverance from these. Have you not sometimes wondered that we are not told of any direct words in which our Lord combated this impression? He might have said at once to the people of Galilee or Judæa, The Kingdom I speak of has nothing whatever to do with those to which you compare it; you only confuse yourselves by thinking of them together. But He did not say so. He used the phrases, 'Thy Kingdom,' 'The Kingdom of God,' 'The Kingdom of Heaven,' on every possible occasion, though He knew that this association was present to the minds of those who heard Him. It is true, that those who had come before Him appealing to the desire for liberty in their countrymen, and holding out the hope of a divine interference to satisfy it, had led their followers into the wilderness to insurrection and to murder. There was that difference, amidst a multitude of others as wonderful, between His method and theirs. What I am observing is, that there was not *this* difference. The Jews generally, the Galilæans more than the rest of their countrymen, looked upon themselves as in an oppressed anomalous condition, such as the chosen people of God ought not to be in. He did not tell them that they were mistaken. They believed that God meant to deliver them out of this condition. His words and His acts confirmed them in the hope. They thought that they must be brought into a different social position before they could attain freedom. He admitted the necessity. Many public acts, besides His last entry into Jerusalem as the Son of David, proved that He claimed to be what Nathanael declared Him to be, 'The King of Israel.' His parables, so far from setting aside common language, from disconnecting His Kingdom with the common relations and feelings of men, affirmed that all facts in nature and social life were testifying of it; His miracles, so far from diminishing the impression that He came to set men free from a galling yoke, were one and all acts of deliverance; of deliverance, not from some bondage of which the sufferers were not conscious, but from the most visible, obvious, bodily torments. These are sufficient proofs, I think, that our Lord did not intend us, when we prayed His prayer, to shut our eyes against the actual confusions and oppressions under which men are suffering, or to think that His Kingdom is of too transcendent a character to take account of them.

Assuredly when we do, we depart from His teaching and example; we bring ourselves into a very artificial visionary state of feeling; we set aside the great truth, that as nothing human should be foreign from those who are partakers of humanity, nothing human *can* be foreign from Him who is the Head of it. The lofty expressions of contempt for the littleness of mere earthly transactions, and the vicissitudes of human governments, which some divines affect, are not learnt in His school, or in the schools of His prophets. *They* rather teach us to be ashamed of the cold indifference with which we trace His footsteps and listen to His voice, in the present and past history of mankind. Surely, then, we are not to condemn those who hope for the cure of the ills which they know to exist, through a larger and wider sympathy in civil governors, through a deeper knowledge of the ends for which the Church exists, and a more faithful use of the powers with which she is endowed, or, lastly, from the manifestation of Him to whom State-rulers and Church-rulers alike owe homage. All these expectations are sustained, not crushed, by the Word and Spirit of God. Without divine succour and encouragement they must have perished long ago, to our great misery, under the pressure of selfish feelings and interests, and of the despondency which experience, not penetrated with a higher principle, brings after it. And wherein then do those who have cherished these expectations, to which we owe so much of all that has been best in the world, seem to have wandered from His guidance who justifies their higher aspirations? In this respect, I think, mainly. Our Lord speaks of His Kingdom, or His Father's Kingdom, not as if it were to set aside that constitution of the universe, of which men had seen the tokens in family and national institutions, of which they had dreamed when they thought of a higher and more general fellowship; but as if it were that very constitution in the fulness of its meaning and power. He who is the ground of the world's order, He in whom all things consist, reveals Himself that we may know what its order and consistency are, how all disorder and inconsistency have arisen from the discontent and rebellion of our wills. Now an opposite feeling to this seems to characterise those who are noticing the present distractions of the world, and are suggesting how, in this day or hereafter, they may be removed. All seem to assume that the constitution of things is evil; not that we are evil in departing from it. With strange unanimity, eager politicians, restless ecclesiastics, hopeful millennarians, seem to take it for granted that the devil is lord of the universe; only that by an improvement in the arrangements of civil life, by a stronger assertion of priestly authority, or by the final coming of the Son of Man, the evil power may be weakened or broken. Which sentiment, by whomsoever entertained, is surely unchristian and ungodly. The holiest men protested against it before our Lord's coming. Though the Kingdom was not yet shown to be a kingdom for the whole earth, they believed that it was; they declared its laws, testified that heathens were at war with their own proper ruler; told the chosen race that by their evil acts as kings, priests, people, they were breaking the everlasting covenant. Any other language since Christ has come is, practically, a renunciation of His authority, and a denial of His incarnation. Those who use it cannot effectually connect the command 'Repent' with the announcement 'The Kingdom of Heaven is at hand;' though our Lord's example forbids us ever to separate them. For they cannot say, 'There has been a holy blessed order among you, which you have been darkening, confounding, hiding from men, by your sins and selfishness; but which must and will assert itself, in spite of you and of all that resist it.' Were this mode of speaking generally adopted by pastors and preachers, their hearers might be led each to ask himself, What have I done to frustrate the ends for which the Kingdom of Heaven has been established upon earth? how can I cease my strife with it, and become its obedient subject? a question which, instead of destroying their interest in the doings of the world generally, would make that interest practical and personal; instead of lessening their hopes of the time when the darkness shall pass away and the true light shall shine out fully, would make them less earnest in guessing about it, than in preparing for it.

II. But if our Lord spoke thus of His Kingdom, did He frown upon the wishes and longings of those who would cast this world behind them, and project their thoughts wholly into a future state? So far as anything in their anticipations is incompatible with an entire recognition of the sacredness of our life here; so far as they imply the Manichæan notion, that the earth, or the flesh, is the devil's creature and property; so far as they utter a merely selfish cry for escape from toil and warfare; He certainly gives them no encouragement, who hallowed all human life, who overcame the Evil Spirit, whose own garments were dipped in blood.

But this, we must all confess, is only the dark and feeble side of a faith which is, in itself, gracious and inspiring. To despair of the present must be bad; to hope for the future must be good. And this hope our Lord cherishes and confirms, as much as He disowns that despair. Think of those words which came with such power to the mind of a scribe who had maintained the doctrine of a resurrection always, but had probably never before felt it to be a reality: 'As touching the resurrection of the dead, have ye not read what was spoken to you by God, saying, I am the God of Abraham, and Isaac, and Jacob? He is not the God of the dead, but of the living; for all live unto him.' What are all speculations about separate states and intermediate existences to this celestial sentence? Those whom you read of in ages gone by, who sometimes stand out in such clear individuality, who sometimes melt into shadows, all alive; for He lives from whom their life came. Nothing of it is departed, only the death which encompassed it. They have lost no personality. Here, there was but the first dawn of it. They were beginning feebly to be conscious of powers; to recognise distinctions; to feel after unity. He was educating their affections through the first stage of infancy; their reason, in its struggles to know its object; their will, in its endeavours to be obedient; who is now bringing them into more wonderful affinities, infinitely deeper apprehensions, a perfect liberty. And what is true of them is true of all who have yielded to the same guidance, who have desired the same light. All live to Him, with not one sympathy impaired or raised too high for human interests. With Him, as the common centre of all their thoughts and adorations, everything which He bestowed specially upon each is, necessarily, quickened and perfected, and finds its relation to the gift of every other. With Him as their centre they must care for all whom He cares for, but still, one would suppose, be knit closest in all bands of attachment and service to those with whom it was His pleasure, by holy pledges imperfectly understood, to unite them below. Such thoughts followed out, not by the fancy, but by the most legitimate reflection upon the state which must remain if the infirmities and sins of earth were purged away, would surely go far to satisfy men who have learnt to mourn over the meanness and incoherency of our earthly existence, considered by itself. And our Lord's own resurrection, and His appearances to His disciples after He was risen, which were so brief, and yet carried with them such a wonderful witness of a perpetual presence—these translate His words into life, and declare that our existence is not rounded with a sleep; or that it is a sleep in Him at whose voice all creation was first awakened, and will awake again. With such thoughts, brethren, we may comfort ourselves when we pray, 'Thy kingdom come.' But we must not think that we are waiting for death to solve a problem which is not solved yet. The death of Him who took away the sins of the world, solved it at once and for ever; we only die to understand how perfect the solution is.

III. But this we shall not understand if we suppose that while our Lord sanctioned the expectations of those who look for a better government of this world, and of those who look for a world after death, He did not include in His gift and promise the satisfaction of those who feel that they want not a visible kingdom, but a Kingdom of righteousness, truth, love; not a future, but an eternal Kingdom. To them and to their hopes we may say that He spoke first. He awakened their longing, He met them before He could respond to the others. 'For now,' said John the Baptist, 'the axe is laid to the root of the trees.' He who is at hand is not coming to deal with external circumstances, but first with the being to whom those circumstances belong. Our Lord spoke straight to the conscience, reason, will, in man, which were asking after the Unseen, which were seeking for a Father. Even by His bodily cures He showed that He was the Lord of the unseen influences which produce the outward signs of disease and decay. When He cast out evil spirits, He bore witness that He was holding converse with the spirit of man, that with the pride, lust, hatred, the powers of spiritual wickedness in high places which have enslaved us, He was carrying on His great controversy. By this victory He accomplished His great work. He manifested forth the true state and glory of man, as the child of God, and the inheritor of truth and righteousness, and built His Church upon that foundation of His own divine Humanity, against which the gates of hell shall not prevail. Here, in this inner region, in this root of man's being, He is still subduing His enemies, He is conducting His mysterious education. To that which He cultivates within us, He promises the great reward, the knowledge of Him who is, and was, and is to come. But be it ever remembered, that while He gives all encouragement to the highest desires of man's heart and reason, He gives none whatever to any mystical conceits and imaginations. 'The axe is laid to the root of the tree: *therefore* every tree which bringeth not forth good fruit is hewn down and cast into the fire.' The Kingdom of God begins within, but it is to make itself manifest without. It is to penetrate the feelings, habits, thoughts, words, acts, of him who is the subject of it. At last it is to penetrate our whole social existence, to mould all things according to its laws.

For this we pray when we say, 'Thy Kingdom come.' We desire that the King of kings and Lord of lords will reign over our spirits and souls and bodies, which are His, and which He has redeemed. We pray for the extinction of all tyranny, whether lodged in particular men or in multitudes; for the exposure and destruction of corruptions inward and outward; for truth in all departments of government, art, science; for the true dignity of professions; for right dealings in the commonest transactions of trade; for blessings that shall be felt in every hovel. We pray for these things, knowing that we pray according to God's will; knowing that He will hear us. If He had not heard this prayer going up from tens of thousands in all ages, the earth would have been a den of robbers. He will so answer it, that all which He has made shall become as it was when He beheld it on the seventh day, and, lo, it was very good.

SERMON IV.

Quinquagesima Sunday, March 5, 1848.

Thy will be done, as in heaven, so in earth.—LUKE xi. 2.

THE prayer we considered last week could not easily be separated from the spectacle which we had just witnessed of a fallen kingdom. Since that time we have been watching attempts to construct a new society out of the ruins of the old. If I do not mistake, many have regarded these experiments with greater impatience, with less complacency, than the events which preceded them, and made them necessary. Such words as these have risen very readily to our lips: ' What a weary repetition is here of a thrice-told tale ! Is it possible that phrases which have been tested and found hollow nearly sixty years ago, are still fit for use and circulation now ? Can it be that we must pass through another series of the same false promises, vain hopes, bitter disappointments, the same dreams of peace realised in blood, which were appointed for the last generation ?' Not to entertain thoughts of this kind is difficult—difficult even not to give them expression. Yet when they are spoken they must drive others to ask, while we harbour them, does not the question present itself to ourselves—Is then the belief a fantasy, that men are intended for a brotherhood? Must the effort to realise it terminate in ridicule or in crime? Supposing that is the fact, should we begin with accusing other men of deception? Have we not a long list of falsehoods to confess which we have been proclaiming ourselves—in pulpits especially—which have been proclaimed throughout Christendom for near eighteen hundred years?

Such an inquiry may no doubt be evaded by the reply: 'Oh! we do not take Christianity into account. *That*, of course, may affect anything. We complain of those who think they can work all good to their species without it.' But our conscience will not be so appeased. It will rejoin: 'And if you take Christianity into account, what then? You know that it will not *of course* set the world right. Do you believe seriously in your heart, that it can set the world right at all, under any conditions? If not, you should not pretend to believe it. Certainly this end will not be accomplished by phrases and professions. These are not the least better when they are coined in one mint than in another. It does not help us more to *talk* of brotherhood on Christian principles, than of brotherhood upon any other principles. The more sacred the language, the more offensive is any trifling use of it. We must not blame our neighbours for trying to make men brothers without the Gospel, if we are not ourselves convinced that the Gospel can make them so.' There is still another resource which I know is commonly adopted by those who seek to escape from this difficulty. They say, 'Christianity declares to us the exceeding sinfulness of the human heart and will. There is the root of all the confusions and miseries of the world. What mockery then to reform it by new schemes of government and society.' Christianity does, no doubt, declare to us, or rather assumes, the exceeding sinfulness of man's heart. But it comes not proclaiming sin, but proclaiming a remedy for it. Do we believe the remedy to be effectual? If not, in what sense do we call ourselves Christians? If we do, how dare we blaspheme Christianity by calling her to prove that evil, social evil or individual, is inevitable? We cannot then avoid the inquiry, severe though it must be to most of us, What have you meant hitherto by this prayer, 'Thy will be done, as in heaven, so on earth'? What have you taken the Will of God the Father of our Lord Jesus Christ to be? How do you suppose it is done in heaven? What is implied in asking, that even so it may be done on earth?

I. It would be a great mistake to identify this petition with that which I spoke of a fortnight ago. The *Name* denotes that which a Person is in Himself, his own character. This is an object of contemplation; it is to be hallowed. A *Will* imports energy going forth; it points to action, to effect; it is to be done. It is very needful for the clearness of our minds, and for great practical results, to remember this distinction. But it is equally needful to remember that the Name and the Will exactly correspond to each other, that at all events in a Perfect Being there cannot be the slightest clashing or contrariety between them. Nay more; if the Name be that which has been revealed to us as the Name of God; if it express goodness, mercy, loving kindness, we cannot think of it at all without thinking of a Will, directed towards other beings, and exercising itself upon them. To identify Will with mere Sovereignty, is to destroy the earlier petition. We cannot hallow the Name of God if we suppose power to be His most essential characteristic, or the manifestation of power to be His chief delight. This notion of Him is evidently fashioned out of our own low appetites and base fancies; it is the notion which lies at the root of the dark fables of heathenism. The whole Revelation which is delivered in the Old and New Testament is nothing else than a continuous protest against it, or rather a continuous unfolding of the truth from which it is a departure. It assaults the natural tendency of our minds, which is to worship all the different shapes and appearances of power that we discern in the world around us; it leads us to feel that we need some power of an altogether higher and different kind to rule ourselves; it shows us that this power must be a *Will*; that it must be moral; that righteousness must be its essence, power its instrument. A God of righteousness and truth, just and without iniquity, is He whom the Bible speaks of, He who presents Himself to the conscience, heart, will, of His creatures, as the Author of all that is right and good in them and in the universe.

When we say, Thy Will, this must be the sense in which our Lord would have us speak the words. To enter into the inmost recesses of that Will, was His only, who perfectly delighted in it. But we are sure, that were it possible for us to know as He knew, we should not discover a difference of purpose, another kind of Will than that which His acts exhibited; we should only behold that infinite abysmal love, which, through our evil and selfishness, had been hidden from us. It would be well for us, brethren, if we were more careful of insulting the Majesty of Heaven in our confessions of ignorance as well as in our boasts of knowledge. We have no right to say, We are such poor creatures, we cannot tell the least what are the designs of God; we can only submit to His irresistible pleasure. It is precisely His design which He has made known to us; what His Will is to the human race and each of its members, is not one of the secrets which He withholds from us and from our children. Nor is there any real awe of Him while we choose to think our own thoughts about it instead of His, whilst we insist upon doing homage to a dreary, naked Omnipotence. For, however we may fancy that there is something at once humbling and elevating in the thought of that which may crush and may uphold us, it is not a contemplation in which we care to abide; the spirit within us soon starts up from the momentary depression it has caused, soon betakes itself to other and more natural ways of realising its own dignity. We want a mightier charm than this; we want the belief and knowledge of a Will that is always originating and effectuating good—good, and nothing else. Before such a Being, the spirit of man trembles; in His presence it feels its own nothingness; to Him it can look up, and be sure that He is raising it. Hence comes a conviction, not of weakness, but of sin; the sense, not that we have been unable to resist, but that we have actually resisted that power which is working for the deliverance and blessedness of us and of our whole race. A power we shall then joyfully confess it to be, when we know that it is not that merely or principally. We could not bear to suppose—it would be the most flagrant of contradictions—that a perfectly Loving Will was ever idle, that it was not continually energising, continually accomplishing its own deep and gracious ends. Where the limit is to their accomplishment, how is it possible that a creature Will can contend with that which has formed it; by what mysterious concurrence, which cannot be understood in either alone, obedience is produced out of rebellion— here is a depth indeed, in which we may be content not to see our way; here *is* that secret which, except in life and practice, we never penetrate. I say, *except in life and practice*; for we can and do know in our own experience the fact of resistance and the law of submission. We do know that every evil act has been one against which there was a divine remonstrance within us; we do know that this act has brought disorder and contradiction after it; we do know that, not we ourselves, but He, who has curbed us and forewarned us of the evil, has wrought the repentance for it; since only when we confessed the wrong and cried to be made right were we brought into our true state. Thus much every man may know in himself; but to generalise from this experience is a more difficult process than we sometimes suspect. The logical terms in which we express our conclusions are even less adequate to describe the subtle operations of spirit than those of nature; we should not, therefore, suffer them to embarrass us either in our dealings with our individual consciences, or in our judgments respecting the purposes of God. Generalities are not accurate enough for the one; they are far too narrow for the other. A man cannot be honest in action if he applies maxims and formulas about the extent of prescience and human power to his own particular conduct; he must be profane and false if he uses them to measure the Eternal Mind. By a strange perversity those who are using their intellects to determine what must be the acts and intentions of God, resent every appeal, though grounded on express revelation, to his moral nature; as if it implied that we were circumscribing Him by our own imperfections. But this appeal is a witness against all such circumscription. We say, that we must acknowledge the absolute goodness of that Will, which was manifested in act by the only-begotten Son, or we shall make it merely the image of our own. We must have an invariable standard to which we can refer ourselves; or we shall make ourselves, with all our variations and contradictions, the standard. We must not let logical formulas, or deductions from our own experience, and the world's experience, or possible dangers, or the fear of losing plausible topics of declamation, come in the way of the strict simple use of this prayer, or force us to mean something less by the words, Thy Will, than a Will of efficient good to every creature; otherwise we shall either be contracting our own love within limits which God commands us to transgress, or blasphemously suppose that it is, at some point or other, greater than His. At all hazards, in despite of all reasonings and all authority, cling to the prayer. That will never do you harm, or lead you astray. The more we use it, in the faith that the Will we ask should be done is the right loving and blessed Will, the more we shall know that it is, the more we shall be sure that it must be done. We shall meet every day with a set of new impediments to that conviction; at times, it will seem the most monstrous and incredible of all convictions; then when it does, the prayer is specially needed to raise us above the plausible lies of our understandings; to place us in a point of view whence we can see the truth which surmounts them. That point of view is obtained when our state is the lowliest; we must sink, not rise, if we would feel our relation to the Will which is guiding all creation; the Cross is at once the complete utterance of the prayer and the answer to

II. For it is the Cross which tells us how this Will is done in Heaven. We should be giving an intelligible sense to this clause, if we took heaven in its simplest, most outward sense, as synonymous with what we call the heavenly bodies; and if we supposed the prayer to be that, as all these silently and calmly obey the law which was given them on the fourth day, so the voluntary creatures of God, who have set His Will at naught, might be brought into a submission as complete, into an order as unbroken and harmonious. There would be a deep significance in such a petition, though we should need great caution to prevent it from turning into the most unchristian and dreadful of all desires—the desire to be free from responsibility, to lose our wills, to become mere natural creatures. And I do not think any one who has prayed the Lord's Prayer ever rested in this interpretation, even if it might be cherished for a moment. The general feeling of Christian people has been that this Will is done in heaven, not by blind agents, but by intelligent spiritual creatures; by wills which might have fallen, but which stood in holy cheerful obedience. Of such beings Scripture speaks often; their existence it assumes throughout; only it does not indulge us with any such account of their condition and circumstances as would lead us away from that one great truth of their history, in which all others are included: 'They do His commandments, hearkening to the voice of His words.' We have, in the Bible, no description of celestial hierarchies, such as the schoolmen of the Middle Ages were wont to draw out: above all, no allusions to the angelic nature, in terms so common in more modern writers, which would lead us to suppose that it was *essentially* different from our own. The more carefully you consider the passages in Scripture concerning angels, the more you will be struck with the use of a language which seems almost to confound them with men. And why, but because Scripture never for an instant contemplates the derangement of man's state, which is the consequence of his disobedience, as determining what that state is. It looks upon the unfallen creature, or the creature renewed after the fall, as the proper representative of humanity—not upon one who is dead in trespasses and sins; it never treats an anomaly as a law. 'Their angels,' says our Lord, 'do always behold the face of my Father in heaven; for the Son of Man is come to seek and to save that which was lost.' The true form of human existence and society has not perished because certain fragments have been severed from it; the flock was not destroyed because a set of sheep had wandered from it: only He, in whom the whole harmony stood perfect, came to reunite the fragments; the Shepherd came into the wilderness to carry home rejoicing the lost one. It is the effect of our sin to make us look upon ourselves as the centres of the universe; and then to look upon the perverse and miserable accidents of our condition as determining what we ourselves are: so all the manifestations of God are treated as if they were merely appropriate to those accidents, till we learn at last to look upon sin, not as that which takes us out of the harmony God has established, but as that which has been able to subvert the harmony; to frustrate the Divine Will. To feel sin, as we are intended to feel it, seems almost impossible while we adopt this scheme; still more, to feel the might and mystery of redemption. But if we contemplate the Son of Man as the Lord of the unfallen as well as of the fallen creation, if we believe that He perfectly fulfilled that Will under all the conditions of temptation and misery upon earth, which He had fulfilled before the worlds were, our minds become quieter and more hopeful. Let science discover to us as many myriads of worlds as it may; let each of these myriads of worlds be peopled with myriads of creatures; we know, if they are involuntary, they are subject to the same Will which rules every animal and vegetable on this planet : if they are voluntary, their state must be one of cheerful dependence upon that Will, or else of rebellion against it. There must be an order for them, and it must be a blessed order. Space and time can make no difference in that which concerns the Eternal government; in the principles of obedience, disobedience, redemption. And however darkly we may see into these things, we are sure of this prayer 'as in

Heaven;' we are sure that we are not presuming when we believe it and offer it up. As we do so the fetters of time and space become more and more loosened through His might who willingly took them upon himself, and then ascended up on high, leading captivity captive, that He might fill all things. It becomes no hard effort to suppose the existence of multitudes of blessed creatures, formed and kept in the image of Him who said, 'Even so, Father, for so it seemed good in Thy sight;' or to believe that mysteries of love have been revealed to them, through our fall and redemption, which they desire more deeply to look into; or to feel that they must rejoice over one sinner who repenteth.

III. And therefore the prayer may well go on, 'Thy will be done, as in heaven, so on earth.' Holding fast the testimony of Christ respecting His Father's Will; believing that it is continually at work to execute its purposes; believing that there are multitudes of wills in whom it does work effectually, triumphantly, who obey it and are free; believing, lastly, that He who guides them, and to whom they do homage, has taken account of this earth for the purpose of restoring those who dwell upon it to submission, liberty, unity, we can ask without fear, that all which resists this Will in one place or another, may be brought to acquiesce in it, and to become its cheerful servant and child. If place makes no difference in the view which we take of those who confess this Will, and yield themselves to it, place can make no difference in its power of reaching and subduing those who have been refractory. There is nothing, surely, in this fair earth to make it an unfit dwelling for all that is pure and gracious. It is the revolted will which interposes the one barrier to all communications from above, to union and fellowship below. The selfish self-seeking spirit says, 'Thy Will be not done;' love shall not have dominion here: supposing that demon cast out, supposing the spirit of man brought to desire that it should serve in heaven, instead of reigning in hell; and the earth, the battle-field between them, which Christ won when He gave up Himself, becomes not potentially but actually God's; by its own acknowledgment, as well as by His victory. And we know, assuredly, that spirits which have yielded themselves to the tyranny of the evil power are, day by day, set free from its yoke; that God, by the mighty instruments which He has wrested out of the hands of His enemies, by individual sorrows, by national calamities, does lead men to feel that it is better to live in their Father's house, than to feed upon husks, or to starve. If we do not think so, why do we use this prayer? what sense is there in it? what hope can we have from it? If we confess so much, how can we ever make it a charge against any people, that they hope for a brotherhood upon earth? To tell them, if that is the case, that they are not resting their expectations on a safe ground; that there is no brotherhood, unless we begin with confessing a Father; that we must attain it by giving up ourselves to do His Will; that if we set up our own, we are enthroning the very principle which has made all unity impossible; this is right, this is benevolent. But we have scarcely a right to dispossess a man of a pleasant dream unless we can give him a reality in place of it; for every hope points upwards: if it does not find an object, it is in search of one; you cannot crush it without robbing your fellow-creature of a witness for God, and an instrument of purification. I do not mean that falsehood can ever do good to a human soul, or be anything except a curse to it; but I mean that hope is a deliverance out of the falsehoods of sense, and that there is a truth always corresponding to it, which is missed, not because the hope is too strong, but because inconsistent elements are mingled with it, which weaken and debase it. Therefore let us labour diligently to clear ourselves of all such mixtures. One I referred to before, and will speak of now. We say that Christianity can bring about a true fraternity among men. But this is an elliptical mode of speech, and may be a misleading one. Christianity, as a mere system of doctrines or practices, will never make men brothers. By Christianity we must understand the reconciliation of mankind to God in Christ; we must understand the power and privilege of saying, 'Our Father—Thy Will be done in earth as it is in heaven.' No notion, or set of notions, will bind us together; He binds us who has given his Son for us all, that we might not live for ever in separation from Him and from each other. There is another error which is, perhaps, in practice, even more fatal. We are apt to say, 'These large schemes of the universe, which we hear so much of, are vain; what good can come of them? let us try to do our duty each in his own sphere.' An excellent resolution: but too often adopted merely in spite, and therefore leading to no result. We exalt the little for the sake of disparaging the large; presently we grow weary of not doing more; we fly back to great schemes which we have pronounced abortive; because we find them so, we do nothing. This prayer meets us at each point; it will not allow us to escape by one pretext or the other. It does not treat the projects of men for universal societies, unbounded pantisocracies, as too large. It overreaches them all with these words, 'As in Heaven.' It opens to us the vision of a society in which angels and archangels, and the spirits of the just made perfect, are citizens, and in which we too have an inheritance. It does not look upon any homely individual task of self-sacrifice as insignificant: 'So upon earth' meets every such case, and reminds us that the lowliest tasks beseem the disciples of Him who 'took upon Him the form of a servant, and was found in fashion as a man.' 'Thy Will be done' reconciles the high and the mean; the Will of Him who created the heavens, and stretched them out; the Will of Him who was born in the manger; the Will of that Spirit of Holiness in whom they are eternally one.

SERMON V.

First Sunday in Lent, March 12, 1848.

Give us this day our daily bread.—MATTHEW vi. 11.

THERE are many points of view from which this season of Lent may be regarded. One of them is given us in the beginning of the Gospel for to-day. The tempter said to Jesus, 'If thou be the Son of God, command that these stones be made bread.' He answered, 'It is written, Man shall not live by bread alone, but by every word that proceedeth out of the mouth of God shall men live.' If these last words had declared that man does *not* live by bread, they would have been naturally construed to mean that he has a higher, more mysterious life than that of his body; one requiring a diviner nourishment. But this sense, though it may be latent in the answer, has not generally been felt to arise immediately out of it. That the most perfect man does, in some sense, live by bread, was shown by our Lord's hungering. He did not exalt himself above the conditions of creatures with bodies, dying bodies; those conditions He entered into. It was to His weakness, to His suffering, that the tempter spoke. And the reply did not move the question to a different ground, but met it on its own ground. Man's *body* lives not by bread alone, but by the Word which proceedeth out of the mouth of God. This was, obviously, the first intention of the language when it was used by Moses. The manna proved to the Israelites that their support came from the Word of God. That Word did not sustain them without visible food; but it conferred upon the visible thing its power of sustaining them. Take away the life-giving Word, which proceeded out of the mouth of God, and the little round thing which lay upon the ground would have been useless. This lesson they were to lay to heart; the pot of manna in the tabernacle was to remind them of it when they were come into the promised land, and were eating bread made by various processes from the corn which they had themselves sown and reaped. They were not to think that this derived its nourishing power less from the Word of God than the manna which their fathers ate in the wilderness. They were not to suppose that this bread had any virtue of its own more than the other. Its virtue lay in its fitness for the creature whom God had endued with a life incomparably more wonderful than that of the corn, wonderful as that is; wonderful as is its capacity of growth, maturity, conversion into a material quite unlike itself; wonderful as is the whole relation of the vegetable to the animal substance. Rightly reflected on, this bread contained a deeper, more comprehensive, revelation of God than the manna But, because deeper and more comprehensive, therefore less adapted to an infant nation, which had been sen sualised and debased by animal and vegetable worship, and by the slavery which must accompany it. Such a people have to begin at the alphabet; they must be taught by the falling of food from heaven, that they depend upon an invisible Person, a sure Friend who cares for them; not upon the hard material thing which will not come to them when they ask for it; which they will be least able to procure when they treat it with most reverence. But that truth had need to be fixed in their hearts, again and again, in different stages of their history, by methods adapted to those stages. In the city as much as in the wilderness, when they had grown old in a settled independence, as much as when they had just escaped from the flesh-pots of Egypt, in the monotony of ease, as much as when everything around them spoke of famine and drought, they would be assailed by materialism and unbelief; they would be in danger of losing all thought of an unseen Protector. Therefore the heavens would become brass, and the earth iron, the locust and the palmerworm would eat up the fruits of the ground, the Philistine, or the Assyrian, would lay it waste for the same reason that the manna had fallen in the sight of their fathers; to show them that they lived by the Word which proceeded out of the mouth of God, and not by any necessary fertility in the soil, or special exemption from the plagues of Egypt, or any strength in their hands or in their wit. There might come, in the latter days of the nation, even a harder and more desperate condition than that which is the result of men's natural inclination to trust in things seen, and in the works of their own hands. A stiff religious formalism, a comfortable conceit that they were going on with suitable decency through a round of appointed services, or, were acquiring merit by acts of voluntary supererogatory devotion, might make the heavens brass and the earth iron in another sense. All real communication might be cut off between them ; the Lord of all might be exhibited as a tyrant to be won over by presents and bribes ; the heart which should receive His grace might become utterly impenetrable. In such a period of the history of the Jews, our Lord appeared among them; at such a time the voice from heaven said, 'This is my beloved Son,' and the voice from hell, ' If thou be the Son of God, command that these stones be made bread.' At such a time, He claimed to be the Son of God not because He could make stones bread, but because He could stand on the old promise, ' Man shall not live by bread alone, but by every word that proceedeth out of the mouth of God.' And having thus asserted his own filial dependence and filial faith, and having claimed the privilege of dependence and faith, not for Himself but for man, He, who came as the firstborn of many brethren, could say to the band of fishermen, His disciples, 'After this manner, therefore, pray ye : Our Father—give us this day our daily bread.' That childlike petition was the fruit of His Baptism, Fasting, and Temptation.

The forty days then which bring that Fasting and Temptation to our mind, are given us especially that we may be taught how to pray this prayer. Those who find it quite easy, in all circumstances of indulgence and comfort, to believe that they receive their bread from God ; who, when it is most abundant, ask Him to give it—meaning what they say—have not, perhaps, any call to self-restraint. But there are some who know, in their consciences, that they are apt to mock God when they speak these solemn words, apt to take food and every other blessing as if it were their right of which no power in heaven or earth except by sheer injustice can deprive them. Something which shall tell them of dependence, some secret reminiscence, insignificant to others, that all things are not their own; some hint that there are a few million creatures of their flesh and blood who cannot call any of these things their own, is needful for *them*. If it comes in the form of punishment sent specially to themselves, they cannot say it was not wanted; if it is a voice addressed generally to the whole Church, a season returning year by year, they cannot pretend that there are any satisfactory reasons why they should close their ears to it. What they ought to desire is, that they may keep the end in sight: so they will never reckon means, of whatever kind they be, of any value for their own sakes; they will not fancy that to abstain from food is more meritorious in God's sight, than to eat it; if in either case, equally, they are desiring to recollect that it is a good which He bestows. Above all, they will feel that, whatever else Lent is, it is certainly a time of confession, and their great hope of being ever able to use this prayer more faithfully must be grounded on an examination of the causes which have made it so unreal in times past. Let us look manfully at some of these causes this afternoon; if we study the petition, we shall not be long in discovering them.

I. It may seem strange that I should put first of all, our unwillingness to acknowledge God as a Giver; our inclination to think of Him rather as an Exactor. Such a charge will, I know, sound to some most paradoxical. 'What!' they will say, 'do you affirm that people in this day like especially to be reminded of the duties that are required of them, and dislike to be reminded of the gifts and mercies which they may expect with or without the performance of those duties? Is not precisely the opposite error that to which our age is prone? Are we not most restless and impatient when we are told, Such things you ought to do, such men you ought to be; most eager to receive the comfortable assurance that we may rest, for that God's grace is everything—man's energy nothing?' Those who make this objection, show that they have considerable experience, both of other men's infirmities and of their own. That a certain languor, not incompatible with much fever but one of its symptoms, is characteristic of our time, I should indeed be afraid to deny. We cannot feel it ourselves without being conscious that it is abroad. That when we are indisposed to strenuous effort, we often take refuge in theories, religious or philosophical, which disparage it, or represent it as needless, is also indisputable. We try stimulants first, then opiates; and each empiric who would suggest a new one may reasonably speculate upon the failure of the last. But where did this listlessness begin? what is the root of it? Our Lord puts this interpretation of it into the mouth of one who had exhibited it and wished to justify it thus: 'I knew thee that thou wert an hard man, reaping where thou didst not sow, and gathering where thou didst not straw: therefore I hid thy talent in the earth; lo! there thou hast that is thine.' If we can trust Him who knew what was in man, the two accusations are not inconsistent; we may be very slow in listening to calls of duty, and the reason may be that we regard

Him who calls us an Exactor, not a Giver. I press this confession before all others, not only because the first word of the Prayer suggests it, but because I believe we, the ministers of God, are more bound to make it than other men. We have thought, it seems to me, that our chief business was to persuade and conjure and argue and frighten men into a notion and feeling of their responsibilities: whereas our chief business is, assuredly, to proclaim the name of God; to set that before our fellow-creatures in its fulness and reality; *so* to convince them of their sin; *so* to teach them how they may be delivered from it. Being very eager to make out a case against mankind, comparatively indifferent about the assertion and vindication of the Divine character, we have failed in one object quite as much as the other. We have not dared to speak of God broadly, simply, absolutely, as a Giver, lest we should thereby weaken His claim upon man's obedience; whereas this is His claim upon their obedience: in this way He enforces His claim. Thus we have begotten in men a feeling that they are obliged to do something which they cannot do. A struggle ensues, passionate, irregular, hopeless, after an unattainable prize; then bitter discontent and murmuring against Him who seems to have created us for vanity and wretchedness.

See how this consideration affects the petition for daily bread. If we dared to look upon God as a Giver in the full, free, intelligible sense of the words, we should, in asking for bread, feel that we were asking for the power and energy wherewith to work for it. We should say to ourselves: 'This is the law under which God has put the universe, a merciful and good law, which if man is able to evade as he is in some regions of exuberant fertility, the seeming privilege turns out to be his curse. It is desiring a stone, and not bread, to desire that we may have all we want without the sweat of our brow; and such a stone the Father will not give us. But when we desire the will to toil, and the wisdom to toil, and the strength to toil, and the fruit of toil, we plead as men with Him who desires that we should subdue the earth and replenish it, because He has made us in His image, and would have us share His work and His rest. Then we ask according to His will, and He heareth us. Then does the earth bring forth and bud, and God, even our own God, blesses us. We are not the creatures of chance; we are not the slaves of a Pharaoh; we are doing the blessed command of Him who created the ground and man to inhabit it.' How entirely then does the life and sense of this passage depend upon those which have gone before it! If we misrepresent the Name of God, and the Will of God, how inevitably does this petition for bread turn to evil instead of good. If we will think of Him, not as the Scripture and the Church teach us to think of Him, as the Author and Giver of all things, but only as one who demands so much work of us, and offers so much pay in return, we fold our hands in indolence and despair; we cannot love that which He commands, or desire that which He promises. Let us confess, then, this sin first, that we have slandered His holy Name, not believing that He gives to all men liberally, and upbraideth not.

II. If we think of God as an Exactor and not a Giver, exactors and not givers shall we be. And so the word *us* acquires a very contracted signification indeed. The prayer will express a hope that we, who are sufficiently well supplied with all necessaries and comforts, may never be stinted of them; it will express a lazy half-formed wish that people, who have none of our comforts and little of what we call necessaries, may not quite starve. Think what meaning it must have had when it was offered up by that band in Jerusalem, after the day of Pentecost, who were of one heart and one soul, eating their bread with joy and singleness of heart. They will have understood it to be indeed a petition to the Father, who had so loved them as to give His only-begotten Son for them, and who had filled them with His own Spirit, that He would give them that which they needed for body and soul; would give it them under that condition of which I spoke just now; and under this further condition, that each, upon whom the Lord bestowed superfluity, should hold himself a steward, and distribute his bounties. As the first principle which united bread and work together had been proved, by a long experience, to be a blessed one, so the second they will have felt to be the fulfilment of Christ's promise, that they should be children of His Father in heaven; that they should be gracious and merciful as He is. Without the one the Church would have been a hive of drones; without the second it would have been a collection of separate bees, each working for itself, bringing in its contribution to a common stock, but wanting the sweetness of affection, sympathy, subordination. Will it be said that the law of that Church was never intended to be perpetual; that even in apostolical history there are few vestiges of it after the Church had diffused itself beyond a single city or province? I answer: the accidents of that Jerusalem Church were indeed transitory; more transitory than the fall of the manna in the camp of Israel: but the law which those accidents made known was as permanent a law as that which the manna revealed. The selling of houses and lands was only one exhibition of a state of mind, an exhibition never enforced, as St. Peter told Ananias. But the principle implied in the words, 'No man said that which he had was his own,' is the principle of the Church in all ages; its members stand while they confess this principle, they fall from her communion when they deny it.

Property is holy, distinction of ranks is holy: so speaks the *Law*, and the *Church* does not deny the assertion, but ratifies it. Only she must proclaim this other truth, or perish. Beneath all distinctions of property and of rank lie the obligations of a common Creation, Redemption, Humanity; and these are not mere ultimate obligations to be confessed when the others are fulfilled. They are not vague abstractions, which cannot quite be denied, but which have no direct bearing upon our actual daily existence; they are primary, eternal bonds, upon which all others depend; they are not satisfied by some nominal occasional act of homage; they demand the fealty and service of a life; all our doings must be witnesses of them. The Church proclaims tacitly by her existence—she should have proclaimed openly by her voice—that property and rank are held upon this tenure; that they can stand by no other. Alas! she has not spoken out this truth clearly and strongly here or anywhere. She has fancied that it was her first work to protect those who could have protected themselves well enough without her, provided she had been true to her vocation of caring for those whom the world did not care for, of watching over them continually, of fitting them to be citizens of any society on earth, by showing them what is implied in the heavenly filial citizenship into which God has freely adopted them. Failing in this duty, she has become powerless for the one she ignominiously preferred. She can give but feeble help to the rich in their hour of need, because she ministered to them with such sad fidelity in their hour of triumph and prosperity. She can scarcely make her voice heard against schemes for reducing all things to a common stock, for establishing a fellowship upon a law of mutual selfishness, because she has not believed that the internal communion, the law of Love, the polity of members united in one Head, of brethren confessing a common Father, is a real one—has left people to fancy that it is only a fine dream, a cruel mockery, incapable of bringing any tangible blessings. If she can yet avert such a calamity, it must be by calling upon all of us her members to confess the insincerity with which we have uttered these words, 'Give us our daily bread.' If we had understood that we were children of one Father, and were asking Him to bless all the parts of His family, while we were seeking blessings for ourselves, that, in fact, we could not pray at all without praying for them, we should have found the answer in a new sense of fellowship between all classes, in the feeling that every man, in every position, has an office and ministry which it is his privilege to exercise for those over whom he is set; in a clearer apprehension of the relationship between the master of a household and his domestics, the landlord and his tenants, the farmer and his labourers, the manufacturer and those who work at the loom or the mill, the tradesman and those who serve in his shop; between these and then between all of them and the outlying mass, which seems to be beyond the bounds of all ordinary civil relationships, but which, as it has the great mark of human relationship, may be adopted into these, or be fitted to take a part in the establishment of new societies elsewhere.

If we meet continually in the streets creatures of our own flesh and blood, who have a look of hunger and misery, without being able to determine whether it is a greater sin to withhold that which may save them from death, or to give what may lead to the worst kind of death; if a thousand social problems which we once supposed were of easy solution, present themselves in new and embarrassing aspects, tempting us to pass them by altogether, and then forcing upon us the reflection that they must settle themselves in some way, whether we forget them or not; if we hear masses of creatures spoken of as if they were the insects we look at in a microscope, and then are suddenly reminded by some startling phenomenon that each one of them has a living soul; then, before we become mad, or escape into an apathy that is worse than madness, let us ask ourselves whether we have yet prayed this child's prayer as we would have a child pray it, in simplicity and truth. And if we are conscious that we have not, let us confess the sin, and see whether He to whom we confess it does not shed some light into our minds which makes our path clearer—a light which we may believe He will vouchsafe to our brethren in this land, and in all lands, for their practical guidance, when their large theories are found to be reeds, upon which, if a man leans, they will go into his hand and pierce it.

III. But the prayer is only for *this day*. Hence it is often thought that the spirit of the Gospel is adverse to foresight. How can the command, 'Take no thought for the morrow,' be reconciled with the kind of anticipation and preparation which seem to distinguish the civilised man from the hunter of the woods? The answer lies in our own experience. Have we found that anxiety about possible consequences increased the clearness of our judgment, made us wiser and braver in meeting the present, and arming ourselves for the future? Is it this kind of temper which enables a man to plough the ground, to sow the seed in the appointed month, to wait patiently for the harvest? Is it the temper which would have enabled any sailor, any merchant, to venture himself or his goods upon the deep? We know perfectly well that the most opposite habit of mind to this, a simple and hearty reliance upon a power whom the ground, and the seasons, and the winds, and the waves obey, could alone have made such acts and enterprises possible. Clearness of vision, providence, discovery are the rewards of the calm and patient spirit. The cases are rare indeed where they have been given to any other. Out of that care for the morrow which our Lord denounces, spring the fever of speculation, the hasting to be rich, endless scheming, continual reactions of fantastic hope and deep depression in individuals, of mad prosperity and intense suffering in nations. If we had prayed for this day's bread, and left the next to itself, if we had not huddled our days together, not allotting to each its appointed task, but ever deferring that to the future, and drawing upon the future for its own troubles which must be met when they come, whether we have anticipated them or not, we should have found a simplicity and honesty in our lives, a capacity for work, an enjoyment in it, to which we are now, for the most part, strangers. Here, I believe, we shall all find abundant matter for confession, if we look faithfully into our lives. This part of the prayer too has been unfaithfully repeated; we have been wearying ourselves in thoughts of what would be, because we have no confidence in Him who is.

IV. But it is our daily bread we ask for, τὸν ἄρτον ἡμῶν τὸν ἐπιούσιον. This word ἐπιούσιον gave rise to one of the controversies between Abelard and Bernard in the twelfth century. The former, following a hint of Jerome, adopted the translation *panem supersubstantialem*, and taught Heloise and the nuns in her convent to use it in repeating the prayer. It appears that the practice was not a new one there; at all events, Bernard had no right to accuse his opponent of wilfully perverting Scripture, when he was following the guidance of the most approved Latin Father. We shall all probably agree that he *was* right in objecting to a phrase which, even if it had more philological plausibility than really belongs to it,* would be entirely out of harmony with the tone and spirit of the prayer. It is less easy to say what exact word we should adopt; we have no analogy to help us, for the word does not exist in any classical author. The balance of evidence seems decidedly in favour of those who derive the word as Jerome did, but take it to mean 'bread for

* It confounds ἐπὶ with ὑπέρ.

subsistence.' Our translators followed a different course, but they arrived nearly at the same result. Bread for subsistence defines accurately what we intend by daily bread, when we intend anything. We ask for bread to sustain us, bread that shall be enough for our needs. What is enough we are happily not called to fix; the act of prayer throws the decision of that point upon a wiser judge. No one, therefore, could infer from the use of this expression that a rigid sumptuary law is involved in the petition; that one has, of course, the same needs as another. The Bible admits the distinction of rich and poor; in commanding hospitality, it assumes that there are some who have the means of exercising it, and others towards whom it may be exercised. But the words are not the less cutting because they do not reduce all expenditure to a level. They may dilate to take in a great variety of cases, but they can never lose their proper original signification. Bread for subsistence will not, under any circumstances, be bread for mere display, for waste, for rivalry. The prayer asserts a broad, palpable, everlasting distinction between the different reasons for seeking wealth, the different ways of using it; though it leaves every man's conscience to determine in the sight of God which reasons govern his acts, which ways he is taking. Honestly offered up, therefore, it will, I conceive, make us very uneasy in that kind of ostentation which men in each class of society are apt to affect for the purpose of not being distanced by those of the same grade, and that they may assert their right to a higher. Moralists, satirists, divines, have long been using their different weapons against this folly apparently with little success. It is now coming before us in a new form. Competition is denounced as a monstrous evil, which a new organisation of society is needed to remedy. How numerous and weighty are the facts which the advocates of this theory are able to allege! how much excuse does there seem for the root-and-branch schemes which they suggest! Yes, if they were root-and-branch schemes; if they did find out the source of this evil, if a reconstruction of civil life could prevent its renewal. But we trust neither in satirists, moralists, divines, or communists. Another hand than ours is needed to deal with a disease which has penetrated so deeply, which has so nearly reached our vitals. What we can do is to tell men that this hand is stretched out, that any secret corruption which has been cherished in the heart of individuals, or in the heart of society, will be brought into the clear light; that national judgments will purge away those of which the removal is not first sought by national repentance. What we can do is to say, He who sends these judgments is willing to give that repentance. He invites us now at this time to acknowledge the sins that we know, to ask Him to search our hearts, and discover those which we know not. He bids us believe that the most inveterate cancer, as in ourselves, so in the body-politic, may be taken from us by His knife, if we will submit to it. He exhorts us not to wait till the dark and evil day actually comes upon us, till the house is left desolate of His presence, and stript of every good gift which we have received through it. He calls upon us this day to turn to Him with thanksgivings, as to the great Giver of all blessings, with confessions as to the Father whom we have grieved by disbelieving in

His love, and not showing it forth to our brethren; with prayer that He will give us and them all we need, and most of all, the heart to receive it from Him as His stewards, for the good of those who are dear in His sight.

SERMON VI.

Second Sunday in Lent, March 19, 1848.

Forgive us our debts, as we forgive our debtors.—MATTHEW vi. 12.

WE should be sorry, I think, to lose the word 'trespasses,' which we use in our ordinary repetition of the Lord's Prayer, and which is translated, no doubt, from the word ἁμαρτίας in St. Luke. Yet St. Matthew's expression presents a more distinct image to the mind; it interprets itself more easily. Therefore I have chosen it this afternoon, not wishing you to consider it alone, but believing that it may help us to a clearer apprehension of a word which for many, at least, has lost its brightness through continual attrition. The idea which the petition embodies, results, I suspect, from the union of that which is peculiar in each of these forms. We find it so generally, when we take the pains to examine different expressions evidently answering to each other, or different reports of the same transaction in the Gospels. From the comparison of them there proceeds a fuller and more profound meaning than we could have obtained from either separately. What is called the study of parallel passages, may in this way be really profitable; it is often made into a very childish exercise, one which involves no reflection; sacred words being turned into an irreverent game; all sense of their unity and relation being lost in the eagerness to hunt out the precise places in which they occur, or their most superficial and insignificant resemblances.

That there is something in the word 'debts,' which we are bound to keep in mind when we consider this prayer, is evident from the use of the cognate verb by St. Luke, in the other clause of the sentence. 'Forgive us our trespasses, for we also forgive every one that is indebted to us.' It is evident also from the word ἄφες, 'send away' or 'remit,' which is common to both Evangelists. Every one feels the appropriateness of such an expression to a creditor's release. We have no need to go beyond the very simplest notion of such a release; we are not bound to think of deliverance from a prison, or from any infliction consequent upon the failure in the fulfilment of an obligation. Discharge from the debt itself is that which the verb suggests. Perhaps we may find that this sense gains, instead of losing strength, when we apply it to trespasses—to sins. Still we should first fix our minds upon that which stands in the most obvious connection with it.

I. Our Lord then bids us pray, Remit, or send away, or discharge, these debts or obligations of ours. Whatever they are, He bids us ask Him for this; this and nothing less. He who tells us to pray, Our Father, says also, Ask for this full remission. He must mean that it is such a request as a child should make of a father, and a father could grant to his child. He who teaches us to say, 'Hallowed be thy Name,' bids us ask for this remission. He must mean that God's Name is hallowed in our making the petition, and in His hearing it. He who taught us to say, 'Thy Kingdom come,' bids us say, Grant us this remission. He must mean that it is consistent with His Royalty, and part of it, and a proof of it, that we should desire and receive this release. He who desired us to pray, 'Thy will be done on earth as it is in heaven,' tells us also to ask for this sending away of debts. He must mean that this is the Will which is obeyed in heaven, and that so, we are obeying it on earth. He who taught us to look up to God as a Giver, not as an Exactor, and to pray for the bread which is needful for us, further commands us to ask for this freedom. He must mean that rain and fruitful seasons are not more a sign to men of what He is, than remission; that one is as much an utterance of His disposition and purpose as the other; that one is at least as much needed by His creatures as the other. He who came down to declare the Name, the Kingdom, the Will of God, and to bring all good gifts to men, must have wished us to understand Him thus; or He could not have trained us to the use of a word so precise, and yet so unlimited.

II. The objects of this prayer must be those who were united with us when we said, 'Our Father,' and, 'Give *us* this day our daily bread.' If there were any for whom we did not pray when we said those words, they will be excluded from these. If there are any human beings whose nature we suppose Christ did not take, any for whom we suppose the Father does not care, for those we do not ask the remission of trespasses. Where such limitations begin, where they must end, I have had occasion to consider while I have been commenting on the former clauses of the Prayer. They begin in a feeling that we must, for our own safety, establish certain boundaries beyond which the divine compassion cannot go; they proceed to the invention of securities and exclusions which compass their end so little, that their places must be presently supplied by others; they end in the discovery that we have destroyed the ground under our own feet, while we have been making it untenable for our fellow-men. I need not repeat the evidence, but I must repeat the warning. When the publican prayed, 'God be merciful to me a sinner,' he claimed for himself a place among the whole body of sinners; he would not say like the Pharisee, I am not as other men are. If in literal imitation of his example, in real contempt of it, any one chooses to say, Forgive me my debts, rather than, Forgive us our debts; he will not go down to his house justified; he will feel that the petition has not been granted.

III. And yet when we come to consider what these debts are which we crave should be put away, it does not seem wonderful that we should choose individualising language rather than that which is more general. For each man says within himself, Are not these debts *mine* in the strictest sense? Are they not obligations which *I* have contracted, and which *I* have violated? Upon me lies a burden which I cannot shift upon any other human creature—the burden of duties unfulfilled, words unspoken, or spoken violently and untruly; of holy relationships neglected; of days wasted for ever; of evil thoughts once cherished, which are ever appearing now as fresh as when they were first admitted into the heart; of talents cast away; of affections in myself, or in others, trifled with; of light within turned to darkness. So speaks the conscience; so speaks or has spoken the conscience of each man. In some it may be a feeble voice, soon lost in the noises of the outward world, or silenced by violent efforts, or choked by the senses, or bribed by the fancy. In others, it is loud and stormy to-day; then comes a reaction of fierce merriment or a temporary lull, which will be followed again by new blasts of passion. In some it is a low but perpetually sounding knell, witnessing of a death begun and going on in themselves; of the past accursed, the present withered, the future vaguely terrible. But each one who has ever known what conscience is, feels that it is upon his own very self these obligations lie. They may sometimes present themselves to him in dark outward visions, they may be associated inseparably with certain places and persons. But they sit like nightmares upon him; they stop his breathing; they hold him chained. How often would he persuade himself that they are only phantoms! How often would he task his understanding to prove that he has himself brought them thither by some strange conjuring! Why cannot he cast them aside as dreams of the night? Are they anything more? They come back with fearful distinctness; the very act of which conscience testifies, every circumstance, look, tone, clearly recorded; it is no dream of the night. The voice, be it from heaven or hell, is a real one, which says, 'It is done, and cannot be undone,' and, 'Thou art the man.' What signifies it that years have passed away. The act is gone, but thou art still the same. The act is gone into Eternity, and there it will meet thee.

These are the debts; are they to ourselves? Often it seems so. We have suffered by them more than all others—our bodies and souls. But if they are to ourselves, we cannot release them. The more we try, the more hopelessly the coil is twisted round us. Are they to our fellows? Often we think so. We were bound to them by sacred ties which were forgotten; the friend repulsed, because we did not understand him, or his opinions seemed dangerous, or because we took a cry of agony for a mocking laugh; the child petted and fondled into sin, or driven into it by roughness and what we call parental authority; those who looked to be raised and purified by us, degraded through our weak and grovelling ways; those who would have entered into the Kingdom of Heaven hindered, because we cared not that they should be wiser and better than ourselves. But if our debts are to our fellow-creatures, they cannot discharge them. If we could hear each one distinctly saying out of the grave or from heaven, 'I forgive,' though the words might be unspeakably delightful, we feel they would not penetrate deep enough, they would not set us free from that which has seemed to become a part of our own being.

Are they debts to God? The first vague consciousness of such a belief, how terrible it is! All the former aspects of the debt seem mild to this one; yet all were surely prophetical of this one. That sense of permanence of Eternity being bound up with our acts and the results of them, what was this but a witness that they had a relation to God himself? He surely was speaking that voice which we thought came from ourselves, and which was echoed by everything and every person in the world around. Yes, *Debts* are

Trespasses; we have not only forfeited an obligation, but committed a sin; we have broken a law which was not formed on earth, and cannot be repealed on earth.

But at this point of despair hope begins. It is sin; sin against God. These very feelings we are groaning under are sinful; this sense of evil is evil. For has it not brought death into the soul? Is not this torpor, this incapacity for action, feeling, loving, Death? Assuredly it is. And He willeth not the death of a sinner. He cannot be pleased that I should continue in a state of sin. He is not pleased with it. Then come dim recollections of words heard in the nursery, of doctrines which had been reduced into mere phrases and stored away in the memory as lumber, or more courageously cast aside as absurd contradictions of human experience and ordinary logic; doctrines which had perhaps been associated with the remembrance of some hard comfortless teacher, who first imparted them to us in traditional shapes and moulds, or who mixed them with views of the Divine character from which the conscience and reason revolted; doctrines, however, which do not sound now as if they were unsuited to our necessities or unworthy of One who cares for His creatures; the doctrine of reconciliation, of a Father who so loved the World as to give His only-begotten Son for it; of a Son who came down from heaven not to do his own Will, but the Will of Him who sent him; who did that Will by laying down his life for the sheep; who was manifested to take away sin, and in whom was no sin; by faith in whom a man may rise out of himself, cast away the slough of death, and become a new and righteous creature. Such words, however imperfectly understood, yet carry in them an amazing power for one who has felt his debts and known them to be sins. But they acquire a newer and a fuller meaning for him when he finds that what seemed to him an entirely isolated experience is that of numbers of his fellow-men; when he hears of publicans and harlots who, through the same storm, have sought and found the same haven. Then he learns to say, and not to say in vain, 'Forgive us our Trespasses.'

IV. There perhaps he stops; the words which follow are either forgotten or they give him no present anxiety. In the spring-tide of wonder and enjoyment, at the discovery that there is a communication between Earth and Heaven, and that the Angels of Heaven and the God of Heaven rejoice over every sinner that repenteth, it does not strike him that there is the least difficulty in remitting to other men any debts they may have incurred to him. But the first fervour of these convictions dies away. He seeks to keep them alive by association with those who are or have been sharers in them. By mutual encouragement, that which is feeble and flagging in each may be invigorated. Everyone has realised something which another might be better for knowing; the barter and interchange of thought will make all richer. It should be so certainly; but those who make the experiment often suspect that the reverse is true. While they are discoursing of that which is passing within, it seems to be within no longer. In the commerce of feelings, notes and bills which there is nothing to meet soon circulate rapidly from hand to hand. And then the latter words of the prayer suddenly assume a disagreeable significance. 'Forgive as we forgive;' surely here is a condition appended to that which we thought absolutely free! Does it mean that our forgiveness is the *cause* of God's forgiveness—that He expects so much of us before He dispenses to us out of His infinite treasures? Or does it mean that our forgiveness is the *measure* of His; that the acts of us fallible creatures determine the kind and degree of the Divine Mercy? Surely if this be so, the Gospel cannot be large and infinite. Forgiving is not *forth*giving as we have been used to think; a narrow and clumsy derivation must take the place of this; it must import the giving *for* an equivalent. Accordingly a great part of men, even of religious men, are content to sit down without determining what the words which they repeat so often actually signify. They cannot mean *that*, therefore it is better to suppose that they have no distinct meaning at all. 'Of course,' thinks the Christian, who is trying hard to be at peace with himself, 'in a sense, I do forgive everyone who is indebted to me. I should not be deserving of the goodness I receive if I did not; and if I come short, I ask to be forgiven. Is not that the very use of prayer?'

There are, I am sure, thousands and tens of thousands who repeat this petition in spirit and truth, and upon whom it brings down blessings unspeakable, though they could not express to others what they mean by this clause, and though their own minds are probably far from clear about it. Prayer seeks that which lies below all words: it aims at the light whereof that which shines in our understandings is but the dim reflection. From those who pray as children one desires only to learn; their lives are better and more beautiful commentaries upon their prayers than any the schools can furnish. But it is altogether different with those who try to explain away words upon which our Lord dwells with special carefulness; those words to which He drew His disciples' attention, as if they contained the spirit and essence of the whole form. 'If ye forgive not men their trespasses, neither will your Heavenly Father forgive you your trespasses '— this is His own express language, which He illustrates again and again in His other discourses, always strengthening not diminishing its awfulness; making in one case the significant addition, 'if ye *from your hearts* forgive not everyone his brother their trespasses.' It will not do surely to make light of such solemn oracles, or reduce them into nullities, because they do not accord with a notion we have formed about the freeness of Christ's Gospel. But as little ought we to part with our belief in that freeness or with any deep conviction which has been given us, because something which we have not yet understood seems to contradict it. We need, for our practical life, that the apparently inconsistent principles should be reconciled; and if we are honest with ourselves we shall not be long in discovering the reconciliation.

How is it that persons who have had that lively sense of mercy and forgiveness to which I referred are not able to retain it? They know in their consciences that they do not; they continually confess it; they are sure that they ought to retain it, but it will not stay. The feeling of a debt grows up in the mind again, after they supposed it was cancelled; they refer to the evidence upon which they rested their confidence; it is as satisfactory as ever; they assure themselves that all must be right, and yet their hearts say there is much wrong. Then they resort to theological distinctions and formulas: this sense of debt and sin is very tormenting, no doubt, but it is inevitable; it must stay with us while we are in this bad world. Perhaps so; but must it be ever multiplying, nay producing fresh sin? Must the consciousness of it make me sour to others; often make me false in dealing with myself? Will theological terms and distinctions, or the recollection of bygone experiences, or a general apprehension that God is at peace with us, make ill-temper gracious or self-deception truth? Must there not be some other more excellent way than this of bringing the facts of our own lives into coincidence with the truths of the Bible? One would think that the most obvious, the most excellent, way was to study our Lord's own interpretation of the case. He says that when a servant who had been pardoned the debt of ten thousand talents went out of his lord's presence, he found a fellow-servant who owed him a hundred pence, and that he took him by the throat, saying, Pay me that thou owest, and would not listen to his cry, 'Have patience with me.' This, he says, was the cause that his own debt came back to him heavier and more hopeless than ever. Is there not a clear light thrown on the dark passages of our lives by this parable. Only think how we are wont to speak of the obligations which other men are under to us, of the debts they have incurred to us, of the demands which we have a right to make upon them. Only think how exactly our Lord's language represents our eelings, how it is uttered in all our daily actions.

'Pay me that thou owest, servant, child, poor dependent, friend, wife, brother:' is not that the first natural thought of our hearts? Do we not encourage it, justify it to ourselves and others? have we not a host of religious excuses for tolerating it till it becomes the habit of our souls? There is abundance of good-natured charity afloat in the world, charity for all sorts of people, for all forms of distress. But this is the ornamental part of our existence, the capital or fretwork of the building. The substantial part, the pillars of it, we seem to think are our *rights*; rights to position, property, rank, the homage of others, their gratitude. If these are withheld—the hundred pence which each man has a claim upon from his fellow—with what indignation do we repulse the claims which we had acknowledged that mercy and charity have upon us!

Now, brethren, if this be so, is it very wonderful that the sense of divine forgiveness, the apprehension of perfect unclouded mercy, should not be very clear and strong in our minds?

It is surely the most fantastic of all dreams, that a man can cut his being into two portions, call one of them religious and the other mundane, and administer them on directly opposite principles. One or other must come to naught. If we believe that the world is governed by a forgiving Being, His forgiveness must be recognised as the Law of the Universe; the Law of our being. If we believe that Individual Right is the great principle we are to assert in all common transactions, that principle will be carried to the highest ground of all, and so far as we acknowledge a Divine Being at all, we shall regard Him as one like ourselves; we shall feel that His main desire is to assert His rights over us. I say, *so far as we acknowledge a Divine Being at all*; for I cannot help perceiving that Atheism is the natural, almost the necessary, refuge from such a notion of the Lord of all as this. The naked contemplation of one who has no will but self-will is so intolerable, that the conscience which remains in human beings, in spite of all their theories, shrinks back in horror from the belief that such a one can be he to whom the name of God, *the good*, was once ascribed. Yet what avails the denial? If self-will do govern the world, if we confess it to be our lord, we may or may not attribute to it personality; but it does, all the same, hold us in its iron bonds; we are in prison, the evil spirit is our jailer, and we cannot come out till we have paid the uttermost farthing.

Brethren, it is this which makes the consideration of our times so profoundly awful. We cannot avoid the conviction that the maxims upon which we have been acting will come forth into full display; that they will be thrown back upon ourselves; that the rights we have asserted against our fellow-men will be asserted by them against us. We have had and we have warnings enough of this catastrophe; let us hope that they have not been wholly lost upon us. Even yet the dark image of mere selfish power, in one or in a multitude, is not revealed; it struggles strangely, wonderfully in the minds of those who seem most ready to fall down and worship it with the belief of a love which must rule at last, which we are permitted to obey now. Oh! if we might interpret to any that strange conflict of two opposing principles

—two Kingdoms—in the womb of humanity! Oh! that some voice might be heard declaring clearly and mightily: 'The elder shall serve the younger. He who won the battle in the wilderness, proved that His Father and not Satan, love and not self, is the King of kings, and Lord of lords.'

But if that proclamation is to be heard on the house-tops, it must first be spoken in the ear in closets. It must come forth as the interpretation and fulfilment of this prayer, 'Forgive us our trespasses, as we forgive them who trespass against us.' We must thoroughly believe and understand that what seems to be a limiting condition of the request, is really an enlargement of its scope and power. We ask to be forgiven, and the revelation of God's mercy in Christ, of the love which is in Himself, of the perfect atonement made once for all, is an answer. It seems to be transitory; we try to fall back upon it, and feel that that which we trusted in yesterday is not so strong to-day. Why? Because we asked too little, because we did not enter into the fulness of the word, 'Remit,' 'Send away.' If we had, we should have prayed not for a momentary sense of Forgiveness, but for the spirit of Forgiveness; not merely that we may know what God is and is to us, but what He can accomplish in us; that we may understand in Him and show forth in ourselves that mercy which is no tolerance of wrong but the tormentor of it, which does not reject stern discipline, but makes it an instrument; which is a fire to consume the evil of all in whom it dwells, of all to whom it reaches. Forgiveness is not forgiveness when it is turned to our ease and comfort. It is in its nature expansive, diffusive; it cannot be cooped up in the heart of any creature; it must go forth into the open air, or it dies. The debts, we know it well, cannot lose their penal hold upon the conscience, their present and future terror, till love comes in to fulfil them and transfer them; till the man who in his pride thought that all nations owed him homage, learns to say '*I* am a Debtor to Jew and Greek, to Barbarian and Scythian, to bond and free.' The sense of sin—sin itself—does not finally depart from the conscience till love its great enemy possesses the ground which it once occupied, till He who was crushed under the sense of powerlessness and evil— 'To will is present with me, but how to do that I will I find not,' can exclaim, 'He worketh in us both to will and to do of His good pleasure,' and, 'I can do all things through Christ which strengtheneth me.'

Wherefore, as it should be one of our saddest subjects of confession this Lent that we have not lived as if we were under the law of Forgiveness which God has established for us and for all, so also let us earnestly believe, whensoever we pray, that we are praying to a Forgiving and Merciful Father, who can yet do for us more than we ask or think; even inspiring us with His own love, and enabling us to walk in love and to forgive all who are indebted to us, as He for Christ's sake hath forgiven us.

SERMON VII.

Third Sunday in Lent, March 26, 1848.

And lead us not into temptation.—MATTHEW vi. 13.

I SAID that the words of our Lord, 'It is written, Man shall not live by bread alone, but by every word that proceedeth out of the mouth of God,' were a ground for the petition, 'Give us this day our daily bread.' Lent, above all seasons, might teach us the sense and power of it. 'Forgive us our debts, as we forgive our debtors,' had surely as close a connection with these forty days. To be delivered from a heavy burden, this is the blessing of confession: a blessing which (as the prophets so often told the Jews) we cannot realise by any prayer or fast unless we seek to set others free from their burdens. The subject of *Temptation* might seem even more than either of these, to embrace the whole history and purpose of this time in its relation both to our Lord and to ourselves. But here a difficulty presents itself. We are told by the Evangelist, that our Lord was 'led up by the Spirit into the wilderness to be tempted of the devil.' We are taught to pray, 'Do not lead or bring us into

Temptation.' Must we not infer from this opposition, that there is not that close resemblance between his struggles and ours which we have sometimes imagined; that our spiritual life is not under the same law as His; that we are to deprecate that kind of trial to which He cheerfully submitted?

There are some, perhaps, who will not feel even the semblance of perplexity here. They will say, 'Certainly; there are multitudes of perils into which it was fitting for the Son of God to enter, and which it would be madness for His followers to encounter. He stood in the might of his impeccable divine nature; how can sinners, nay, even mere human creatures if they were not sinners, ever forget their own readiness to fall?' Persons who use this language cannot be aware what practical heresies they are uttering, how completely they are demolishing the whole intent of the Gospel, the very ground of man's trust and hope. If there are some parts of our Lord's example that we are not to follow, what authority is to tell us which? Does not the assertion that he stood by the strength of a nature in which we are not sharers, exclude us as much from communion with one of His acts as with another? We make void the doctrine of his having taken our nature: it is too little to say that we lessen the perfectness of the relation; it becomes imaginary.

And surely no record of our Lord's life is so entirely outraged by this hypothesis as the record of His Temptation. If He had asserted an independent standing ground, He *would* have listened to the words of the Tempter. He would, because He was the Son of God, have made the stones bread, have cast Himself from the pinnacle of the temple, have taken to Himself the Kingdoms of the world and the glory of them. He refused to do this, He would simply stand by faith and dependence on His Father; thus and thus only would He assert his filial character. He did put Himself upon a level with those whom He called His brethren; He did claim for them a right to depend as He depended, to trust as He trusted. Dependence and trust are *not* inconsistent with the condition of creatures who are human, and who have sinned. Because we depend and trust so little, we prove that we are still trying to be gods—*that* is our sin. Just so far as we depart from our Lord's example, we show our pride, not our humility, our self-confidence, not our fear of ourselves.

The prayer then cannot be justified on this plea; it cannot bear a construction which would make it a separation between the creatures who offer it, and Him in whose name it is offered.

Indeed, if we reflect, we shall perceive that such a notion of it would be as much at variance with what we know of ourselves, as with what we believe of Him. Is it not the fact that we, too, are led up into one place or another—a wilderness or a city—to be tempted? Is not this whole life of ours one continual succession of temptations? I say, advisedly, of *Temptations*: for we shall gain little, I think, by changing that word for '*trials*,' as if every trial did not of necessity involve a temptation. When we speak of undergoing 'trials,' we do not mean merely 'troubles;' we mean that in some way or other we are proved, that we have an opportunity given us of doing wrong or right. When we speak of Temptation, we look at the same fact from another side; we wish to indicate, not merely that we have the good and evil set before us, but that there is a power biassing us to the evil. But this is implied in either form of expression. And therefore, if we suppose that God has brought us into this world, and that we are dwelling in it under His guidance, and that all trials are ordained by Him; we must suppose that He just as much intended *us* to be tempted as He intended His Son to be tempted. If we make out a difference, we do it wilfully. Our consciences, and Scripture, equally oppose the attempt.

But why then should we pray, '*Lead us not into Temptation?*' I answer, Because this, and no other, is the prayer which, if we believe the Scripture account of our Lord's forty days in the wilderness, He must Himself have prayed at the very time when He was led up to be tempted, and when He was going through the Temptation. His first act of dependence and obedience was to go whithersoever He was led; not to choose His circumstances for Himself; to be equally ready for the desert or the market-place. His second act of dependence was in the desert or market-place, in the full sight and foresight of the Temptations which beset Him to say, 'Father, bring me not into them.' And the prayer was heard. That wicked one touched Him not. The Tempter had no power over Him, not because He exalted Himself in His own strength, but because He would not exalt Himself in it; because in all things He glorified Him whose will He came on earth to do. It may seem a subtle and shadowy distinction to make; and subtle and shadowy must be all verbal distinctions which concern the Will and its acts. If you would realise the distinctions which words try to embody, you must leave them and turn to facts. There you will find how substantial are these subtleties; that in them lies all the difference between the best and the worst man; between an angel and a devil. To be incapable of temptation is the privilege of involuntary creatures; a man, or an angel, dares not desire it. So long as he feels who it is that has made him capable of such danger, who has given him a will, he is safe; for his life is a prayer that he may not be left to his own guidance. The moment he ceases to offer that prayer he is brought into temptation, he comes under the Tempter's power; because he has lost trust and allegiance and claimed independence. Then he tries to say that he was tempted by God; but he is conscious that he lies; he knows that his act was one of submission to another than God; that it was a secret defiance of Him. He had a right to believe that God placed him in the circumstances which his own will has made destructive; but that belief, if he had hallowed the Name of God, if he had cried, 'Thy will be done on earth, as it is in heaven,' would have been a security against the temptation; it would have given him confidence to cry, 'Thou, Father, art leading me; bring me not into this temptation, but through it.'

The deflections and eccentricities then which sin has introduced into our lives do not make the life of our Lord, which exhibits to us humanity in its orderly state, in its perfect harmony, a less practical standard; on the contrary, they oblige us to look for such a standard: we cannot measure or interpret our own acts without it. In the sunlight of His history, our relations to the Father, and to all which opposes Him, stand out clearly and distinctly revealed; though it is only in prayer and in action that we can fully appropriate the lesson, and feel the truth as it is in Jesus to be also a truth in us.

However strange it may be to affirm that God is leading us every day into some circumstances of temptation, and that here lies the very strength and warrant of the prayer that He will not bring us into it—will not suffer our enemies to prevail against us—we can boldly adopt that paradox, and find the blessing of it in all ordinary events and in all terrible emergencies. Riches, we know, are temptations; poverty, we know equally, is a very great one. The king in the Proverbs might be judicious in desiring a mean; but therein too lies a peril of its own; a kind of secure hardness, self-indulgence comforting itself with the assurance that it is not luxury, the rich and the poor man's sins both regarded with abhorrence because they interfere with us and there is no knowledge of either. What wild pride and recklessness there is in the sense of health; how miserably are those deceived who fancy that a sick-bed is in itself a cure for natural infirmities, and not an aggravation of them and an excuse for them! What selfishness is there in possession, but oh! how it turns inward, how gnawing it becomes in the hour of deprivation and loss. Various gifts and endowments we speak of as full of danger, and yet the man in the Gospel hid his talent in the earth because he had only one. The physician, lawyer, divine, may each suspect that the other has some especial means of usefulness, some exemption from evils which he has felt; but the heart knows its own bitterness; not one of them is wrong in saying that his position is full of snares; and that what seem to the on-looker securities, are really dangers. If the busy man is every day tempted to worship the *idola fori,* how many *idola specûs* are there which continually seduce the contemplative man from his allegiance! How easy it is for monks to bring evidence that marriage makes the soul less free; how utterly they fail when they would praise the safety of celibacy. When the characters of those who are bound together are unsuitable, what irritation and restlessness! if they perfectly accord, what fear that each may confirm that which is wrong in the other! How free from all debate and turmoil the halls of philosophy may be thought by one who has only known the region of politics: sometimes men escape from both for security to the religious world, and find that there they are in the midst of more fierce and implacable contentions.

The last discovery seems appalling. Can religious habits, a religious atmosphere, tempt us into evil, into falsehood, into Atheism? Experience answers, Yes! It tells us not only that no sect, no Church, is free from these dangers, but more, that sects and even Churches directly or implicitly, by the idolatries or self-righteousness which they encourage, or by the reaction against them, by pious frauds, or the unbelief which follows upon their detection, may lead us into utter ruin. It is most necessary, in our day especially, to know that fact, and to keep it in our recollection. There may be a Protestantism, a Catholicism, a Christianity without a God; all that sounds most religious, all that really is full of deepest worth, of divinest meaning—confessions, ordinances, the Bible—may be used to make us in practice and ultimately in theory, deniers of Him from whom they have proceeded and of whom they speak. Where then lies the security? In this, that He *is,* that

He lives, and that in one condition or another we are still led by Him. Into what perils soever we have come, into what perils soever we may come, let us be sure it was not the Evil Spirit, but God Himself who ordered the whole frame and condition of our lives, and that this frame and condition is not the worst but the best possible for us, the best possible though—yea, because—it is one of tremendous temptation. Let us be equally sure that He is not our tempter; that He never tempted any man to evil; that we fall into it only when we think He is not with us to deliver us from it; that to think so is to believe a lie; that at all times, and in all possible states, this is a right and true prayer which He inspires and which He hears. 'Bring us not into temptation.' Those old words, 'The Lord is my Shepherd, therefore can I want nothing. He prepareth a table for me in the midst of mine enemies. Though I walk through the valley of the shadow of death, Thou art with me; Thy rod and Thy staff they comfort me;' these words have lasted three thousand years, and they are just as living and as good now as they ever were; as adapted to the temptations of every Englishman in the nineteenth century as to those of David.

The words 'Lead us not into temptation,' are of the same kind; equally reminding us that we are in the midst of enemies, that we may have to pass through a valley of the shadow of death, through a state of utter darkness; equally telling us that there is One who provides us a table now, and will be with us then. But it is a prayer which goes down more deeply, for He taught his disciples to use it, for whom the table had been prepared in the wilderness where there was no bread, but only stones; who was Himself to pass through the valley of the shadow of death, and to feel all that can be felt of desertion and solitude there. He bids us say, 'Lead *us* not into temptation,' assuring us that God is not merely the Shepherd over each lonely man, when passing through hours and days of gloom and doubt and anguish which no other creature knows of, but that He is also the Guide of the whole flock, of His own Church upon earth, and of the great human family, out of darkness into His marvellous light. 'Lead *us* not into temptation,' said He who is the Head of the whole body, intimating that though it consists of many members, and each has its own special trial, which would not be precisely such a one to any other—though it often seems as if this were the greatest hardship and misery of all, that sorrow is incommunicable, that each person understands so little of his neighbour's—yet in spite of this seeming diversity and solitude, there is the most intimate relation between all the parts of the body, that what affects one, of necessity affects all. We know it to be so, and in our different ways express the conviction. We talk of family likenesses, of national feelings, of a particular age having its characteristic tendencies, its own special good and evil. The observation of these sympathies is one of the necessary qualifications for conversing with men and describing their acts; we may have made comparatively small progress in the inquiry, but all confess it to be real and full of interest. Our hearts bear witness to the Scripture assertion, that we have a common Tempter and a common Deliverer; that all things, though made the instruments of one, are yet actually and truly the instruments of the other; that there must be such a cry from all hearts as this, and that it must be the most helpful and uniting of all cries: 'Lead us not into temptation.' O strange and mysterious privilege, that some bedridden woman in a lonely garret, who feels that she is tempted to distrust the love and mercy of Him who sent His Son to die for the helpless, should wrestle with that doubt, saying the Lord's Prayer; and that she should be thus asking help for those who are dwelling in palaces, who scarcely dream of want, yet in their own way are in peril as great as hers; for the student, who in his chamber is haunted with questions which would seem to her monstrous and incredible, but which to him are agonising; for the divine in his terrible assaults from cowardice, despondency, vanity, from the sense of his own heartlessness, from the shame of past neglect, from the appalling discovery of evils in himself which he has denounced in others, from vulgar outward temptations into which he had proudly fancied that he could not fall, from dark suggestions recurring often, that words have no realities corresponding to them, that what he speaks of may mean nothing because to him it has often meant so little. Of all this the sufferer knows nothing, yet for these she prays—and for the statesman who fancied the world could be moved by his wires, and suddenly finds that it has wires of its own which move without his bidding; for her country under the pressure of calamities which the most skilful seek in vain to redress; for all other countries in their throes of anguish which may terminate in a second death or a new life. For one and all she cries, 'Lead us not into temptation.' Their temptations and hers, different in form, are the same in substance. They, like her, are tempted to doubt that God is, and that He is the Author of good, and not of evil; and that He is mightier than the evil; and that He can and will overthrow it, and deliver the universe out of it. This is the real temptation, there is no other. All events, all things and persons, are bringing this temptation before us; no man is out of the reach of it who is in God's world; no man is intended to be out of the reach of it who is God's child. He himself has led us into this wilderness to be tempted of the devil; we cannot fly from it; we cannot find in one corner of it a safety which there is not in another; we cannot choose that we shall not have those temptations which are specially fitted to reach our own feelings, tempers, infirmities; they will be addressed to these; they will be aimed at the heel or head, at whatever part has not been touched by the fire, and is most vulnerable. We must not crave quarter from the enemy: to choose for ourselves where we shall meet him, is to desert that guardianship in which is all safety. But we may cry, 'Lead us not into temptation:' and praying so, we pray against ourselves, against our evil tendencies, our eagerness for that which will ruin us. Praying so, that which seemed to be poison becomes medicine; all circumstances are turned to good; honey is gathered out of the carcase; death itself is made the minister of life.

Away then with that cowardly language which some of us are apt to indulge in when we speak of one period as more dangerous than another; when we wish we were not born into the age of revolutions; or complain that the time of quiet belief is passed, and that henceforth every man must ask himself whether he has any ground to stand upon, or whether all beneath him is hollow. We are falling into the temptation, when we thus lament over it. We are practically confessing that the Evil Spirit is the Lord of all; that times and seasons are in His hand. Let us clear our minds from every taint of that blasphemy. God has brought us into this time; He, and not ourselves or some dark demon. If we are not fit to cope with that which He has prepared for us, we should have been utterly unfit for any condition that we imagine for ourselves. In this time we are to live and wrestle, and in no other. Let us, humbly, tremblingly, manfully look at it, and we shall not wish that the sun could go back its ten degrees, or that we could go back with it. If easy times are departed, it is that the difficult times may make us more in earnest; that they may teach us not to depend upon ourselves. If easy belief is impossible, it is that we may learn what belief is, and in whom it is to be placed. If an hour is at hand which will try all the inhabitants of the earth, it is that we may learn for all to say, 'Lead us not into the temptation' of our times; that so we may be enabled with greater confidence and hope to join in the cry of every time, 'Deliver us from Evil.'

SERMON VIII.

Fourth Sunday in Lent, April 2, 1848.

Deliver us from evil.—LUKE xi. 4.

WHEN a man prays, 'Lead us not into temptation,' he prays against himself; prays that he may not go where he has an inclination to go ; prays that neither he.nor his brethren may have what they have a false taste for, even though God's hand seems to offer it them. Such a prayer, till we know something of ourselves, something of His purpose in placing us here, must needs appear strange and perplexing. Is not the one which follows it altogether different; the simplest, most spontaneous utterance of the heart; one which all the world has been pouring forth; which we should certainly have learnt, though no one had taught it us ?

It would be idle, indeed, to deny the universality of this prayer. Wherever men are visited by any storm, or fire, or earthquake ; wherever they are plagued with any bodily sickness; wherever they are oppressed by their fellow-men ; wherever they have a vague sense of being crushed by fortune ; wherever they have learnt to look upon custom or law as an incubus; wherever they are stifled by systems; wherever they are conscious of a remorse which stays with them and moves with them; there is a cry ascending to some power, known or unknown, 'Deliver us from evil.' The question what evil is, and whence it comes, is for such sufferers of easy solution; they know well what they mean by it; they know or guess generally what brought it to them; at all events it *has* overtaken them. They may suppose that some fellow-creature can rescue them from it, or chance, or themselves; they may look to the physician, the priest, the legislator; to alterations in government; to new dispositions of property; to a friendly executioner; to suicide. But a deliverer there must be; something or some person to hope in. If once we believe evil to be omnipotent, or suppose that it was intended for us, and we for it, I do not think it is possible to conceive of human society or human life. Recollect the worship of every country you ever heard of, how many names or characteristics of the different divinities had relation to deliverance of some kind, or to the averting or avenging of wrong. If you took these away from the mythologies, you would find that there remained a mere *caput mortuum*; all that had held them together and appealed to human trust and sympathies would have escaped.

Now it would surely be a very hard and stoical doctrine to proclaim that what these different creatures of our flesh and blood have cried to be saved from, were not really evils, but only certain conditions of existence, which they fancied to be such. No one, I should think, can imagine that he served truth by maintaining such a proposition against the sense of mankind, and against the witness of his own heart. That from which men have revolted as utterly unnatural and inconsistent and unreasonable, that which they have felt to be in positive disagreement with their constitution, they have a right to call an evil; and all the theories, political, philosophical, religious, in the world, can never deprive them of the right. Nor can these theories, so far as I see, prove even the most extravagant hopes that our race has indulged to be utterly vain and delusive, or take from any man the right to seek deliverance from human helpers, kings, lawgivers, shepherds of the people; from his own strong arm, from invisible helpers, from some fate that is higher, sterner, more inflexible than all other powers. There was a warrant for all such hopes, even for hope from the last resource of self-destruction. We have no right to take away such refuges until we can provide a better; and it is at least probable that if a better be found, we shall find some explanation of all the rest.

We may readily grant them, not only that the prayer has been offered in all places and in all ages, but that in all places and in all ages a deep truth has been expressed in it. But do we, therefore, say that the prayer had no need to be taught, that it sprang up naturally in the mind of man without any inspiration from above, that it was not like the former, the petition of a man against himself, but altogether one from and for himself? I rather think the evidence, if it is well considered, will lead us just to the opposite conclusion; that the prayer was, *in all cases*, taught and inspired from above; that what was contributed to it by the natural heart of man in his different circumstances and positions, was just the false, confused element of it, just that which narrowed its scope and divided its object; that in its true sense and purport it is in perfect accordance with the cry against temptation; that He who imparted it to men in the old time, was He who gave it to His disciples in its clearness and purity, in its length and breadth, when He said, 'After this manner, therefore, pray ye: Our Father—deliver us from evil.'

I. Other portions of the Lord's Prayer have led me to remark, that there is a fearful tendency in us all, which has infused itself most mischievously into our theology, to look first at our necessity or misery, only afterwards at our relation to God, and at His nature. The last are made dependent upon the former. We are conscious of a derangement in our condition; simply in reference to this derangement do we contemplate Him who we hope may reform it. We have just been tracing this process in heathenism. A mischief is felt; if there is a mischief, there must be a deliverer. Undoubtedly the conscience bears this witness, and it is a right one. But the qualities of the deliverer are determined by the character or locality of that which is to be redressed, or by the habits of those who are suffering from it. From this heathenish habit of mind the Lord's Prayer is the great preserver. Say first, 'Our Father.' This relation is fixed, established, certain. It existed in Christ before all worlds, it was manifested when he came in the flesh. He is ascended on high, that we may claim it. Let us be certain that we ground all our thoughts upon these opening words; till we know them well by heart, do not let us listen to the rest. Let us go on carefully, step by step, to the Name, the Kingdom, the Will, assuring ourselves of our footing, confident that we are in a region of clear unmixed goodness; of goodness which is to be hallowed by us; which has come and shall come to us, and in us; which is to be done on earth, not merely in heaven. Then we are in a condition to make these petitions, which we are ordinarily in such haste to utter, and which He, in whom all wisdom dwells, commands us to defer. Last of all comes this 'Deliver us from evil.' When we are able to look upon evil, not as the regular normal state of the universe, but as absolutely at variance with the character of its Author, with His constitution of it, with the Spirit which He has given to us, that we can pray, attaching some real significance to the language, Deliver us from it. Then we shall understand why men looked with faith to the aid of their fellow-men; to princes, and chieftains, and lawgivers, and sages. They were sent into the world for this end, upon this mission. They were meant to act as deliverers. They were to be witnesses of a real righteous order, and to resist all transgressors of it. We can understand why strong men felt that they had better act for themselves than depend upon foreign help. For the father of all put their strength into them, that they might wield it as His servants in His work; it was His Spirit who made them conscious of their strength, and of that purpose for which they were to use it. We can see why these hopes were so continually disappointed, though they had so right a foundation; why they were driven to think of higher aid, of invisible champions, because those upon the earth proved feeble, or deserted the cause and served themselves. It is true that the hosts of heaven are obeying that power which the hosts of earth are commanded to obey; that they are doing His service by succouring those who are toiling below; it is true, because He who rules all is not a destiny, but a loving will; not an abstraction, but a Person; not a mere sovereign, but a Father. All creation is ordered upon this law of mutual dependence and charity; but it is only in the knowledge and worship of the Highest that we can apprehend the places and tasks of the lower; when He is hidden these are forgotten; society becomes incoherent; nothing understands itself; everything is inverted; the deliverer is one with the tyrant; evil and good run into each other; we invoke Satan to cast out Satan. See, then, what a restorative, regenerative power lies in this prayer! See what need there was that the Son of God should come from the bosom of the father, to make men know that they were not orphans, to show how they might be in fact, and not merely in idea, children!

II. For now it is not any longer by this or that man, or unseen power, by this or that subordinate agency, by this or that alteration of events and circumstances, that we are forced to bound our plans and prospects of deliverance. We have not to work our way upwards by stairs winding, broken, endless, to an indefinite shadowy point, which we are afraid to reach, lest it should prove to be nothing. We begin from the summit; we find there the substance of all the hope men have drawn from the promising, but changeable, aspects of the cloud-land below; we see that all the darkness of earth, all its manifold forms of evil, have come from the rays being intercepted, which would have scattered it and shall scatter it altogether. Therefore we pray boldly, 'Deliver us from evil,' knowing assuredly that we are praying to be set free from that to which the will of the Creator is opposed, against which all the powers of the universe are engaged: that which all natural things, doing Him quiet homage, are punishing; that against which all voluntary creatures by the law of their being are pledged to co-operate. We are praying against that which men have not been praying against in vain for six thousand years, but rather which they have been stemming, overcoming continually; each of their prayers, if offered in ever so much dimness and confusion, opening a vision out of the darkness, because each of them derived its first impulse from Him, who through them and in answer to them was preparing the full discovery of Himself, and of that strength whereby all that resists Him shall be broken. I say the prayer offered with this recollection, becomes one full of cheerfulness and confidence. The difficulty is, to offer it in that recollection. God forbid that I should speak lightly of that difficulty! knowing how great it is; how hard, when evil is above, beneath, within, when it faces you in the world, and scares you in the closet, when you hear it saying in your own heart, and saying in every one else, 'Our name is Legion,' when sometimes you seem to be carrying the world's sins upon yourself, and then forget them and yourself altogether—which is worse and brings a heavier sense of misery afterwards —when all schemes of redress seem to make the evil under which the earth is groaning more malignant, when our own history, and the history of mankind, seems to be mocking at every effort for life, and to be bidding us rest contented in death; oh it is hard, most hard, to think that such a prayer as this is not another of the cheats and self-delusions in which we have worn out existence! But courage! if the evil were less pressing, we might have leisure to doubt the remedy; when all possibilities are exhausted, we begin to understand that here is certainty; we must believe on some ground or other that evil is not absolute, not victorious; we must believe it honestly, and without a trick, not pretending that it is nothing, when we feel inwardly that it is only not all. And we can believe it honestly with our whole hearts, while we say, 'Our Father—deliver us from the evil.' Then that which seemed so terrible, because it was so manifold, is condensed into one; it means in all its forms that which is opposed to the mind and will of Him who so loved the world as to give His only-begotten Son, that we might be His children, and brethren one of another.

III. This truth, that evil, though by its nature multiform and contradictory, has nevertheless a central root, our Lord teaches us by his temptation in the wilderness, and again by the prayer, 'Deliver us from *the* evil.' He, for the first time, made it fully evident that mankind has not merely enemies, but an enemy; that neither the various external torments which seem to make up evil, nor the desires and appetites of the man himself, upon which we often charge it, create or constitute the mystery of iniquity which is at work. Most blessed was this discovery; it justified the thoughts which had been in a number of hearts; it justified the ways of God. I said that the stoical denial of external evil is an artificial doctrine, at war with conscience and reason. Our Lord never for a moment yielded to it; He acknowledged palsies, and hunger, and leprosies to be plagues and curses from which men should seek deliverance. But He did at the same time explain wherein the truth of stoicism lay. He showed that these sufferings are not *the* evils of man; they belong to a wrong condition, but they are not the causes of it; nay, their sting may be taken out of them, they may become instruments for the cure and destruction of evil. He Himself underwent them; He felt them as none ever felt them; so He showed that men are intended to feel them. He exhibited love and mercy in them, and through them; so. He showed that they are not the masters of the will; that they may be its servants. Equally does He prove that the good things of life, the riches and beauty of the universe, are not the origin of its evils, as men have wickedly imagined; and if not, then that the desires and appetites of our heart, which correspond to these, and which they address, are not the origin of evil, and carry in them no necessary corruption. And yet He does bring the sense of evil nearer to us than it was ever brought before; He does explain by His words, by His life, why we must feel that evil to be actually bound up with ourselves, why it is the most difficult of all things, not to identify it with ourselves. For He by bidding us deny ourselves, He by giving up Himself in every thought and act, He by presenting Himself as the one great Sacrifice to the Father, makes us perceive that the setting up of self, the worship of self, is *the* evil from which all others flow, from which we are to pray, 'Deliver us.' Here is the wonderful Gospel-mystery which meets all the mysteries of our own hearts and of the world, and expounds them. Here is that which makes that last refuge of man in self-murder intelligible. It is self he wants to get rid of; he has sought evil elsewhere, and not found it; he has it in his own being; that must perish. What a sense of solitude must be in the spirit before it can dream of such an act! what a feeling that all which it has seen without is centred within! And yet what it feels in that hour, all the world is feeling in a measure; this self is the curse of each, as much as it is his. Oh if he could rise for a moment to that perception, if he could feel 'It is not *I*, it is the spirit of self-will, who is counterfeiting me! it is this from which I must be delivered, it is this from which my race must be delivered! That each may be himself, that the universe may be what the Lord of all created it to be; this must be overcome for each, for all.' With what a new and wonderful feeling would he then turn to the words, ' Behold the Lamb of God, which taketh away the sins of the world!' 'Lo, I come (in the volume of the book it is written of me), to do thy will, O God; thy law is within my heart;' and to this, ' By the which will we are sanctified, through the offering of the body of Christ once for all.' Such words may have seemed hitherto quite vague, the fragments of an obsolete theology. Seen in the light of this discovery respecting the nature of Evil, seen in the light of that other more glorious discovery respecting the infinite charity of God, how they harmonise with all that our hearts had prophesied of, with our consciousness that we have capacities of sympathy and fellowship, which are destroyed by self-will; with the conditions of a world, created for brotherhood, destroyed by the same self-will. How little a man, who has learnt this lesson, wishes any more to resolve the evil spirit into the feelings and passions of the individual heart! How he abhors such implicit practical Manicheeism, against which Christ's temptation, and the history of His redemption, extending as it does to every thought and movement and appetite of our souls and bodies, as well as to the whole outward universe, is the protest! How he must rejoice to think—'I can pray, I will pray, Deliver us from the evil. I will pray to the Father of our Lord Jesus Christ against myself, against my inclination to make self the object of my existence, of my worship, against every act and thought which involves that inclination. I will pray to Him, whose will is that I should be in submission to Him, that I should be His servant in all the powers and affections of my spirit, soul, and body; who would use all these for the manifestation of His love, for the deliverance of His creatures. I will pray to Him in the confidence that He has accepted the perfect sacrifice of His Son for me, and for all mankind, the sacrifice which He had himself prepared, the sacrifice which was the fruit and perfect setting forth of His own love, the sacrifice which was presented to Him by the Everlasting Spirit. I will pray in the confidence that He will receive the sacrifice of myself and of all to Him in that Name. I will pray in the certainty that He is maintaining a conflict with the self-will which is the curse and dislocation of the world, and that every plague, pestilence, insurrection, revolution, is a step in the history of that conflict, tending towards the final victory. I will pray that we may not be cast down and lose faith, because change after change only seems to bring out the evil more fearfully, to exhibit some darker and more inward form of it. I will pray that we may not acquiesce in any evil about us, or within us, because we fancy that a worse might come from its removal. I will pray to feel that our only safety is in the God of truth and love, to recollect that self-will, as its different veils and bandages and rags of borrowed finery fall off, must be displayed more nakedly and horribly; to give thanks, nevertheless, that its resources are nearly exhausted, that its rage will be fiercest when its hour is shortest; to make, therefore, no truce with it; to wish none for my fellow-men; to act and live in the confidence that if we wait the appointed time, the travail-hour of creation, He who overcame the principalities and powers of evil in the wilderness, in the city, on the cross, in the sepulchre, and who ascended on high, making a show of them openly, will fully deliver us and our race from them, that we may serve without fear Him, the Father, and the Holy Ghost, the one God, world without end.'

SERMON IX.

Fifth Sunday in Lent, April 9, 1848.

For Thine is the kingdom, and the power, and the glory, for ever'
Amen.—MATTHEW vi. 13.

As this Doxology occurs in only one Evangelist, the Church, in her repetitions of the prayer, omits it at least as often as she uses it. The idea contained in the words has been expressed already; it is involved in all the petitions. But the distinct utterance of it at the close of the prayer teaches us some lessons which the prayer might fail to teach us, and yet which we must always remember if we would say it truly.

I. The words, 'Thine is the kingdom,' certainly assume that it is not *ours*. Now if by 'kingdom' we understand the kingdom of Nature, the courses of the planets, the succession of day and night, of seedtime and harvest, perhaps the temptation to say, 'This is ours,' may not be very great. Some *Opifex Mundi*, or Intelligent Principle, or Demiurgus, or fixed law, may be admitted to preside over these arrangements. But if we apply 'kingdom,' as I suppose most of us would, to the order and conduct of human society generally, or in some of its particular divisions, the feeling is very different. Here we have a claim to be masters; over this order man exercises a most evident influence. Is there anything monstrous in the notion, that he established it, and that he upholds it? There can be nothing strange in it, for we all drop into it most easily and naturally. True, there are old forms which denote a belief the most opposite of this, forms which indicate that the highest ruler of the land, and every subordinate magistrate, derives his authority from an Invisible Person, to whom he is under a fearful responsibility for the fulfilment of his duties. The recognition of an actual King of kings, and Lord of lords, of One not only interfering at certain crises to disturb an existing monotony, but present at all times, the real source of government, through whatever hands it may be administered—this recognition enters assuredly into the institutions and laws of every nation in Christendom; I might say, of every nation in the world. But we have become more and more convinced that these witnesses are, as to their real and original intent, obsolete. They belong, it is said, to a theocratic period of the world's history; when that had passed away they lingered still, and are even now not without their use in enforcing obligations, the true ground of which cannot be apprehended by the people at large, in giving an historical sacredness and mystery to that which would else seem a creature of the present, in sustaining the force of laws by sympathies and affections, by the terrors or hopes of another world. But all these explanations and apologies clearly assume, that the schemes for upholding society, be they religious or secular, are of our creation; that society itself is. Some would throw a decent veil over its origin; some would lay bare the savage contests, victories of cunning and terror, contests of the weak many and the strong few, out of which it arose; some would find a resting-place in the physical conformation and mental temperament of different races; ultimately, the great majority of those who think for themselves, and of those who are thought for, subside into the conclusion, that man is an absolute sovereign over his own social relations; or, at all events, that there is merely a reserved right dwelling with some other power, which in ordinary calculations hardly needs to be taken into account. It may happen, undoubtedly, that this claim of sovereignty assumes a shape which we find startling. We may be suddenly required to recognise, not the abstract phantom, but the practical exercise of popular supremacy. Then we begin to observe, that whenever that which is in conception so sublime takes a concrete form, it is a very coarse and very narrow one; the most ignorant part of some city or district embodying the great idea. We may begin to ask, Whether that which seems to be the highest achievement of liberty does not involve a perpetual alternation of despotism and servility; whether that which is the last and highest effort of reason does not lead to incessant contradiction? Such expressions may be true, such doubts amply justified, but do not they come too late? Have we not already admitted the principle, sanctioned the contradiction? If this ultimate sovereignty resides in *any* creatures, surely there must be a law of gravitation which will make it settle at last where we dread to think that it is settling now. That law cannot for ever be resisted by mere prescription, or tricks of diplomacy, or arms which may lose their edge and change their object; or, lastly, by spiritual influences which we resort to for a purpose, which we wish to be effectual for others but can trifle with ourselves. Surely all these things must come to naught; all, that is to say, which interposes between us or any country, and the abyss of self-willed mob dominion, if these words which we utter so often have not a reality in them above all realities, a depth beneath all depths. 'Yours,' says our Lord, 'is not the kingdom, though you may be called to sit down in it, and occupy honourable places in it; though each of you has *some* place in it; some work and office assigned you by the Great King, a rule over a portion of His subjects. Yours is not the kingdom; nor, as so many of you come to think, when all your plots have failed, and you are desperate of overcoming evil and establishing good in your fashion, is it the devil's kingdom. He claims it; he says to you, as he said to Me, "It is mine, and I give it to whomsoever I will." On the strength of that assertion he bids you, as he bade Me, fall down and worship him. He asks you to traffic with him for the means of regenerating your fellow-creatures, and getting the kingdom out of his hands. But you can answer him as I answered: "It is written, Thou shalt worship the Lord God, and Him only shalt thou serve." You can say, "Thine is the kingdom; thine it *is* now; not thine it shall be hereafter. Thine it is who art our Father, and hast called us to be thy children. Thine it is, whom we have asked according to thy will to deliver us from the evil."'

Now, my brethren, in making this ascription, we do not affirm Theocracy in the sense which some persons give to that word, and which may well have made it hateful. We do not say, 'Thine is the kingdom,' meaning that it belongs not really to an invisible Father, but really to certain visible priests, who claim the homage due to Him for themselves, and bring men into bondage by the perversion of that truth which is alone able to set them free. We do not mean, according to the Filmer and Sacheverel doctrine, that the divine power is transferred to certain visible kings, in whom it rests absolutely and indefeasibly. We do not mean, according to the fifth-monarchy teachers, that this kingdom resides in a certain body of saints whom God has authorised to claim the world as their possession. All these doctrines we should reject, not as exaggerations, but as evasions; not more for their folly than for their profaneness. If the words, 'Thine is the kingdom,' are true words, priests, kings, saints, must say as much as any, yea, more than any: 'It is not ours. We exist only to testify whose it is, only to bring all whom we can reach within the experience of its blessedness.' They are to make it manifest that their consecration is not a falsehood; that all the services by which we hallow our civil acts are not horrible mockeries; that all the forms of human discourse which unconsciously witness of a divine order and government, need not for the sake of honesty be cast out of it, till it is reduced to little more than the chattering of savages. They are to declare—we all of us, brethren, are pledged by our baptismal vows to declare—that there is an actual eternal ground for what we have treated as fictions, for what men declare, and declare rightly, if we could by our lie make God's truth of none effect, to be worn-out fictions. We are bound to affirm, that a Fatherly kingdom is established in the world; that to be members

of it is our highest title, and that the beggars of the
land share it with us; that in it the chief of all is the
servant of all; that under Him all may in their respective
spheres reign according to this law; that all ranks
and orders stand upon this tenure, and are preserved or
overturned by their honour or contempt for it; that all
offices, the highest and lowest, have hence their responsibility
and dignity; that this kingdom has its highest
throne over the human will, and its secret impulses and
determinations; that it reaches to the most trifling acts
and words; that not one of the suffering myriads in a
crowded city is forgotten by Him who is its Ruler, any
more than one of the spirits of just men made perfect;
that when all the subordinate vassals of the kingdom
shall confess their dependence upon Him, shall know
that He is, and shall feel towards those who are
beneath them and to one another as He feels towards
them, then His kingdom which *is* now, will indeed
have come in power.

II. And so it shall come; for *Thine is the Power*.
Different words from the last, however closely allied to
them; and I think harder words to say in perfect sincerity.
Here we are not limited, as in the other case.
We were obliged to confess that we did not call the
Kingdom of Nature into *existence*. But we do put
forth a great and notorious *power* over that kingdom;
men can say, with much apparent justification, 'Ours
is the power,' even there. Accordingly they did say
it. The students of Nature went forth, like the Persian
king, with the chains wherewith to bind her, with
the magical sounds which were to make her do their
biddings. But then the humbling maxim was pro-

claimed, which has been the foundation of all real discovery and victory in this department: 'Man, the servant and interpreter of nature, knows nothing, can do nothing, except what he had first observed in her.' All the boastings to which two centuries of wonderful success might have given birth are stopped by the recollection that obedience to this canon has been the single secret of success, that any one who would resist it, and determine to conquer without stooping, has gone away discomfited. Nature, even when she seems most confessing the dominion of man, is saying with all her voices: 'Yours is not the power; you are learners, interpreters, receivers; you can use the strength which you have first asked for, that is all.'

Yet how wide a field remains, if this is denied us! Ours is surely the power, in some way or other, to affect our fellow-men. There is the direct power which lies in relationship, station, age; the power of outward attractions: the power of wealth; the power of conversation; the power of moving crowds by speech; the power of written words and of song; these, with all the innumerable subtle mysterious agencies which are only known in their operation. Surely whatever may be said of the objects to which these powers are directed, their existence must be admitted. It cannot be said that they are not put forth by human beings, that they are not human powers. Can it be pretended that they would be in any respect better if they were less vigorous, that there is in power itself an inherent curse? Such a proposition would, I believe, be a denial as great as there can be, of the truth which this ascription affirms. But upon this point experience has its own testimony to bear, which must be listened to, and which cannot be at variance with that which comes from any true authority. These exercises of power do not only bring *with* them pain, which might be easily understood, but *after* them, disappointment. And this not only when the end sought for has been mean, but when it has been glorious; when it has been the triumph over wrong and the setting up of right. A bitter wail is heard again and again, that weak insignificant men do the work of the world, and that those who could do it are kept back or crushed; a wail which they who make it are half ashamed of, but which, nevertheless, they cannot suppress. The thing that was aimed at is not achieved; hopeless obstacles from the force of circumstances and the ignorance of mankind are said to stand in the way. What is stranger still, those in whom no power is apparent, who are not conscious of its existence in them, are seen to exert it; the meek people whom the world does not regard, whom the men of power have been used to look upon with scorn, effect what they cannot; at some time or other that influence reaches even them and overmasters them. Strange facts, but recurring continually, making up the history of mankind! How can they be explained? They are not explained, I think, to any person who has much vaunted of his own powers, till he is led to perceive that man, the servant and student of the ways of God, knows nothing in morals, can do nothing in influencing his fellow-men, except what he hath first perceived in Him after whose image he is formed. In other and much better words he learns to say, 'Thine is the power. Thine are all those powers which I have found in myself and call mine. From Thee they came, by Thee they must be sustained and directed. That perpetual restlessness which I have experienced, which sometimes made me curse the world, sometimes myself, sometimes thy gifts, was the effect of my claiming that which did not belong to me, trying to wield armour which was too weighty. Those whom I complained of because they were set in high places, with so little right to be there, were less mischievous than I should have been, because they did less, struggled less, and left more room for Thy working. Those whose strength I was forced to admit, though naturally I despised them, might have fewer powers than mine, but what they had were submitted to Thee, were confessed to be Thine; therefore they had Omnipotence with them. And now, since Thou hast taught me, by sore and tremendous discipline, that I cannot strive with Thee, I believe, indeed that Thine is the power; the power to make this will conformable to Thine; the power to use what thou hast endowed me with as Thine own; the power to make all circumstances, which have no virtue of their own, and which, whether sad or happy, may be my plagues, really blessed; the power to bring order out of the chaos within me; the power to change selfish remorse into gracious repentance; the power to quicken the bodies of Thy saints, to restore the age, to renew the earth, to subdue even all things to Thyself.'

III. For lastly, Thine is the glory. To what is this kingdom tending? What is to be accomplished by this power? 'Though we admit,' it is often said, 'that there is some Being who formed individuals and human society, and who is continually directing both, still, if we hold Him to be a gracious and benevolent Being, we cannot conceive Him to have any object but the happiness or well-doing of His creatures; we must not dream that self-glory is ever His aim. But if not, then surely the blessedness and glory of humanity may be *our* ultimate aim, we need not, cannot look higher.' This statement you must all have heard frequently, in one form of words or another, and we shall hear more of it yet. We ought not to overlook the important truth which is contained in it, or to be unthankful for the confutation it contains of a deadly doctrine which divines have been too ready to propagate. If the glory be His, whom we have called our Father, whose Name we have desired to hallow, whose Kingdom we have prayed might come, whose Will is to be done on earth and in heaven, who is the Giver and the Forgiver, who guides us through temptation, and brings us out of evil; we dare not believe for an instant that it is a Self-glory of which we are speaking. It must be that which is the eternal opposite and contradiction of Self-glory; the glory of a Being whose name and nature is Love. That such a Being must seek the good of the creatures He has formed, we are all agreed. What we say is, that He would not be seeking the good of His voluntary creatures, if He did not raise them above themselves; if He did not give them a perfect absolute object to behold, and to dwell in. Those of our age who speak so much about the glory of humanity, affirm that man wants no such object, or cannot attain it if he does. Either it is really the satisfaction of all his wants, or else the only one he can hope for, to be a Narcissus, ever beholding his own beauty and becoming more and more enamoured of it. I am aware that many who use this kind of language, would protest strongly against the notion that a man becomes necessarily a *self*-worshipper, a seeker of his own glory, because he seeks the glory of his race or kind. I admit the distinction; it is a very important one. What I desire earnestly is, that they would ask themselves how it may be practically realised. Humanity cannot be contemplated merely as an abstraction; it must be seen in someone. For a time we may choose a favourite hero, and think that he embodies all we covet to behold. Imperfections appear in him, or he does not meet the new cravings of our mind; he is discarded, another is raised up, who has a shorter reign. We discover that we must not exalt one against another; each one carries in him the nature of all; each man has that nature very near to him. A great and wonderful conviction! but if existing alone, sure to turn into that state of mind which I just now spoke of. Around, beneath, above, the man finds no object so worthy of his delight, admiration, adoration, as himself.

It is very possible, that those who put forth a theory which justifies, as it seems to us, this mournful result, are not practically nearer to it than we are, who denounce it. God forbid that I should exaggerate their danger, or our safety! I believe that we are one and all haunted by this tendency to self-glorification every day and hour of our lives; that no religious systems, no religious practices, are a protection against it, nay, will, if we trust in them, infallibly lead us into it. It signifies not under what pretext, philosophical, political, theological, we build altars to ourselves; the worship is in all cases equally accursed. To throw down these altars, to destroy the high places in which men are burning incense to divinities that will prove at last to be fouler than Belial or Moloch; this must be our work. But if we have commenced this process, where it always should commence, in our own hearts, we shall know that we can only drive out the false by turning to the true. It is only God who can break the yoke of the tyrants under whom we have fallen from forgetfulness of Him.

Therefore I have desired that we should meditate upon the prayer of our childhood, in which lies, I believe, the charm against all that has assaulted us in our manhood. Within the few weeks that we have been considering it, as many events have been passing before us as might fill many centuries; it has seemed to meet them all; to be the best and fullest language, in which we can express our fears, hopes, longings, for ourselves, our nation, the world. We have not found that the wants and sorrows of Humanity were forgotten in it, because it begins from a higher ground, because it starts from a Father, because it acknowledges all the highest and lowest blessings as proceeding from Him. If we believe that this Father beholds Humanity, created, redeemed, glorified, in His beloved Son; if we believe that in that Son we may behold it and behold Him; that being members of His body we may see Christ in each and Christ in all; we cannot think less nobly of our kind than those do who shut their eyes to the facts of its corruption and misery, or who will not acknowledge that this corruption comes from our refusal to retain God in our knowledge. If we believe that the Holy Spirit, the Spirit of the Father and Son, is given to us that we may be united to each other, that we may be fitted for all knowledge and all love, we cannot have less noble anticipations of that for which man is destined than those who speak most loudly of his emancipation from all thraldom, and of his infinite capacities. But what we desire for ourselves and for our race—the greatest redemption we can dream of—is gathered up in the words, 'Thine is the glory.' Self-willing, self-seeking, self-glorying, here is the curse: no shackles remain when these are gone: nothing can be wanting when the spirit sees itself, loses itself, in Him who is Light, and in whom is no darkness at all. In these words therefore we see the ground and consummation of our prayer; they show how prayer begins and ends in Sacrifice and Adoration. They teach us how prayer, which we might fancy was derived from the wants of an imperfect suffering creature, belongs equally to the redeemed and perfected. In these the craving for independence has ceased; they are content to ask and to receive. But their desire of knowledge and love never ceases. They have awaked up after His likeness, and are satisfied with it; but the thought, 'Thine is the glory,' opens to them a vision which must become wider and brighter for ever and ever. Amen.

THE END.